T0348652

Klopp's Last Stand

Red Odyssey IV

Klopp's Last Stand

Red Odyssey IV

JEFF GOULDING

First published by Pitch Publishing, 2024

Pitch Publishing
9 Donnington Park,
85 Birdham Road,
Chichester,
West Sussex,
PO20 7AJ
www.pitchpublishing.co.uk
info@pitchpublishing.co.uk

ISBN 978 1 80150 749 3

Printed and bound in the UK on FSC® certified paper in line
with our continuing commitment to ethical business practices,
sustainability and the environment.

Typesetting and origination by Pitch Publishing

Printed and bound in Great Britain by TJ Books, Padstow

Contents

A New Beginning and the Battles Still to Fight
Liverpool FC May–October 2021

The Reds Go Gathering Cups in May
Liverpool FC October 2021–May 2022

The Promise of Immortality
Liverpool FC March–May 2022

The Final Push and a Tale of Two Cities
Liverpool FC May 2022

The Long and Weary Road
Liverpool FC July–December 2022

Liverpool 2.0: Reinventing Klopp's Reds
Liverpool FC August 2023–January 2024

Reds Buckle Up for Klopp's Last Stand
Liverpool FC January–June 2024

This book is dedicated to the memory of my beloved mum, Pauline Goulding, Nan, Sally Goulding, my aunt and uncle, Rene and Tommy Mills, and our dear friend, Mary Coffey, who are all now gone but never forgotten. They are forever part of my personal odyssey, and I will always be grateful for the chapters we shared together.

And, to Ian St John, Ray Kennedy and David Johnson. They gave us the best of days. They will never walk alone.

Acknowledgements

This is my seventh book with Pitch Publishing, the fourth in the Red Odyssey series. And, assuming we manage to get it across the line, my eighth title, another collaboration with the excellent Kieran Smith, will find its way to you all on 30 September. I'd like to acknowledge here the support I've had from Pitch over the last seven years. It has been a very easy and relaxed relationship, and the flexibility I've often needed on deadlines is particularly welcome.

Thank you to Jane Camillin, who, to my surprise, answered a speculative text from me pitching the first Red Odyssey book. I'd been given her number by another Pitch author back in 2017, but I never expected a reply. That exchange set me on the path to becoming a published author, a dream come true.

I'll never forget travelling to a European game at Anfield some weeks later, in the back of a taxi. It was late and I was stuck in traffic on Priory Road and wondering whether I'd make it in time for kick-off. Rummaging through the contents of my phone, I decided to check my emails. I'll never forget the sense of disbelief and excitement when reading Jane Camillin's words, which went along the lines of: 'Dear Jeff, find attached your author contract. Please read carefully before signing.' It's genuinely not false modesty to say that I thought Pitch had made an error and sent the email to the wrong person. I've been anxiously waiting for the call to tell me it's all been a terrible case of mistaken identity ever since. Thankfully, that call still hasn't arrived, yet. Thanks Pitch for backing me and helping me to fulfil a lifelong ambition.

I must also acknowledge the work of Graham Hales, whose efforts have managed to turn a sow's ear into a silk purse on so many occasions, and for also putting up with my constant stream of amends. To Alex Daly, a big thanks for working with me on cover copy, press releases and for being patient when I don't reply the first and sometimes second time.

Thanks also to the editors and proofreaders who have worked with me on my books: Ivan Butler, Gareth Davis, Dean Rockett, Andrea Dunn, and anyone else I may have forgotten. I must admit my heart sank when I received that first email from each of you containing your notes. I imagined pages of corrections and critique. Not a bit of it, you've all been extremely professional, understanding and supportive.

I've always been incredibly impressed – blown away in fact – by the cover designs used on my books. Each of them has captured the essence of the story brilliantly, which I'm sure makes them even more appealing to readers. Not to mention the fact that they all look great on a bookshelf or in a shop window. Every time I think I've found a favourite, the next one blows me away. The credit for that goes to Duncan Olner. If you haven't seen the cover for the upcoming *Red Dawn* yet, you're in for a treat.

As always, the Red Odyssey books wouldn't be as rich in story, emotion and authenticity without the first-person perspective, knowledge and passion of so many supporters and other contributors who have helped enrich all four books. As ever, there are so many, and I'm bound to forget someone here. You all know who you are, and I'm grateful to all of you:

Mark Platt, Joe Blott, Chet Muraji, Johnny Stokkeland, Steven Done, Kieran Smith, Tony Zeverona, Peter Simpson, George Scott, Kieran Smith, Chris McLoughlin, Susan Taylor, Steven Scragg, Gareth Roberts, Alan Kennedy, Ian Byrne MP, Dan Carden MP, Councillor Lena Simic, Phil Thompson, Jamie Carragher, John Barnes, David Maddock, the late and truly great Dan Kay, Matt Ladson, Joanna Durkan, Henry Jackson, Jack Lusby, James Nalton, Dave Usher, Paul Salt, George Sephton, Lizzie Hoare, Linda Ellston, Peter Kenny Jones, Andy Knott, Paul Amann, Darren O'Connor, John McMenemy, David Moen, Niall Cull, David King, Dermot Nolan, Alicia Lorena McDermott, Arngrimur Baldursson, Ian Golder, Jeremy Latimer, Kevin Woods, Gerard Kenny, Joe Goulding, David Goulding and David Wilkinson.

And ...

Steve Hunter, John Pearman, Emma Case, Prof. Stephen F. Kelly, Jordan Moore, Lee O'Connor, Peter Carney, Tracey Murray, Gary Shaw, Mike Holt, Keith Salmon, Ian Salmon, Chris Peers, Les Jackson, Frank Carlyle, John Kennedy, Paul Moran, Jacqueline Wadsworth, David Webber, Yumiko Tamaru, Paul Maychin, Carl Clemente, Mook San Lim, Lee Tracy, Ted Morris, Jo Goodall, Les Lawson, Garry Williams, Raul H. Cohen Llaguno, Kim Olthof, Rado Chmiel, Keith Williams, John Stulberg, Paul Coppell, John Whitehead, Spion Kop 1906, Andy Marsden, Neil Mulvaney and Jacob Hansen.

Finally, to my family. My wife Angela and my kids, Joe, Mollie, Lucy and Sophie, a heartfelt thanks for your support, putting up with my silences and moods when I'm writing and for your endless encouragement. Thanks to my dad, Billy Goulding, for buying everyone he works with a copy of my books, sometimes two. He even buys his own, even though I give him a copy for free. And he reads them. Every kid wants to make his dad proud; I hope I have.

Thanks also to my sister, Yvon Wardale, the Blue in the family. She may not share my football allegiances, but she always shares and promotes my books to her friends. Love you, Sis. I should also acknowledge my sister-in-law and mother-in-law, Julie Stephenson and Anne Colquhoun for the same reason. A mention also to my in-laws and friends, Harry, Dave and John Colquhoun, Paul and Robert Coppell. They're all Blues, so may not thank me for this, but thanks lads for buying and sharing the books, coming to my book launches and, in the case of Dave, setting up and driving me to radio interviews. It's much appreciated.

In truth, there are too many people to thank here. Nobody achieves anything in life without the help and support of a wide network of people, and I'm certainly no exception. To all of you, you have my eternal gratitude. I have never walked alone.

Foreword

The longer you're in the game, the more aware you are that the final whistle will eventually sound. If you're clever, you don't dread the end, you revel in every moment you have left in and around the field of play. This is what supporting Liverpool has been like for me ever since a certain German coach became our manager. I've lost track of the number of times in the last nine years when I've been able to revel in the gifts football gives us, despite the results not always falling into line with expectation.

Glorious moments like Dejan Lovren's winner against Dortmund in the dying embers of a tie that burned with emotions of every hue will always outshine the outcome of the Europa League Final in 2016, and Alisson Becker's headed goal against West Bromwich Albion in 2021 will be talked about far longer than the Reds third-place finish that season, and the way Liverpool's kids stuck out their chests and thrust forward their chins against Chelsea in the 2024 Carabao Cup Final and drove us across the finish line will live longer in my memory than any game of that season. It's always about the journey, our odyssey, than it is about the destination. That's Klopp's Liverpool, that's life.

Yet that's not always how I or we have felt. For 30 long years we allowed football to be all about the outcome, we allowed the past to dominate the way we thought about the present and the future. We failed to enjoy the moments, and fixated on a fear of failure, of not living up to impossibly high standards. And we became gripped by envy at the success of rivals. Not even a treble under Gérard Houllier in 2001 or a Champions League win in 2005 felt sufficient to erase the nagging sense that it wasn't enough to shut up the detractors or silence the doubts in our own minds.

We'd lost sight of ourselves, of who we were and why we feel we're different. As a student of the history of Liverpool Football Club, I can tell you that every successful period in our history would not have been achievable without unshakeable belief, a self-confidence bordering on arrogance and an unbreakable connection between players, supporters and the manager. That was true when Tom Watson led the Reds to their first league title in 1901, it was true when Bill Shankly finally brought the FA Cup to the Anfield trophy cabinet, and those same prerequisites for glory have been almost ever-present throughout the Jürgen Klopp era.

Only a community blessed with those qualities could have suffered the pain of conceding the Champions League trophy to Real Madrid in 2018, only to rise again and win the competition the following year, just as their leader – amid the agony of defeat – had predicted they would. To repeat the feat by winning the Premier League title a year on from missing out on the prize by a single point, despite a record-breaking season.

And only the truly faithful could dream of giving Barcelona a three-goal start in a Champions League quarter-final in 2019, before running them ragged in the return leg. 'Normally, I'd say it's impossible,' said Klopp in his pre-match speech to his players, 'but because it's you, we have a chance.' 'NEVER GIVE UP' screamed an injured Mo Salah's T-shirt during the pre-match warm-up, and in the stands we roared. As one, we believed that the impossible could be achieved and not even Lionel Messi could prevent the inevitable outcome.

We came together in the moments; we suffered the defeats together and shared the joy as one club. The output of all that is a sense of belief that has sustained us through the hard times and drove us on to new heights. Here's what I wrote at the end of *Champions Under Lockdown*, the third instalment of the Red Odyssey series:

> As I bring down the curtain on this volume, I am mindful of the words of our famous anthem. We walked through a storm with our heads held high. We deserve this golden sky and can rightly revel in the sweet silver song of that lark. Our team has journeyed from flatterers to deceivers to a bastion of invincibility. We have all abandoned doubt and embraced belief and we have all earned our rewards.

It's a paragraph dripping with a faith restored. That I could write like that after living through the ravages of Covid-19 and the social and economic collapse of the country, after a concerted campaign to curtail a historic title-winning season, declare it null and void or emblazon our achievement with an asterisk speaks to how hard fought Jürgen's achievements have been and how important they are to me, and to all of us.

Like the great generational managers who went before, Jürgen Klopp is more than just the manager of our club. In so many ways he transcends it, and in doing so he has captured the *zeitgeist* of the city of Liverpool itself. Again, this is a quality he shares with the greats of Anfield history. Klopp is not only in tune with the city's spirit of struggle, but he also embodies it, as evidenced by this quote: 'If you're from here. You're probably not just ready to fight, you actually want to fight.'

The boss has frequently weighed in on the big issues of the day, supporting LGBTQ+ fans, championing multi-culturalism and speaking passionately about social justice. These factors have helped to cement his legacy every bit as much as his achievements in the game. Little wonder that in 2022 Jürgen was awarded the Freedom of the City of Liverpool. These comments to the BBC prior to the ceremony were particularly pertinent. When asked what he thought about the ancient title conferring the right to drive sheep through city's streets, he said, 'I've read a little bit about this, what it means. I read something about sheep in the city and stuff like this, I'm not 100 per cent sure, but one of the duties is to defend the city, or in the past it was. I know they meant it differently, but I will, with words, forever.'

It's a sentiment he repeated on his departure: 'I don't think the club will need me in the future. But if the city ever does, I am there. Always.'

Klopp understands that football doesn't exist in a vacuum, the lives of the people who sustain the club are fraught with challenges, and he believes it's his duty, his players' calling to alleviate their struggles at least for the duration of a game. Or as he puts it, 'Football is not the most important thing in the world, but for 90 minutes it can feel like it.'

In this book I'll explore how Jürgen has not just shouldered the football club for almost a decade but, like Shankly and Dalglish before him, he has led the city's people through some of their greatest challenges.

I make no apology for the fact that this Red Odyssey will reflect both the lives of the people who support Liverpool Football Club – including my own – as well as those who play for or work for it, in equal measure. After seeing the Reds come agonisingly close to winning the lot on two separate occasions in the last few years, memories of how hard it was living through the aftermath of our title win in 2020, still battling a global pandemic and wrestling with a sense of isolation and grief, may have faded for some.

In reading through pages of notes dating back to the 2020/21 season, as I researched the early chapters of this book, I'm struck by how far we've come since those dark days, and I'm determined to deal with that here. As with the previous instalments, this is a social history of our club and I make no apology for straying into the subjective when I feel it's appropriate.

I'm eternally grateful for readers' comments and reviews of this Red Odyssey series. So many of you are incredibly generous and honest. I value that honesty even when it includes criticism. We can disagree and still be friends, and we can always learn from each other. I know that most of you enjoy the subjective nature of my writing, particularly when it comes to the great moments in our history. I'm always pleased to hear that a reader has felt close to the action, even imagining they could hear the noise of the crowd when reading my words. This is what I set out to do. That's obviously impossible to achieve when covering games played behind closed doors. Yet those games are part of the journey and I hope to illuminate them by providing context from my own life and the events that surround them.

I'm also aware that some of you would prefer it if I 'stuck to the football', leaving the politics out of the story. I honestly understand that desire to see football in isolation. For many of you the game is a release, an escape from the trials of daily life. You read because you want to celebrate your love of the club and relive the great moments. I promise that you'll always be able to do that when reading my books. They'll always be a love letter to our club, to all of you and to the city of Liverpool.

However, I don't feel I can do justice to our odyssey without dealing with the whole story, warts and all. Bill Shankly famously talked about politics and politicians and understood the impact of politics on football and on life itself. He knew that the experiences of those stood on the Kop shaped the attitude and behaviour of the supporters he described as 'a great community, united together in an arrogance that says, we are the people, we are Liverpool'. Bill knew that football alone couldn't explain that outlook alone. He understood that social factors had given rise to a community used to struggle and who understood the power of the collective. Hailing from a small mining community in Scotland, Glenbuck, Shankly was cut from the same cloth as those Scousers who sang his name with more reverence than they'd show any politician or religious leader.

For Bill Shankly it was all about everyone working together and sharing the rewards at the end of the day. Crucially, he said, 'That's the way I see politics, it's the way I see life.' Six decades later, and we have a manager who says and embodies those same values, both in terms of his approach to both football and life.

Contrast Shankly's socialism with Jürgen's philosophy: 'If you're not doing well, vote for someone who can make your life better. If you are doing well, vote for someone who can make everybody else's lives better.' For both men, individual reward comes from collective effort, and football and politics are intrinsically linked.

Who makes decisions about how our club is run is a political question, as is whether I or you can afford to attend games. And, despite our best efforts sometimes, we can't always leave life's struggles on the streets outside the turnstiles when we take our seats in the stadium or sit down to watch on television.

For me, there's another reason to illuminate the life and struggles of the people who support and follow our football club. As someone who has spent years researching and writing about the history of Liverpool FC, I can tell you that the records are littered with testimonies as to the prowess of our players, and details of games won and lost are not difficult to find. The challenge has always been to place events and people in context, to understand them and what drove them more clearly.

The heroes of the past didn't win trophies or suffer crushing defeats in splendid isolation. They lived lives that were rich, held views that were both agreeable and disagreeable and they were supported in the stands by people who were equally fascinating and who lived lives that deserve to be remembered. The history of our club is about more than the games we've played, and I want Red Odyssey to reflect that.

If I'm lucky enough that these books are still in print or available in some form or another to the football historians of the future, I hope they help illuminate the lives of the people who played and worked for Liverpool FC. But I also want them to understand the lives of the people who followed and sustained the club through this period in its history, so they can properly place the facts and the figures into context.

So, please enjoy this volume. Feel the passion in the words and allow them to transport you to the moments in our history when we believed again and dreamed again. Allow your ears to hear the sounds, allow your eyes to see the colours and breathe in that atmosphere. Experience the joy and the pain, and understand the full social, cultural and political context in which all of this took place.

Any odyssey is all about the journey. That's the way it has always been. Ours is far from over, of course. However, as we pause along the road to say farewell to a great leader, let's reflect on the ride. The Klopp era may be over, but his achievements will live long in our hearts and minds for as long as we live. His reign has been a wild one, a far from normal one.

Klopp's Last Stand and Me

A Sort of Introduction

Like all of you, I'll remember where I was and what I was doing the day I heard Jürgen Klopp was leaving the club. It's this generation's Shankly moment. I was too young at six years of age, in 1974, to remember the footage on Granada TV of a young kid being told by a young Tony Wilson that the great man had retired. I've seen it many times since, of course, and I'm always struck by what is, to all intents and purposes, a portrait of grief and loss. Not of a family member, of course, but of a football manager who just happened to feel like one.

'Yer joking aren't yer, came the response in that 70s Scouse accent. 'Who said?' It was as if the news was too painful to be true, it must surely be a wind-up. Fast-forward to 1990, and the resignation of Kenny Dalglish, and it was me in utter disbelief and totally bereft when my supervisor hung up on a call from a friend and announced to the entire office, 'Dalglish has resigned.' You could hear a paper clip drop as jaws hung open.

Now, 34 years later, I found myself back in that same state of utter shock and bewilderment as a colleague (thanks, Brian) held up his mobile phone to me. He needed no words, the image on the screen was enough. It was BBC Sport's breaking news page: 'Jürgen Klopp to leave Liverpool at the end of the season.'

'What! Yer joking aren't yer. No way' was all I could manage.

The video of Jürgen announcing his departure revealed a man utterly exhausted and whose mental and physical batteries were dangerously close to empty. He'd given everything for nine years, shouldered the weight of a club and city's expectations, lifted us from mediocrity and propelled us to glory. Like Shankly and Dalglish before him, he meant more to all of us than someone who was the manager of our club; he'd come to feel like one of us, a leader and an inspiration.

Football managers like that don't come round that often, maybe once in a generation if you're lucky. We've been so fortunate; I have been blessed. And, although I was genuinely shell-shocked at the news, desperate for it to not be true or for the boss to change his mind, one look at that haggard expression told me everything I needed to know about Jürgen's state of mind, and I completely identified.

I believed I knew what it felt like to juggle so much in terms of the expectations of others and have nothing left in the tank. I had experienced digging deeper into resources that were so low and sometimes empty in order just to keep going, and feeling that I was at breaking point.

I don't pretend to understand Jürgen's mind, and in no way is my experience the same as his, but there was something in his words and his demeanour that I recognised. He was telling us that he had just enough fuel to get him to the end of the current road at full tilt, and after that he was going to have to park up and take a break. To have that presence of mind amid such emotional turmoil is remarkable and not common. It was self-aware and very courageous. It was a powerful lesson for me.

I'm reminded of a quote from Jürgen that I'm sure you'll have heard: 'It doesn't matter so much what people think of you when you arrive. It matters more what they think of you when you leave.' As with many of Jürgen's utterances, it's completely authentic and represents the way he views life, relationships and his work ethic. I'm sure that his desire to leave the place better than he found it and not hang on longer than necessary, potentially risking the progress made, was at the heart of his decision.

On a personal level, the last nine years have been, to quote Jürgen himself, a ride. As a supporter of this great club, I have found it at times exhilarating but also exhausting. Those seasons in which we went into every game knowing that nothing short of three points would do, for an entire season, were both a blessing and a curse. In the years where we fell short, the agony was sometimes difficult to bear, but the journey was always both thrilling and stressful. What must it have felt like for the boss?

In my personal life, it's fair to say there has been trauma. The loss of my mother, stress and strain at work – you may not know that writing isn't my day job – I don't do anything half-heartedly, and I always try to do too much, then I kick myself for not doing anything well enough. Managing work, family commitments and writing professionally has meant that I've almost certainly short-changed the people I love and possibly not given my best at times.

The stress of all that can feel immense at times. And that's without the trauma of a global pandemic and more recently a series of health issues that I'm so far successfully navigating. Our lives may be as different as it's possible to be, but Jürgen and I are both at a crossroads. We're of a similar age, and we've both been going full tilt at the expense of really important aspects of our lives for too long. We're both human beings and it's time to change.

It feels to me that just as Jürgen has taken stock and decided that this season at Anfield will be his last stand, I too am facing a very similar stage in life. It's time to focus on what really matters: our health, our families and the things that bring us happiness. It's okay to do that, for us and for everyone. We're both just lucky we're able to do that.

I feel at this point the title of the book needs some explanation. In my wildest fantasies, I imagine Jürgen holding a copy of this, staring at the title with a confused expression on his face, before erupting in laughter. 'Last Stand,' he might roar through full-throated guffaws, 'I'm not dead yet.'

Of course, the boss has many more adventures and challenges ahead of him, However, I feel that, although we may not realise it, all of us get an opportunity in life to evaluate, take inventory and decide what your last great adventures are going to be, what your 'last stand' will be. These opportunities may arise through introspection, self-awareness or a chance comment from a loved one or trusted confidant, as is the case for Jürgen. Or, for some of us, we're forced to face the choice as a result of a series of life crises and challenges, which is how I realised that I needed to decide where I would make my last stand.

For me that will involve semi-retirement from the day job, and more time with the family. You may or may not be pleased to read that it will also involve more writing, a lot more writing. Sorry about that.

So, this instalment of the series will mix my personal journey with that of the club and the team. I've done that in each of the Red Odyssey books and I hope you're happy to continue to indulge me. There have been painful episodes along the way, as well as joyful ones. We're fortunate, I believe, that there has been far more to celebrate and rejoice in than there has been to commiserate.

This instalment of the Red Odyssey encapsulates another tumultuous period in the history of Liverpool Football Club. Against the backdrop of social and political upheaval, and a public health catastrophe, the club's story has continued to roller-coaster through the depths of disappointment and drama to unimaginable glory. Through it all, one man stood strong against the vagaries of football favour, controversies on and off the pitch, and the strain of managing one of the world's most iconic sporting institutions.

At times Jürgen Klopp has seemed impervious, almost superhuman, possessing an uncanny knack for always saying the right thing. Even when he didn't, he would recover like a punch-drunk boxer in a Hollywood blockbuster, lifting himself from the canvas before pummelling his foes into submission. There was, of course, for him, a heavy price to pay.

We should have known; he always told us he was the normal one. Maybe we were in denial. Maybe. However, if we'd been unable to see how the constant stress was chipping away at Jürgen's resilience, refusing to see he was just an ordinary human being, it's only because everything he has done while at Anfield – indeed throughout his entire career – was nothing short of extraordinary.

Danke, Jürgen.

The Long Dark Season of the Soul

Liverpool FC August 2020–March 2021

The Summer After the Season Before
Reds' Title Hangover

The August sun envelops me as the heavy hum of a bumblebee graces my ear, my eyes blink open and I wince at the sunshine. At the back of my head a dull ache that signals dehydration gnaws at me and I reach for a can of cola on the patio table as a gentle breeze captures the red banner pinned to a fence panel behind me. It's a mere week or so since Liverpool secured their first league title in three decades, and in all the years since that last one in 1990, whenever I dreamed of how life would be when we eventually did it again, the reality was as far removed from the fantasy as it could be.

I'd envisaged various scenarios that ranged from me going on a drunken tour of the Home Counties, carrying a replica league trophy, and rubbing salt into the wounds of our bitterest rivals to, well, going on a drunken tour of European cities and celebrating with Liverpool supporters I met along the way. I'd dreamed of that title parade around the city streets and how the numbers gathered to greet the team and the trophy would have dwarfed anything that had gone before.

However, Covid-19 still stalked the land and lockdowns of varying degrees remained in place. Daily news conferences trotted out a depressing roll call of rising infections, and families ravaged by grief and loss struggled to make sense of the hurricane that had engulfed all our lives.

In football land, the same tribal insanity pervaded as rival supporters of all hues struggled to cope with the fact that Liverpool had actually won the league. Perhaps they'd stop singing their 'Gerrard song', I naively thought. That obviously assumed a degree of imagination and creativity these terrace wits simply didn't possess.

My social media feeds were full of faux outrage at a perceived overexuberance on the part of Liverpool supporters who had taken to the streets in jubilation in the aftermath of the club's historic achievement. It was during these celebrations at Liverpool's waterfront that some drunken idiot had launched a firework at the Liver Building, causing some minor damage.

It was a foolish and embarrassing affair for sure, but did it really justify the waves of memes discussing the cultural significance of the iconic landmark and how this act of generational vandalism was evidence of a lumpen tendency unique to Liverpool supporters? Or was it more like a symptom of youthful irresponsibility fuelled by beer, months of enforced isolation and the kind of elan that only a communal sporting triumph can evoke?

Likewise, the wave of tutting and head shaking that accompanied the celebratory pyrotechnic displays that lit up the night skies above the city streets bordered on the melodramatic. Liverpool fans were, according to Evertonians at least, a threat to both our pets and our civic landmarks.

For my part, I'd steered clear of the party at the Pier Head and had simply donned a face mask and wandered down to the local shops to purchase as much 'Champions' tat as my money could buy. After gathering up enough T-shirts bearing Jürgen's grinning face to clothe me and the entire family, my attention turned to the array of cheap banners and flags on display. None of them were particularly good, to be honest, but I wanted one to hang in the garden and annoy any neighbours of a blue persuasion, so anything would do. Yes, I know if I were a proper supporter, I'd have made my own banner. I have no real argument here and can only offer mild depression and Covid malaise as a vague defence.

It's this banner that's now wafting in the summer air, as the kids enter the garden.

It's fair to say that I've never lived down the embarrassment of this banner, nor will I forget their mocking laughter as they first set eyes on it. As a middle-aged dad, I realise it's my duty to embarrass my children, and here it seems that I've succeeded with flying colours. Literally.

The flimsy piece of cloth is clearly mass-produced, and possibly by someone without the same keen eye for design possessed by the artists on the Kop. Emblazoned on a red background, in gold lettering, is the word 'Liverpool' above an image of the Premier League trophy. So far, so good. Then, underneath that, the words 'Champions of England'. So far, so good. However, from this point on it all falls apart.

The banner's design committee – and it's so bad it must have been designed by committee or even a mysterious algorithm – clearly wanted to create something truly poetic, before failing miserably and settling on the following prose:

WE SAY IT LOUD
WE ARE RED
AND WE ARE PROUD
FORM IS TEMPORARY
CLASS IS PERMANENT

I imagine that more than a few of you will have taken a short break from reading to stop laughing, and have now returned, composed and ready to resume. You may want to take another break. To make matters worse, the committee had opted to arrange the words either side of that image of the Premier League trophy. So, it could now be read as:

WE SAY IT LOUD FORM IS TEMPORARY
WE ARE RED CLASS IS
AND WE ARE PROUD PERMANENT

The suspension of football during Liverpool's championship-winning season had meant that the title wasn't secured until late in July, and that meant the FA Cup Final would take place on 1 August. Arsenal would beat Chelsea 2-1 in an empty Wembley, and strangely nobody refers to that game as the Covid final, there were no demands for it to be declared null and void and there were no calls for an asterisk to be engraved on the trophy. Strange that.

The ensuing summer break lasted just a few weeks, meaning there was no time for the usual meltdowns due to perceived transfer inactivity to evolve into all-out cyber wars. Liverpool would warm up for the season, in empty stadiums, of course, with friendly matches away to VfB Stuttgart, Red Bull Salzburg, and a 7-2 victory over Blackpool at Anfield.

Then, it was as if we all blinked and found ourselves in front of our TV screens watching a Community Shield tie contested by Liverpool and Arsenal in an echoing Wembley Stadium on 29 August.

A Takumi Minamino equaliser in the 73rd minute cancelled out a 12th-minute Pierre-Emerick Aubameyang opener, and the game finished 1-1. A penalty shoot-out followed and, sadly, it would be Liverpool's Rhian Brewster who would miss from the spot for the Reds, leaving Aubameyang to seal the contest for Arsenal.

I could have said, 'It's only the Community Shield, who cares?' But I did care. I wanted us to win the game and I wanted Jürgen to lift that trophy too. I wanted to see him lift them all before he eventually departed Anfield, as an old man if it was up to me. Still, the defeat could do little to dampen the buzz of winning the league.

Liverpool were their usual sensible selves in the transfer window. With a net spend that reflected the economic realities of months without supporters through the turnstiles, and inability to truly cash in on our historic success. Mass job losses in the hospitality and travel industries would soon spread to other sectors and add to the gloom. Meanwhile, Manchester United's Marcus Rashford was receiving criticism from sections of the right-wing media and politicians for – checks notes – campaigning to end child poverty. The National Health Service was creaking under the strain of a pandemic and millions would take to their doorsteps to applaud its workers on the 72nd anniversary of its creation.

The applause was an act of thanks and solidarity on behalf of a grateful public, and no doubt appreciated by those who had risked their lives during the viral outbreak. But the sight of grinning politicians clapping like performing seals in front of compliant TV cameras was a little galling. Decent PPE, a track and trace system that worked and a government who cared would have meant far more.

Liverpool said goodbye to a host of fringe players. Nathaniel Clyne, Pedro Chirivella, Adam Lallana, Andy Lonergan, Dejan Lovren, Ovie Ejaria, Ki-Jana Hoever and the unfortunate Rhian Brewster all headed through the exit door, raising an astonishing £51m. The money would partially fund moves for Kostas Tsimikas, Thiago Alcantara and Diogo Jota for a combined £84m.

We all craved a return to what used to pass for normalcy, but Covid's grip was vice-like it seemed. News of vaccine trials and the lifting of restrictions would lift the spirits, only for us to see our hopes dashed by predictions of a second wave of infections as university and school students returned in September. Against this backdrop, the government introduced 'eat out to help out', and by 'help out' they, of course, meant the struggling hospitality sector and the wider economy.

Even by the standards of the period, this seemed crazy. But such was our desperation that many of us headed to our local restaurants to get our 50 per cent discount and, for many of us, unwittingly spread the virus. We now know that public health officials were aghast at this measure, having argued it would lead to an uptick in infections.

In the middle of all this, the new football season resumed at Anfield on 12 September 2020. Liverpool opened the defence of their crown against newly promoted Leeds United. The scoreline makes it sound like a classic, a game for the ages. However, memories of watching the Reds behind closed doors from my armchair, with crowd sounds dubbed over the commentary, tell a different story.

This was football in 2020.

Liverpool 4-3 Leeds United
Chaotic Opener as Reds Edge New Boys at Anfield

For many the pandemic was a nightmare, and like all bad dreams it can take time to completely shake it off. You'll be going about your business and then you'll see something, catch an odour in your nostrils or hear a word or phrase that takes you right back to those days.

For me, to this day, sitting in the garden on a bright sunny afternoon can transport me back to lockdown. For my youngest daughter the very layout of her bedroom was a permanent reminder of sleepless nights full of worry, and we had to rearrange it. In reviewing my notes for this book, I decided to watch video of the game against Leeds United at Anfield on 12 September 2020, and it left me cold, but also thankful that I don't have to watch the football on my television accompanied by passionless commentary, empty stands and nothing but the echoing cries of the players to entertain me.

The experience was a painful reminder of what we missed. I read that the backdrop to this match included dire warnings from the government's scientific committee, SAGE, that the UK was 'on the edge of losing control' as recorded cases of Covid-19 exceeded 3,000 for the second day in a row. It now seems a fitting description of Liverpool's approach to the game. Imagine this game in a full stadium.

This was a night match, a 17.30 kick-off, so not quite floodlight territory. However, we can be certain that the place would have been rocking as supporters got ready to welcome the champions. The arrival of newly promoted Leeds United and the air of excited optimism from fans crossing the Pennines to Anfield for the first time in 16 years would have added piquancy to the proceedings. Throw in a 4-3 scoreline and what we should be talking about here is a classic for the ages.

Rows of empty seats draped in banners representing supporters who watched remotely tells a different story. This was a sterile encounter, bereft of the pomp and majesty of a season opener at Anfield, and we watched on in confinement.

There was at least the promise of freedom. Around two weeks earlier, 275 miles away on the south coast, 2,500 supporters watched Brighton play out a pre-season friendly against Chelsea. This was the first time fans had entered a football ground since the Premier League retreated behind closed doors.

Despite the misery of being locked out of Anfield, there was still a sense of relief that football was back. I had no doubt that we'd eventually be allowed back into the ground, but my optimism had little to do with the government approach to handling the virus, nor did the ditching of the daily press briefings from Downing Street convince me that it had all gone away.

The source of my faith lay in the development of vaccines, and sure enough we were just months away from a rollout. While I was more than able to understand and to an extent even sympathise with the population's growing sense of mistrust in politicians and 'the establishment', whatever that had come to mean in 2020, I didn't and still don't have time for conspiracy theories around the emergence of the vaccine. Of course, I could be wrong, and Bill and Melinda Gates may well be sitting on their sofas as I write, each laden with buckets of popcorn as they study my every move, monitored via the chip in my arm. Somehow, though, I'm sure they have better things to do with their money and time.

As a healthcare worker I agreed with the experts who argued that our only way out of the crisis was a vaccine, and for me it couldn't come soon enough. I was also happy to wear a face mask. When I was later lambasted in a shop by a guy who was unfeasibly angry with me for wearing a surgical face mask, scolding me for the fact that I was unwittingly breathing in the 'toxic gas carbon dioxide', which he told me was 'far more dangerous than any virus', I couldn't help wondering why surgeons and theatre teams hadn't been dropping like flies all these years.

Anyway, I digress. As I settled into my favourite 'lucky' seat on the couch, I cheered as Mohamed Salah became the first player to score on the opening day for the fourth time in a row. By the end of the game he would become the first in a Liverpool shirt to score a hat-trick in the first game of a league season since John Aldridge did so against Charlton during the 1988/89 campaign. His third would break Leeds' hearts, but before that they'd threaten to embarrass the champions.

Salah punished United defender Robin Koch, who handled the ball in the area just four minutes into the game. The Egyptian was flawless from the spot and the defending champions were off and running.

During the pandemic, Anfield hadn't been the fortress it once was. Without supporters in the stands, the players somehow became careless and lacked the ruthless edge that drove them to their first league title in 30 years, and the 18 they'd won before. Future football historians studying whether the fabled Anfield atmosphere is a myth or reality would do well to look at how the home team fared in the famous old stadium, with and without supporters.

Like many more after them, Leeds would find that going behind in L4 no longer held the same fear it once did. Just seven minutes after Salah put the Reds in front, Jack Harrison powered a right-foot shot past Alisson Becker to equalise for United.

Liverpool relied on poor defensive play by the visitors to retake the lead through Virgil van Dijk's header from an Andy Robertson corner on 20 minutes. However, our Dutch No.4 then gifted Patrick Bamford Leeds' second. This was all so uncharacteristic of a team who had ruthlessly marched to the title in the previous season.

A screamer from Salah restored my faith, albeit temporarily, in the 33rd minute, and the Reds ended the half in front. There had been a time when that would have been enough, and I could have relaxed during the interval, preparing myself for the inevitable rout to follow, as the Reds punished an away team for having the temerity to score not once but twice on our turf. Leeds had other ideas, however.

This was a game full of goals, literally packed with them. Four of them didn't stand but thankfully, of the seven that did, Liverpool edged it. Before they could eventually deliver the coup de gras, though, Mateusz Klich drew his team level on 66 minutes. It was a strike that deserved the adulation missing from the away end. Klich's first touch was sublime, and the resultant volley beat Alisson all ends up. How he'd have loved to knee slide in front of his travelling admirers and milk their adulation. How many moments like that were players up and down the country robbed of?

Salah, whose goals would earn him the title of man of the match, had one last ace up his sleeve, though. A late tackle in the box by Rodrigo on Fabinho left his manager, Marcelo Bielsa, cursing on the touchline, and the Egyptian King ensured an uncomfortable trip home for the visitors with his third goal of the game, and his second from the spot.

Liverpool had secured the three points in the 88th minute. How we'd have celebrated that had we been in the ground. There's nothing like a late winner to have your heart hammering in your chest and send you home with a grin as wide as the mighty Mersey. I celebrated at home, of course, but it couldn't possibly compare.

Under Bielsa, United looked a decent side. Phil McNulty, writing for the BBC, had this to say: 'Leeds got on the ball, were bursting with energy and attacked Liverpool every time they had the chance, playing with confidence and self-belief.' It was the sort of form that would lead them to an impressive eighth-place finish on their return to the top flight.

Liverpool were uncharacteristically shaky at the back, with Van Dijk and Alexander-Arnold both probably grateful that the game was played behind closed doors. Liverpool's No.66 had headed into his own net before being rescued by the offside flag and our No.4, usually so 'calm as you like', was responsible for one of the visitors' goals.

As ever, though, Klopp could rely on one of the most potent attackers in world football, and Mohamed Salah had ridden to the rescue again, more than meriting his man-of-the-match title. For the Reds, this would extend an unbeaten home run to 60 games (W49 D11). As reported by the BBC, this was only the third run of 60-plus unbeaten home games by any top-flight team in English football. The other two were Chelsea with a run of 86 ending in October 2008 and Liverpool's run of 63 ending in December 1980.

However, as the 2020/21 season progressed, fortress Anfield would experience its sternest test ever, and the absence of supporters would take its toll on the Reds' ambitions of retaining their crown.

Chelsea 0-2 Liverpool
Kepa Nightmare as Sadio Mané Demolishes Chelsea at Stamford Bridge

Just eight days later, on 20 September, Liverpool headed to Stamford Bridge to face Frank Lampard's Chelsea. As we now know, Frank had earned himself legendary status among Evertonians by – checks notes – shouting at Jürgen Klopp during a 5-3 defeat to Liverpool, who were about to lift the Premier League trophy at Anfield. The former Chelsea midfielder would, of course, go on to manage our neighbours across Stanley Park, adding saving them from relegation to his CV, but in the autumn of 2020 he still had fantasies that involved the top end of the table.

Refereeing the game was Paul Tierney, a man who would later achieve pantomime villain status at Anfield. However, he proved that even a referee can get things right occasionally, and only at the second time of asking. After initially awarding a yellow for an Andreas Christensen lunge on Sadio Mané, who had raced on to a Jordan Henderson pass, Klopp's future nemesis eventually delivered Liverpool an advantage by serving the Chelsea player with a red card on the stroke of half-time.

In truth, though, this was a comfortable win for the Reds, with Mané in imperious form, Alisson resolute in the Reds' goalmouth and Chelsea porous in defence. Mané grabbed a brace in the game, becoming the third Liverpool player to do so at Stamford Bridge after Steve McManaman in 1995 and Philippe Coutinho in 2015. Alisson, meanwhile, saved a penalty, denying Chelsea an unlikely route back into the game, keeping out Jorginho's effort from the spot.

However, his opposite number, Kepa Arrizabalaga, had a calamitous game. Within five minutes of the restart Mané put Liverpool in front following an assist from Bobby Firmino. Then, just four minutes later, the game was won when the man for whom Chelsea had stumped up £71m, a record fee for a keeper, attempted a clearance that Laurel and Hardy would have been proud of, failing dismally to deal with a Firmino cross and handing Sadio the simplest of headed goals.

The second half started with a debut appearance by Thiago Alcantara, on for the injured Henderson. The Spaniard is a sumptuous footballer whose capture from Bayern Munich for a mere £20m plus add-ons had excited us all; however, a clumsy challenge on Timo Werner in the Reds' penalty area gifted the Londoners a possible way back.

The sight of Jorginho with the ball in his hands felt ominous. Usually consummate from 12 yards, the Brazilian saw his effort saved by Alisson. Although there was still 15 minutes to play, Liverpool were home and dry.

Despite the home side being down to ten men for the whole of the second half, the media and Jürgen Klopp were in no doubt as to Liverpool's dominance. Jürgen hailed the result as perfect, and both the print and broadcast media were unanimous in declaring that Liverpool were back to their old selves. The perspective of time shows that they were all premature in their judgement, but this was a comfortable win for the Reds in the capital.

For the Blues, the performance of their 'star keeper' would convince them to pursue a little-known goalkeeper plying his trade at French outfit Rennes. Édouard Mendy and Kepa Arrizabalaga would trade places in the Chelsea goal in the seasons to come, most notably, and with disastrous consequences, in the 2022 League Cup Final. We'll come to that later.

Speaking to BBC's *Match of the Day*, Chelsea boss Lampard clutched at straws, saying, 'For chances the first half was very even. The red card changes the face of the game, the talk I do at half-time, and it forces me into a reshuffle. It was always going to be difficult after that.'

Surprisingly, Klopp agreed that the red card had been significant, telling BBC Sport:

It's always a tough game here. I liked the first half. It was two teams that wanted to play, create, defend and make things happen. They were the dominant side without goals but then a massive game-changer in the last seconds, which was good for us. We had to adapt to that, and we did.

Generous? Maybe, but a win at Stamford Bridge has always been satisfying regardless of how it arrives. It was now six points from two games, and with a trip to Lincoln City and Sincil Bank in the third round of the League Cup to come, few would have bet against the champions having another memorable campaign. It would be, of course, but not for the reasons we expected.

Lincoln City 2-7 Liverpool
Three Debuts and a Curtis Jones-Inspired Rout

We've reached 24 September and, with the national news continuing to be dominated by the pandemic, Liverpool travelled to Sincil Bank to face Lincoln City in the third round of the Football League Cup. Children had returned to our schools, we were working from home and the UK had just posted the largest daily number of Covid infections since mass testing began.

Meanwhile, a group calling themselves Extinction Rebellion had blockaded printing presses, preventing the publication of several national newspapers as part of their ongoing campaign to wake up a species seemingly sleepwalking towards oblivion. These were crazy times, and it was hard not to feel apocalyptic about the future. Thankfully football rumbled on, albeit still a pale imitation of its former self.

The game against Lincoln was packed with debuts. We've come to realise in the years since just how many young players owe their careers to Liverpool's academy, first and foremost, but also to Jürgen Klopp for having the courage and belief to give them their start in football. In an age in which supporters demand instant success, where our rivals are spending the GDP of small countries to monopolise the sport, it takes great bravery for a coach to put his faith in youngsters. One of those is, of course, Curtis Jones, a player who divides opinion at times and who Jürgen seems to treat as a favourite son, sometimes praising the youngster and sometimes chastising him.

As the final whistle sounded at Sincil Bank, Klopp would be singling the Scouse prodigy out for the plaudits, describing Jones as an 'exceptional talent' and declaring that 'we will have some fun with him, I am pretty sure, in the future'. Of course, his brace of goals and man-of-the-match performance against the Imps was only part of the story.

In addition to Jones, debuts were also handed to Kostas Tsimikas, Diogo Jota and Rhys Williams, while Marko Grujić would grab his debut goal. Xherdan Shaqiri got the ball rolling with a sublime free kick with the game barely ten minutes old. Then, in a game packed with understudies, Takumi Minamino decided that he'd also seize his moment in the spotlight, dispatching a goal of similar quality into the top corner just nine minutes later.

With Lincoln starved of quality, Liverpool were threatening to serve up a footballing banquet, but it was now time to add a little local flavour. As the half-hour mark passed, Curtis Jones unleashed a quick-fire double, obliterating the Imps' dreams in four breathtaking minutes. The Scouser's first was a stunning long-range effort past a bedraggled Alex Palmer on 32 minutes, and he wasn't finished yet. Jones added to his tally with another piledriver from distance. It took a slight deflection but there was no doubting the quality of the strike, his fifth for the club. Jürgen Klopp agreed, stating, 'Both goals were difficult, for the second one the first touch was absolutely exceptional between two opponents and then he opens up and sees the opportunity and finishes it off.'

Liverpool went into the break with a four-goal lead, and for Lincoln it would be a case of damage limitation. Their manager's words would have been ringing in their ears after just 18 seconds of the restart, when Takumi Minamino doubled his tally, after pouncing on a loose ball after another Shakiri effort was saved.

Then in a blistering six-minute spell, Lincoln's Tayo Edun pulled one back on the hour mark, only for Marko Grujić to make it 6-1 after 65 minutes, before Lewis Montsma added a second for the home side. The Sincil Bank crowd were certainly getting their money's worth, and their heroes had given themselves a chance of winning the second half as their manager, Michael Appleton, had urged them to do.

Sadly for them, Divock Origi wasn't ready to surrender the limelight to his team-mates. The Belgian raced on to a Minamino through ball and made no mistake as he fired powerfully past Palmer to seal the tie with Liverpool's seventh. The reward would be a fourth-round tie with Arsenal.

Lincoln boss Michael Appleton tried his best to lift his players and their fans but had to concede that Liverpool had been on top throughout: 'I thought in the first half we had our moments. It was a masterclass of finishing from Liverpool. In the second half we created a lot of opportunities. I felt sorry for the boys because the idea at half-time was to try to win the second half … a simple message. We got punished by one or two errors. The difference in the first half was their finishing.'

Jürgen Klopp told BBC Radio 5 Live: 'We played a really good football game tonight. It was easy on the eye. We passed the ball and finished situations off. The boys wanted to play football and showed an exceptional attitude.'

Bigger tests lay ahead, but Liverpool's second string had proven they had the attitude and work ethic to do a job for their boss whenever he needed them. As we now know, he'd have to call on those reserves with increasing regularity as the season went on.

Liverpool 3-1 Arsenal

Gunners Outclassed as Jota Opens His Anfield Account

As we headed into the last week of opening month of the season, Liverpool appeared to be in reasonable shape. Manchester City had lost 5-2 at home to Leicester on Sunday, 27 September, and in a league in which the Reds had fallen short by a single point in 2019, that felt potentially significant.

For me, working in the health service, the pandemic had become genuinely all-consuming. It dominated both my home and professional life and I was becoming desperate for an escape. I loved and was immensely proud of my time in the NHS. I'd spent almost 30 years in public service, but the sense that my stint was coming to an end was inescapable.

I interviewed successfully for a position at a local university and faced a new challenge outside of the NHS with a heavy heart and a little apprehension. On the plus side, lockdown had given me the gift of time. When the working day was done, there was little else to occupy my whirling thoughts and, as it so often has, writing filled the void. As a result, I'd managed to publish two books in 2020. The first, *Champions Under Lockdown*, the third in this series, had arrived in August and would soon go to reprint. The second, *The Lost Shankly Boy*, written with George Scott, was published on 21 September.

I should have been excitedly looking forward to a new challenge in life, celebrating my success as an author and looking forward to another roller-coaster season with Klopp's Reds. Instead, it was hard to extract much joy or optimism from anything in what was shaping up to be – to paraphrase the late, great Douglas Adams – a long dark season of the soul. My family had suffered great trauma during lockdown. My wife, working on the front line, had to deal with the daily anxiety associated with the fear of becoming infected or passing on the virus to us. My kids had struggled greatly.

For my part, I'd tried to play a supporting role with varying degrees of success. Mostly I was hiding from it all, and hiding from my own feelings, escaping into work and writing but unable to escape a sense of guilt at not really being there for those around me. It was becoming ever harder to escape the realisation that I was drifting into depression. My lifestyle was becoming unhealthy, and stress felt all-pervasive, weighing heavily on my every waking moment. There seemed to be no release.

On Monday, 28 September Liverpool welcomed Arsenal to Anfield for the first of two games in the space of three days. On this day there were just three Premier League points at stake, but it would be a place in the fourth round of the League Cup up for grabs on the following Thursday. Such a situation would normally have provided that vital safety valve, allowing me to escape the pressure for at least a few hours, to mingle with friends before, during and after the games, and share life's burdens. That release was no longer available to me or anyone else.

Football, Shankly said in more innocent times, is much more important than life or death. Jürgen Klopp would describe it as the most important of the least important things in life. We can argue over the merits of these quotes, but both men were scrambling to explain how much the game means to many of us.

The league game against Arsenal on 28 September, played in front of a sea of empty seats, was at least one packed with incident. A goal for new signing Diogo Jota – who had become the 13th player in the Reds' history to notch on his debut – a rare strike for Andrew Robertson operating from the left-back position, and assisted by his right-back, Trent Alexander-Arnold, were just some of the highlights. And Sadio

Mané would ride his luck by escaping a red card after elbowing Kieran Tierney in the face.

Both teams went into the game having won their opening two matches, and it was Arsenal who took the lead through Alexandre Lacazette after just 25 minutes, following an error by Andy Robertson. Mané, who was probably lucky to still be on the pitch, grabbed Liverpool's equaliser just a few minutes later, pouncing on a weak clearance by Bernd Leno from a Mo Salah shot. Robertson then made amends for gifting the Gunners their lead by converting Alexander-Arnold's centre on 34 minutes.

Arsenal had a chance to level against the run of play, with the score at 2-1, but Lacazette's feeble effort when through on goal was easily saved by Alisson. Then, with the clock ticking down, Diogo Jota, making his Anfield debut, ended all doubts as to the outcome by grabbing Liverpool's third, and his first in a red shirt, to seal a 3-1 victory.

Mikel Arteta was magnanimous in defeat, telling BBC Sport after the game: 'They are superior to us in many aspects.'

Liverpool had coped well without new signing Thiago Alcantara and captain Jordan Henderson, both out with injury. We now know that Liverpool had bigger challenges ahead, some they'd fail to overcome. But for now the defence of the championship was looking healthy.

That may or may not have been true of their army of supporters watching from home, but for now it would have to do.

Seventeen Days in Hell
Champions Hit the Rocks

September had ended on a high for Liverpool, with the Reds riding high in the league and looking forward to another pivotal month. However, as Britain entered a rain-soaked October, the country continued to creak under a tiered lockdown system and the Reds' title defence was about to face its sternest test.

After dismissing the Gunners at Anfield, Liverpool faced Mikel Arteta's side for the second time in just a few days. As expected, the Spaniard had learned a thing or two from the humbling his side had faced in the league a few days earlier, and the Reds were frustrated by a more stubborn version of Arsenal and their keeper, Leno, this time out. Klopp had chosen to make nine changes from the team that had recently beaten the Londoners so comfortably.

The game ended goalless after 90 minutes, and the Reds would once again have to try to settle a tie against the Londoners from the penalty spot. With memories of their shoot-out defeat in the Community Shield just weeks earlier no doubt fresh in the mind, Klopp's men once again failed to win the footballing equivalent of a lottery.

Adrián gave the Reds hope when he saved Mohamed Elneny's spot kick with Liverpool 3-2 up. However, the Gunners' goalkeeper, Bernd Leno, proved to be the hero of the day, saving two penalties, those of Divock Origi and Harry Wilson. That left it to Joe Willock to score the winning penalty and dump Klopp's men out of the cup.

This was the first clean sheet by an opposition goalkeeper in eight years, and there was no denying the frustration. The Reds had squandered numerous hard-earned chances created by the likes of Diogo Jota and Takumi Minamino.

Arsenal's reward would be a last-eight clash with Manchester City, in which they'd be well beaten. Meanwhile, for Liverpool it was a case of licking wounds and readying themselves for the next battle, away to Aston Villa.

Jürgen Klopp, ever the pragmatist, sounded philosophical when talking to Sky Sports: 'If there would have been a winner in 90 minutes, it should have been us, but we are not in dreamland, you have to score. I liked a lot of parts of the game, we mixed it up a lot and I saw a proper performance, a lot of things we like on the pitch when you wear this wonderful shirt. A penalty shoot-out is tricky, everyone knows. That is it.'

In truth, the boss probably wasn't too despondent at the prospect of exiting the competition. With injuries stacking up and a busy winter period not too far away, he'd have likely been relieved to see his fixture schedule lighten somewhat. For me, though, a win would have left us two games from Wembley and a chance to win another trophy. I was gutted.

If our exit from the League Cup had left me cold, just three days later an embarrassing drubbing at the hands of Aston Villa would plunge me into the deep freeze. Bad results happen in football. They always have. And the 7-2 mauling at Villa Park probably won't be the last of its kind in the club's history. I'm old enough to remember Joe Fagan's treble-winning Reds get battered 4-0 away to Coventry City in that 1983/84 season.

Perhaps it was the context: mounting injuries, the misery of lockdown restrictions or the absence of key players, but for whatever reason the result at Villa Park felt like a hammer blow, a humbling we might struggle to recover from. And, although that may have been an overreaction, it did signal that Liverpool may not have what it takes to successfully defend their title.

The BBC's Emlyn Begley described it as a 'game that defies all logic', as Ollie Watkins (hat-trick) and future Manchester City substitute Jack Grealish (2) ran riot against a hapless Liverpool defence that, while missing Alisson Becker, boasted a title-winning back four. To make matters worse, Villa had narrowly escaped relegation only the season before. The BBC's hyperbole knew no bounds, describing it as 'one of the most unbelievable scorelines in Premier League history'. It hurt because it was probably true.

This was, after all, the first time the Reds had conceded seven since 1963. It was only the fourth time they'd tasted defeat in the Premier League since 3 January 2019. Not even two goals from Mohamed Salah could save them, a result and performance Villa manager Dean Smith couldn't have imagined in his most fevered dreams.

'We never dreamed of getting a result like this,' he gleefully told the media after the game. 'The performance was outstanding from start to finish. We created an awful lot of chances against an exceptional defence and team. We had to work very hard.'

Villa were at their best and deserved their victory, but it flattered Liverpool to claim they had to work hard to achieve it. The Reds were terrible and got deservedly hammered. The result also handed the army of football pundits a new narrative, that of Liverpool's high defensive line being exploited by the opposition.

There may have been some merit to this, as the Reds struggled initially to implement this new evolution. However, anyone downing drinks every time a former player uttered the phrase 'high line' would have been well sloshed in no time.

Klopp's men would eventually master it, of course, and score many goals as a result of winning possession higher up the pitch and catching the opposition offside more than any other team in the process. Yet it never ceases to amaze me how these tropes gain traction and are repeated slavishly throughout an entire season. The endless droning on about zonal marking under Benítez is another example of this.

After the Villa rout, Jürgen Klopp was left to rue unforced errors, most notably from stand-in keeper Adrián, who had gifted Villa their first goal. He told BBC Sport:

> You have to say that Villa did very well. They were very physical, very smart and very direct, we were not. We had big chances, which we did not use, but when you concede seven, I'm not sure you can say it would have been 7-7. We made too many mistakes and massive ones obviously. It started with the first goal and around the goals we made massive mistakes.

The result skewed Liverpool's goal difference to the extent that this was their worst league start in terms of goals conceded in the opening four matches since the 1937/38 season. Perhaps proving the adage about lies, damn lies and statistics, they'd actually won three of the four league games on offer. However, this result would deliver a psychological blow and meant that Liverpool dropped from second to fifth place as they went into what would be a powder-keg game against their neighbours, Everton, on 17 October 2020, at Goodison Park.

The game ended 2-2, a result celebrated on the blue half of the city like a win. For the Reds, though, it was a match that left us enraged. The scoreline was frankly only half the story in a game that saw the Reds lose their talismanic No.4 for the rest of the season after a horror tackle by Everton keeper Jordan Pickford. The fact that Everton's No.1 didn't see red for wiping out Van Dijk is remarkable enough, but Liverpool were also denied what was a clear penalty despite Stockley Park reviewing the incident multiple times. Another brutal foul on Thiago saw Richarlison red-carded, but this was only a fraction of the controversy.

Sadio Mané put Liverpool in front after only three minutes, but it was shortly after this that Pickford decided to take out Van Dijk with a wild tackle that wouldn't be out of place in a martial arts movie. Virgil hobbled off, replaced by Joe Gomez on 11 minutes. It would be Virgil's last game of the season. The official explanation as to why Pickford wasn't immediately dismissed for such a reckless foul that clearly endangered an opponent is that VAR couldn't review it because of an earlier offside decision, an argument that only adds to the increasing absurdity of the system.

This was always going to be a tough game. Liverpool, still missing Alisson, and having suffered a damaging defeat at Villa days earlier, were facing an Everton side high on confidence. They'd won their previous seven games in all competitions under Carlo Ancelotti, with Dominic Calvert-Lewin scoring in their opening five. However, it was Michael Keane's header from a James Rodríguez corner that drew the Blues level after 19 minutes. That's the way it stayed until half-time.

Thiago was having one of his best games in a Liverpool shirt, and was running things for the Reds in midfield. In the second half it looked like the Reds were regaining some control over their nearest neighbours. Then, in the 72nd minute, a poor clearance by Yerry Mina was hammered in by Mohamed Salah. Liverpool looked back to their old selves and threatened to punish Everton further, only for Jordan Pickford to brilliantly and frustratingly save a Jöel Matip header.

It proved a significant moment for the Blues, as just minutes later Calvert-Lewin rose to head home an equaliser, in the 81st minute. Everton had miraculously managed to keep 11 men on the pitch up to now, thanks only to the vagaries of VAR, but the dismissal of Richarlison for a terrible tackle on Thiago in the 90th minute set up a frantic stoppage time.

The Reds looked to have won the game when Jordan Henderson smashed in a goal that would have broken the Blues' hearts and sent ours soaring, only for Stockley Park to once again ride to the rescue. The drawing of lines by video assistant referees is clearly more of an art than a science and, after a lengthy delay, they eventually found a part of Henderson's body offside, or was it Sadio Mané's? The media couldn't agree and the Professional Game Match Officials Limited (PGMOL) remained vague on the subject. It was, as Phil McNulty, writing for the BBC, said, 'A finish to match the chaotic nature of the game.'

Scrambling for positives and barely managing to hold down the lid on his simmering rage, Jürgen Klopp told *Match of the Day*, 'We were dominant against a flying side.' On the disallowed goal, he echoed how most people in football felt, stating, 'I don't know where the line is where you can do offside.'

We still don't know, Jürgen. Liverpool had at least steadied the ship after a horror thrashing by Villa, but the loss of Thiago for an extended period and Van Dijk for the rest of the season would ultimately prove pivotal to the Reds' title defence.

Anfield's Walking Wounded Mount Recovery
The Reds Remain in Title Hunt

As has so often been the case throughout the post-Shankly era, Europe has provided hope and salvation to Liverpool. In good times and bad, the Reds have usually found a way to thrive in UEFA competition. We have an affinity with continental football that's unrivalled in English football, and this association would once more bear fruit for us in the aftermath of that horrible October.

Klopp's men followed up the calamities at Villa Park and Goodison with a 1-0 win over Ajax in the Amsterdam Arena, before November brought a 2-0 home win over FC Midtjylland, and a 5-0 thrashing of Atalanta put them on the brink of qualification for the knockout phase of the Champions League. The run in Europe also seemed to help Liverpool regain their footing in domestic competition. Victories over Sheffield United (2-1), West Ham (2-1) and a creditable 1-1 draw with Manchester City at the Etihad did much to lift the gloom.

Bizarrely, the victory over Sheffield United had seen Liverpool move level on points with league leaders Everton. Now that probably sounds incredible, especially given the Blues' recent struggles. These were strange days indeed.

A similar scoreline against West Ham a week later put the Reds top, which somewhat masked the fact that they'd now conceded 27 goals in 14 games since becoming champions. There were ominous signs – for those who cared to see them – that Liverpool may not have what it takes to retain their title. I didn't see them. Maybe I just didn't want to.

Many would see the point won at City as a missed opportunity, especially given the fact that the Reds had taken the lead through a Mohamed Salah penalty after just 13 minutes. I was happy to take it, especially as Kevin De Bruyne had squandered the chance to put City in front from the penalty spot.

Klopp, it seemed, was starting to see those ominous signs, and his frequent comments about the demands of a packed season were seized upon by pundits and rival fans alike as evidence of the German moaning and looking for excuses. Jürgen had been arguing for the introduction of a five substitutes rule for some time. This would allow managers to rotate players to a greater extent during games, easing the impact of fixture congestion. Of course, clubs with smaller squads would argue that this gave the 'big clubs' an unfair advantage. For his part, Pep Guardiola claimed that the failure of the Premier League to introduce the rule was a 'disaster'.

As if justifying the cases put forward by both men, the game against City saw Liverpool suffer another significant injury, with Trent Alexander-Arnold leaving the pitch late in the game with a calf injury. The Reds' already porous defence had been weakened still further.

When Liverpool lined up against Leicester City at Anfield on 22 November they did so minus the talents of Jordan Henderson, Virgil van Dijk, Trent Alexander-Arnold and Mohamed Salah (rested). That meant veteran James Milner as captain and Fabinho in the centre of defence. Still, looking at a front three of Firmino, Mané and Jota, I had enough confidence that the Reds could outscore their opponents. In the end Klopp's men would be perfect in both defence and attack, winning 3-0 and making a mockery of Brendan Rodgers's 100 per cent away record.

Diogo Jota became the first player in the club's history to score in his first four appearances at Anfield, adding to a Johnny Evans own goal and a Roberto Firmino strike. In doing so Jota helped send Liverpool back to the top of the table, joining Tottenham, who were the latest of the also-rans to fleetingly ascend to the summit.

Jürgen Klopp, speaking to Sky Sports, expressed his satisfaction with the Reds' performance:

> We deserved it 100 per cent and the boys played an incredible game against a top, top opponent. Playing like we did tonight, I don't take this for granted. The boys were on fire, football-

wise, played and played and played. Jamie Vardy was much deeper than even last season, so that made it more tricky, as we had to bring Gini into possession as well. How the whole team defended from the front was incredible. We should've scored more goals, and that's a top sign for a good game.

Klopp's Liverpool were now undefeated in the league at Anfield since April 2017, an achievement that eclipsed a record set by Bob Paisley's Liverpool in the 70s and early 80s. The Reds were continuing to make a mockery of their injury crisis and defensive woes. And, where other managers would use such challenges as an excuse, Jürgen Klopp was finding ways to overcome them.

Crisis, what crisis?

Liverpool 4-0 Wolves
Emotion and Reverie as Supporters Trickle Back to the Terraces
With the final whistle blown and the players trudging towards the tunnel, having shown their appreciation to the supporters on the Kop, a grinning Jürgen Klopp made his way to that famous old terrace.

The sound of the applause grew, and shouts of approval filled the cold night air. We all knew what was coming, we'd waited so long to see it, and with great smiles on our faces we greeted each fist pump with a giant roar. The boss touched his hand to his heart and signalled his delight that this communion had finally returned.

It was the perfect end to a magical evening in L4, lit up by a few fine performances and, of course, four goals. However, it was our return to our spiritual home, Anfield, after so long away that would dominate our thoughts as we made our way home in the cold night air. No wonder that Klopp would describe the game as a 'goosebumps moment', and the sound of George Sephton playing the song 'Oh Happy Day' by Edwin Hawkins couldn't have been more pertinent.

This was, of course, Liverpool's first game in front of supporters since the Premier League went into lockdown several months earlier. It felt momentous and the first step on a long road back to normality. Whatever that means.

Yet earlier, with barely an hour to go before kick-off, Anfield's streets were a bleak affair, save for the flicker of Christmas lights dancing in the windows of Skerries Road. The sight of Homebaked with its storefront shuttered and The Park pub standing silent and lonely on Walton Breck Road were dark reminders that this was no ordinary matchday.

On flagpole corner, where the Kop meets the Sir Kenny Dalglish Stand, a solitary stall selling scarves and badges had been erected, and in the faint glow of the turnstiles a small group of Kopites had assembled, clutching not their season tickets or fan cards but their mobile phones as they waited for stewards brandishing thermometers to carry out temperature checks. It was yet another reminder that, although we may have been climbing out of the Covid nightmare, we were merely at the foothills of our ascent.

The arrival of December had brought with it the country's first vaccines, and despite the shrieks of anti-vax protests and a wave of social media posts, memes and videos that mixed legitimate questions about the safety of this new inoculation with wild conspiracy theories that – as I've mentioned – sometimes involved Bill Gates and microchips, the vast majority of us rushed to be inoculated.

On the national scene the prime minister was expressing confidence in a home secretary facing allegations of bullying. Meanwhile, locally the news had been dominated by the arrest of the Liverpool mayor on charges of conspiracy to commit bribery and witness intimidation. Both denied the charges, of course.

As I wandered around the ground, taking in the old haunts, the Shankly statue, the Hillsborough Memorial and Anfield Road, before finally completing my circuit of the stadium, it was hard to escape the conclusion that society was a creaking wreck that could come crashing down around our ears at any moment. We were all hanging on for dear life, and against that backdrop it seemed strange that something as comparatively trivial as a football match could provide a degree of comfort and relief. Yet that's exactly how it felt.

I remembered those conversations in the Cabbage Hall pub, when the nagging voices at the back of our minds, telling us that our lives were about to change irrevocably, were at their loudest, and the only concern we had was whether a potential league title would be stolen from under our noses by a bloody virus. That was obviously naive, but it spoke to how important football had been then and still was.

It all seemed like an eternity ago to me on that cold December night in Anfield as I passed through the turnstile. There was no quietening the excitement in my belly. Like many of us, after nine months – 270 days, or thereabouts – without going to the game, I'd buried the longing deep down, convinced myself that I could find joy in watching the Reds from my couch and settled into the now clichéd 'new normal'.

But that had all been a lie. Denial is so often the first stage of grieving, and as I passed through that turnstile and on to the concourse, leaving behind the gloom of the streets outside, I felt a wave of emotion. I realised that, despite my attempts at optimism, the fear that this day would never arrive hadn't been completely vanquished. What I was feeling was joy, but mostly relief.

The brightness of the concourse and the staircase to Block 207 were calling me home. This was Anfield, not as I'd come to know it, for sure. But it was still our place, and it had never looked or felt better.

Liverpool's form had been indifferent in the lead-up to this game. They'd followed up a disappointing 2-0 home defeat to Atalanta in the Champions League with a frustrating 1-1 draw with Brighton at the Amex, in which Jürgen Klopp raged at TV broadcasters, demanded the introduction of five substitutes and referred to his opposite number, Graham Potter, as selfish.

Liverpool had dropped two points after Diogo Jota had put them in front, thanks to a 93rd-minute penalty awarded by VAR against Andy Robertson, for reasons only apparent to Stockley Park. To be fair to the boss, we were all raging. It was the softest of penalties that only a man in front of a TV screen searching for a moment to make himself relevant could award.

A 1-0 victory over Ajax on 1 December provided a crumb of comfort and the prospect of floodlit European nights at Anfield. As I gazed out across the lush turf and awaited the arrival of the teams, it was enough to make my heart soar.

Supporters had each been given a scheduled time to arrive so that meant many of us were in early to greet the players as they ran out to warm up, just like the old days. When the goalkeepers and their coaches appeared in front of us, they were practically blown over by rapturous applause. The roars of approval were so loud they made a mockery of the socially distanced gaps on the Kop and the swathes of empty seats in the remaining two thirds of the ground.

With so many local postcodes represented in those red seats, this was also a time for in-jokes of a more local flavour. 'Free the Lobster Pot One!' shouted one Kopite, a reference to Liverpool's embattled mayor, who was 'cooperating with the police', and his apparent love of a chippy tea. But it would be a chant of 'bring on the champions!' that would send a shiver down the spines of everyone in that old stand and all those watching from afar. How long we had waited to sing that, our pain extended long into a new season. To bellow that out from the Kop, finally, after 30 years of waiting, was a small reward for our patience.

For all the pain and grief of the previous nine months, the Kop could breathe again. And although we were just 2,000 strong, you'd have had to go back a long way to hear our anthem sung with more passion and joy.

This was once more a makeshift Liverpool squad, a team selection made from necessity but, as it turned out, no less effective than the one that marched to an unassailable lead in the previous campaign. No doubt our presence played a part in that.

The frequent applause and shouts of appreciation for the likes of Neco Williams were in stark contrast to the noise dished out by the anonymous keyboard crowd on social media. And, as the young lad jogged off the pitch in the second half, he turned to acknowledge his admirers. He looked like he'd grown a few inches in stature. I'm sure he felt the same.

In goal, Klopp had opted once more for Caoimhín Kelleher. Against Ajax five days earlier he'd been in inspired form, and here he showed he was no one-hit wonder. He may not have been called into action often, but whenever he was needed he rose to the occasion magnificently. Chants of 'Ireland's number one' would one day prove to be prophetic.

However, it was on the half-hour mark that the crowd showed the football world and one player in particular what we'd been missing. The Kop's rendition of 'Si Señor', an ode to Bobby Firmino, was as emotional as it was enduring.

We may say that football without fans is nothing, and we're right to do so, but it's worse than that. Without our songs, our flags and banners, football had been a soulless affair. The game against Wolves may have marked a new beginning but was also, mercifully, the end of a kind of zombie football, with its canned crowd noise and empty seats.

This had been a Liverpool team full of heroes. Yet they'd been reduced to rubble in the wake of behind-closed-doors action that barely got the pulse racing. Now they seemed energised, rebuilt. Not since the days of the 60s and the 70s has the power of the collective been so evident at Anfield.

Missing a host of superstars, including a £75m defender and a £65m goalkeeper, they somehow grew closer together. Liverpool under Klopp were at times more than resilient, they were anti-fragile. Klopp teams on occasion do not simply withstand pressure, they seem to grow stronger under it. But at least some of that power has always come from the relationship and bond with the crowd.

The Reds survived a penalty appeal when a VAR review overturned the initial decision to award the visitors a spot kick for handball. Then, magically, gloriously, Mohamed Salah opened the scoring for Liverpool in the 24th minute. We drank that goal in, and time seemed to be racing by.

Georginio Wijnaldum added a second close to the hour mark. It was a great strike from the edge of the box and in front of the Kop. They kept going, but, in truth, Wolves' fate had been sealed as that shot rippled the net. Then, Jöel Matip, absent for so long and plagued by a series of injuries, rose to head home a brilliant Salah cross, claiming Liverpool's third and bellowing his joy at us as he celebrated his goal like it had just won us the title.

The evening was rounded off with a Nélson Semedo own goal in the 78th minute. Trent Alexander-Arnold, on for his more-than-able deputy, Williams, picked up a pass from Curtis Jones and raced down Liverpool's right flank. Mané charged into the box and Trent spotted him, before whipping in a perfect ball. The resultant chaos in the Wolves defence saw the hapless Semedo poke the ball past his own keeper. It was a goal that guaranteed smiles on every face as we filed out of the light of Anfield and into the gloom of the streets beyond.

This was a performance that would warm us all through the days and nights to come. How apt that once again George Sephton, whose voice has been the soundtrack to so many great days and nights as a Kopite, should find the most fitting of swansongs for the game. George's musical selections are sometimes controversial, occasionally acerbic, but always on point. After the magic of the Barcelona fightback, he chose Lennon's 'Imagine'. That was a masterstroke, but his playing of 'All Things Must Pass' as 2,000 of us filed out of the ground, marshalled by hi-vis Covid stewards, seemed to capture the Anfield *zeitgeist* to perfection.

The scoreline of 4-0 was the least Liverpool deserved for a night of endeavour, grit and sheer bloody-mindedness. With Klopp's men continuing to show undiscovered depths of endurance and belief, I left in search of a taxi home, wondering just how far this team could go in a season that had so far proven something of an anticlimax.

Reds Mourn the Death of Gérard Houllier
One of Liverpool's Truly Great Managers

On 14 December 2020, Liverpool bid a final farewell to former manager Gérard Houllier, a man who has more than earned his place among the pantheon of great Liverpool managers.

Whenever I think of the Frenchman, my mind inevitably drifts back to one summer in 2001 and the incredible season that preceded it. It was and remains one of the greatest campaigns I've ever witnessed as a Liverpool supporter, and I'll be forever grateful to the man who made it so. Come with me as I relive that glorious campaign.

It's Sunday, 20 May 2001, in Liverpool. The summer sun beats down on the thousands of faces gathered at the junction between Queens Drive and Prescott Road. Hundreds of thousands have lined the streets of the city, to celebrate Liverpool Football Club's return to trophy glory.

Just 24 hours earlier the Reds had thumped Charlton Athletic 4-0 at The Valley. That win would be enough to clinch third spot and a place in the Champions League the following season. It signalled the club's return to Europe's top table for the first time since the 1980s. However, for the multitude who have turned out to see their heroes take a well-earned trip on an open-top bus, the Champions League is just a bonus in what had been an incredible season.

The Reds, having won two cups in the 1990s – their last coming six years earlier in 1995 – had just won three trophies in the first season of the noughties.

As I strain my neck to catch a glimpse of the bus, emblazoned with the words 'Tell Yer Ma We Did It!' along with those three shiny pieces of silverware, I feel like my city and my team is on the cusp of another incredible era of footballing excellence.

The Reds had played a mammoth 63 games in what was a gruelling season. They'd played every game of every competition entered, and they'd emerged with the League Cup, the FA Cup and the UEFA Cup. Only the league title itself had eluded them. There was more to follow too, with the European Super Cup and a Charity Shield making it five trophies in a single calendar year.

By any standard, the Frenchman had delivered an epoch-defining season. And, in the May sunshine of 2001, as far as I and countless Liverpool supporters were concerned, he could do no wrong.

This was Houllier's second full season in charge. He'd joined the club as joint manager alongside Roy Evans, in 1998. That partnership failed, perhaps predictably, and, in the November, Roy resigned, leaving Gérard in sole charge. He dispensed with the likes of Paul Ince, David James, Steve Harkness, Rob Jones and Jason McAteer. The Frenchman's transfer activity would have broken social media, if it had existed back then, as he proceeded to bring in eight new players.

Sami Hyypiä, Dietmar Hamann, Stéphane Henchoz, Vladimír Šmicer, Sander Westerveld, Titi Camara, Erik Meijer and Djimi Traoré all arrived as Houllier began to reshape the squad. There was also an overhaul of Melwood. The modernisation of the club was in full swing, with players given new rules on discipline and diet.

There was further progress the following year with Liverpool climbing to fourth place in the league table. And the manager would add further talent to an already improving squad – Markus Babbel, Nicky Barmby, Pegguy Arphexad, Grégory Vignal, Emile Heskey, Gary McAllister, Igor Biščan and Christian Ziege all arriving at Melwood in a continuous revolution. The departures of David Thompson, Phil Babb, Dominic Matteo, Steve Staunton, Brad Friedel and Stig Inge Bjørnebye ensured a paltry net spend of just £5m and brought a degree of balance to the wage bill.

The arrival of Barmby drew great hostility from across Stanley Park, as this was the first direct transfer between Everton and Liverpool in decades. When Walter Smith – the Blues boss – revealed that Barmby had agitated for a move to the Reds – Everton fans chanted 'Nicky die!' and daubed graffiti on walls around the city, declaring their rage at the transfer. Houllier, who perhaps should have better understood the city's culture, having worked as a schoolteacher here in the 1960s, joked that he didn't understand the reaction of Everton fans. After all, he said, 'He hasn't changed his religion.'

That may have been true, but, as far as any Blue was concerned, he'd done something much worse. Barmby, along with fellow signing Gary McAllister, would go on to heap even more misery on Evertonians during this season. But more about that later.

The stage was now set for a momentous campaign. Gérard Houllier, alongside his assistant Phil Thompson, was about to lead Liverpool into one of the most remarkable seasons in the club's history.

Among the highlights of that season was the return of the full-blooded derby encounter, in which the games became a throwback to the old days, full of skill, passion, flying tackles, blood and thunder. And the first encounter of the season at Anfield epitomised that above all. The *Liverpool Echo*, under the headline 'DERBIES AREN'T MEANT TO BE LIKE THIS', had this to say:

> Amid the frenzied atmosphere and tension, creativity is usually stifled, and raw aggression wins the derby day. But this was a superb spectacle in which both sides played their part to produce a quality yet hugely passionate game of football.

The Reds were a little tentative to start with and gifted Everton a host of chances, which they squandered, before Liverpool settled into their stride. By the 12th minute the atmosphere in the stands was at boiling point. Barmby, understandably, became the target of blue ire. Amid the crescendo of songs, cries of Judas could be heard. As if egged on by the travelling support, Mark Pembridge threw himself into a lunging late tackle on his former team-mate, earning himself a yellow card in the process. The home crowd growled, and the red majority responded in kind. A huge chant of 'blue-and-white shite!' filled the air, before Barmby provided the perfect answer to his detractors, heading in a cross-come-shot from Christian Ziege.

The goal detonated an explosion in the Kop and a shock wave of frenzied celebration travelled around all four corners of the ground, causing scenes of jubilation among the Reds, and striking the Blues mute. Barmby celebrated it like a title win. The Reds ran out 3-1 winners after Kevin Campbell had briefly given the away fans hope.

Liverpool had risen to third in the league, while the Blues had slumped to 14th. The season was just getting started, though.

Houllier would lead his men to their first cup final since 1996, when the club reached the final of the Worthington Cup (Football League Cup), where they'd meet Birmingham City on 25 February 2001. And, as Wembley was being rebuilt, the tie would be held at Cardiff's Millennium Stadium.

The game exploded when Robbie Fowler unleashed a delightful shot from distance that put Liverpool in front on 30 minutes. However, Liverpool failed to build on their lead and paid the price when Darren Purse levelled at the death.

Extra time failed to separate the teams, and if Liverpool were to clinch their first trophy in six years, they'd have to win a penalty shoot-out. They hit a perfect five, while Birmingham squandered one of theirs. Houllier had delivered his first trophy and the stage was now set for a historic run-in.

March saw Liverpool reach the semi-finals of the UEFA Cup and FA Cup with victories over Porto and Tranmere Rovers respectively. Wycombe Wanderers were edged out 2-1 in a surprisingly tight FA Cup semi-final at Villa Park, with all three goals coming in the final 12 minutes of the game. The Reds took a 2-0 lead before Wycombe made for a tense finale, grabbing a late consolation in the 88th minute. Houllier had led his players to their second final of the season.

Three days earlier Liverpool had left the Camp Nou with a creditable goalless draw in the first leg of the UEFA Cup semi-final. Now it was back to Anfield for an emotional and incredibly tense encounter, which saw a Gary McAllister penalty beat future Reds keeper Pepe Reina, and send Houllier and Liverpool to their third final of the season.

However, the prelude to that momentous European night at Anfield would see Houllier's men duke it out with Everton, at Goodison Park, in one of the greatest derbies of all time. With Liverpool's hopes of a

Champions League place still in the balance, they couldn't afford to drop points to their arch-rivals.

In a rancorous match, played close to the anniversary of the Hillsborough disaster, with emotions raw and the game boiling, Gary McAllister became an immortal. It was level at 2-2 as the game went into injury time. It looked for all the world like the Reds would fall short. Then a young Frenchman named Grégory Vignal made a surging run into the Everton half, drawing a tackle and winning a free kick more than 30 yards from goal. McAllister lined up the free kick, stealing several yards in the process. Still, the ball seemed too far out to trouble the Blues' goal.

Then the wily midfielder appeared to indicate that he was going to cross it, as he had earlier in the game. Everton's entire back line fell for the trick. But instead of curling a pass into the box, McAllister shot low and hard from distance. It flew into the net like a rocket. The Liverpool end could scarcely believe what they'd seen.

The Reds' bench erupted on to the pitch, and the look of sheer disbelief on Houllier's face spoke volumes. Liverpool had won the game 3-2 and broken blue hearts in the process. There's no better way to win a derby, and it would send Liverpool into their semi-final showdown with the Catalan giants in fine fettle.

Nothing said 'big time' quite like the visit of Barcelona to Anfield. After years in the wilderness the Reds were back, and the stadium sizzled. After holding the Spaniards to a goalless first leg at the Camp Nou, the stage was set for a nerve-shredding evening.

The Reds took the lead thanks to a Gary McAllister penalty on the stroke of half-time. The game stands out in my mind as one of those moments when you knew, you just knew that the club was on the brink of something truly magical, and I recall the celebrations at full time vividly. Of course, the game also featured a Pep and a Pepe, two men who would go on to have significant roles in Liverpool's future.

Pep Guardiola would become Moriarty to Jürgen Klopp's Holmes, and Pepe Reina would replace the hero of Istanbul, Jerzy Dudek, becoming Rafa Benítez's No.1 at Anfield for eight years. However, both would trudge from the Anfield soil as vanquished souls that night.

If you're a Liverpool supporter and you're planning to watch a replay of the 2001 FA Cup Final against Arsène Wenger's Arsenal, my advice would be to fast-forward through the first 75 minutes. There's frankly nothing in the first three quarters of that game for Liverpool fans to enjoy. Arsenal were totally dominant and deserved more than their 1-0 lead.

However, Michael Owen had other ideas. Many of us have mixed views on Owen these days. His decision to leave Liverpool for Madrid, then snub us for Newcastle before joining Manchester United means he'll always be judged harshly by Reds. However, there's no denying he won the cup for Liverpool that day, all on his own. It was daylight robbery but who cared. The Reds had secured a domestic double. However, there was no time for the players to celebrate. They had a UEFA Cup to win just four days later.

The final against Alavés, at Borussia Dortmund's Westfalenstadion, has gone down in history as the greatest UEFA Cup Final of all time. Alavés were a tiny Spanish team. In comparison to Liverpool's pedigree, they were European minnows. Yet they gave the Reds a huge fight.

At half-time Liverpool were 3-1 up and, in commentary, Alan Hansen compared them to a pub team. They were anything but. In an eerie foreshadowing of the Reds' comeback at Istanbul four years later, the Spaniards were level within six minutes of the restart.

With just over an hour gone, Houllier rolled the dice, bringing on Robbie Fowler for Emile Heskey. The Scouse marksman made an immediate impact, forcing Alavés back and giving their defenders no time to think. Then, just nine minutes later he scored the Reds' fourth.

However, the Spaniards wouldn't lie down easily, and in the 89th minute, Jordi Cruyff drew Alavés level. Extra time beckoned and the spectre of the golden goal hung over both sides.

Houllier had been a vocal opponent of the new rule change that meant whoever scored first in added time won the game. He could have no complaints, however, when a Gary McAllister free kick was diverted into the Spaniards' goal by Delfi Geli in the 117th minute.

A historic treble had been won. In just four days' time, the Reds would seal Champions League football with that win at Charlton Athletic, setting up an epic homecoming. We'd waited six years for a trophy and Gérard Houllier had delivered three and the promise of Champions League in the coming season.

I can't help but feel a tinge of sadness that Houllier's legacy isn't celebrated more today. To me, he'll always be a significant figure in the history of our club, and he deserves to take his place among the pantheon of great Liverpool managers.

That banner on the Kop, the one we call the Scouse Mount Rushmore, it has Shankly, Paisley, Fagan, Dalglish, Rafa and Klopp on it. Well, it has one missing. Instead of a super six, it should be displaying a magnificent seven, with the Frenchman taking his rightful place alongside Liverpool's greatest managers.

Rest in Peace, Gérard.

Mourinho Fuming and Hodgson Crushed
Reds Dispatch Spurs and Palace to Claim Top Spot

With the disappointment of two points squandered to Fulham behind them – thanks in no small measure to another VAR debacle – Liverpool looked to the visit of Jose Mourinho's Tottenham and a trip to Selhurst Park for a chance of redemption. Neither could be described as 'gimmes', especially heading into deep winter with a casualty list that brought a tear to the eye, and facing the kind of Christmas fixture congestion I've grown up loving but Europeans struggle to understand.

The Spurs game offered a chance to remember a fallen former manager, and the Palace game pitted us against one we'd sooner forget. Gérard Houllier was honoured before kick-off at Anfield on 16 December, with a mural on the Kop designed by the brilliant Andy Knott, architect of so many wonderful displays down the years. Just three days later, at Crystal Palace, Roy Hodgson would cut a dejected figure as his side was trounced by a Liverpool team he could never hope to have built.

Liverpool and Mourinho's Tottenham were vying for supremacy at the top of the table, and a win for the Reds would leapfrog them into top spot. And, with football continuing its tentative steps out of the pandemic restrictions, there were 2,000 Liverpool supporters in the ground to cheer them on.

Liverpool took the lead on 26 minutes through Mo Salah, who'd become the Reds top scorer in Europe a week earlier with a strike against FC Midtjylland, eclipsing former captain and talisman Steven Gerrard in the process. However, Son Heung-min's equaliser just after the half-hour mark dampened the spirits a little and set up a tense encounter with the Londoners, whose battle plan under their Portuguese manager was typically one based on the counter-attack.

Liverpool had controlled the game for the most part, but Spurs would leave Anfield ruing two glorious opportunities that should have broken the hearts of those 2,000 supporters on the Kop. First, Steven Bergwijn hit the post with a fierce shot that cannoned back into the danger area, only for Curtis Jones to clear it over his own bar. Then it was Harry Kane who came close to sealing a win for Spurs. However, it was the irrepressible Bobby Firmino, heading in a corner from Andrew Robertson in the 90th minute, that sent those supporters home with a smile on their faces, and the Reds back to the top of the league.

Liverpool had won the game without turning to their bench for reinforcements for the first time since Gérard Houllier's last game as manager on 15 May 2004. That's 908 games. Quite a stat, given Jürgen's demands for a five-substitute rule, and the backdrop to the game.

Klopp celebrated Liverpool's winner as you'd expect him to, with all the zeal of a kid on Christmas morning. He'd spent the game remonstrating with his players, the referee and presumably the gods of football, who'd forsaken him time and again this season. When Firmino headed home the winner at the death, the resultant release of emotion looked like relief bordering on exultant joy, edging close to fury.

Jose Mourinho wasn't happy. Obviously, he'd never let his emotions get the better of him in the technical area. He told Klopp that 'the better team lost', and Jürgen respectfully disagreed.

On 19 December, Liverpool travelled to the capital to face Roy Hodgson's Crystal Palace. Hodgson is to Liverpool fans what Voldemort is to Harry Potter and the Hogwarts gang – he who must not be named. I've got mates are in denial as to whether he ever managed Liverpool at all. For them, his brief reign at Anfield has been airbrushed from history. For me, I still shiver when I think of those days, but mostly I feel pity for the man. He simply should never have been put in that position; he was hopelessly out of his depth at Liverpool.

That turned out to be an apt description of his Crystal Palace team when Liverpool came to town. We now know that the Reds were flattering to deceive when they pummelled Palace 7-0 that day, but when they left the pitch they looked every inch a team capable of retaining the league title.

Palace fans may have been grateful that with London in Tier 3 Covid-19 restrictions, none of them were allowed in the arena to witness their gladiators thrown to the lions. Only the players' cheers, echoing around empty plastic seats, greeted the seven goals Liverpool scored, but I enjoyed the display from my armchair, nonetheless. This, after all, was a Premier League record win (because results secured before 1992 don't count).

Klopp, though, claimed not to be satisfied and felt his charges could have performed better. No doubt. They'd barely got out of second gear. The record books will show that Takumi Minamino, Sadio Mané, Roberto Firmino (2), Jordan Henderson, Mohamed Salah (2) were the goalscorers, but there was so much more to this display than that. Liverpool were at times so comfortable that they could have sent their keeper for the paper and still kept a clean sheet.

It was a performance that would make a mockery of what was to come over the festive period. Nevertheless, the Reds would now spend Christmas Day on top of the table for the third time in successive seasons. And, when Gary Lineker tweeted 'Liverpool go top of the league, and they might just stay there', I agreed with him. How foolish we both were.

Roy Keane's 'Bad Champions' Jibes
Reds Face Months of Purgatory

Liverpool supporters throughout the land got ready for a socially distanced festive period, still basking in the afterglow of that demolition job in London. For me, it was a case of counting blessings. Yes, the country was a shambles, ravaged by a pandemic and run by the political equivalent of the Three Stooges. But the Reds were top of the league, the family and I were healthy – if a little traumatised – the fridge was well stocked, the Christmas decorations were up and, despite the restrictions imposed on everybody but Boris Johnson and his acolytes, I was determined to make the most of it.

It was at this point in their campaign that Liverpool decided to press the self-destruct button. That's probably a little unfair; they were after all carrying injuries, and maybe the season just caught up with them. Whatever it was, the fall-off from that victory over Crystal Palace was remarkable. The Reds were unrecognisable over the Christmas period and would plummet new depths in the New Year.

A sloppy display that bordered on the criminal saw Liverpool throw away three points at home to West Brom on 27 December. After Sadio Mané had put them in front after just 12 minutes, we could all be forgiven for thinking that we were in for a comfortable evening. However, a combination of Sam Allardyce's team sitting deep to frustrate Liverpool, sometimes playing six at the back, and some terrible passing by the Reds meant the Baggies were able to stay in the game far longer than they should have.

When the inevitable equaliser came, it was less disappointing than it was infuriating. Klopp fumed, at his opposite number and at the profligate nature of his own players' approach to the game. They then followed that up with a turgid display and a goalless draw at Newcastle on 30 December, guaranteeing a miserable New Year for us all.

With players of many teams going down with Covid and games being cancelled, Liverpool had squandered a chance to tighten their grip on the title. They were still top but there were ominous signs now that all was not right.

Despite the hope of the vaccine, the country was still struggling. And, with areas of the country seeing rising levels of infection and games being cancelled, some, like Steve Bruce, were claiming the season should be halted, and that it was 'immoral' to continue. Jose Mourinho raged when his Spurs side's game against Fulham was called off just three hours before kick-off, due to an outbreak of the virus.

With 2020 finally over, the Reds travelled to St Mary's on 4 January 4 2021 to take on Southampton. Thiago Alcantara made his first start since October, after that reckless Richarlison tackle put him out of action. He could do little to lift the Reds, and Klopp's men faltered again. To add insult to injury, it was a former Liverpool striker, Danny Ings, who applied the killer blow after just two minutes. Liverpool had no reply.

With players looking decidedly jaded and with the squad struggling with infections and injuries, the risk of descending into a spiral from which we couldn't escape felt very real. Then came some semblance of salvation in the form of the FA Cup. It would prove short-lived but, in the circumstances, we were happy to take it.

With the team crying out for reinforcements, Liverpool ended an extended January transfer window with the addition of Ben Davies from Preston North End for a fee of £1.6m, and a loan deal that saw Ozan Kabak arrive from Schalke 04. To many of us that seemed negligent in the extreme, and it was hard to see this patched-up squad mounting a serious challenge for honours this year.

Once more, Liverpool, it seemed, had failed to capitalise on the success of the previous campaign, and if they were going to achieve anything this season, they'd need every ounce of reserves they had in the squad, Klopp's genius and, of course – particularly at home – the crowd. However, they'd have to manage with just two out of the three. The results would be almost catastrophic.

Across the Atlantic, just two days before Liverpool travelled to Villa Park in the FA Cup, I and many others were transfixed by images streaming in from Washington as an angry mob, seemingly egged on by Donald Trump, attempted to mount an insurrection. Men and women erected gallows outside Capitol Hill, occupied America's seat of power for hours and, in doing so, exposed the fragility of democracy. We were, and still are, living through strange times and it was difficult to escape the feeling of collapse and existential threat.

At times like this, football seems trivial, yet it still dominates my thoughts. Stubbornly it competes for my attention, governs my moods and is both exhilarating and exhausting in equal measure. As Liverpool entered a new decade, it was one of a shrinking list of pleasurable distractions in my life, and it was doing a poor job.

In what was becoming a rare respite, Liverpool dispatched Villa comfortably, 4-1. In doing so, they set up a fourth-round tie with Manchester United in a little over two weeks. The scorers at Villa Park were Sadio Mané (2), Georginio Wijnaldum and Mohamed Salah. It was a win that lifted spirits, but it would be short-lived.

In a run that extended from December 2020 to April 2021, Liverpool suffered nine defeats in 17 games, including six consecutive defeats at Anfield. Think about that, six times in a row a visiting team left Anfield with all three points. When I look back on that now, I can still barely believe it. It was unprecedented.

If ever anyone needed proof of the power of that bond between the 'holy trinity' that Shankly spoke of – the players, the manager and the supporters – then look no further than that almost four-month spell when supporters were no longer able to add their fire to the mix. During this epic collapse, Liverpool fell from fifth in the table, were dumped out of the FA Cup, having already exited the League Cup, lost to Everton at home for the first time since 1999 and, after losing away to Real Madrid, stood on the brink of leaving the Champions League too.

To rub salt into gaping wounds, an almost gleeful Roy Keane – or as close to gleeful as his expressions allow – goaded Reds everywhere, stating that Liverpool had been 'bad champions'. We would, of course, later get the chance to ram those words right back down his throat, but during that horrific run of games, they felt fair, and they hurt.

Farewell to the Saint as Klopp's Spring Offensive Captures Europe

Liverpool FC March–May 2021

Reds Bid Farewell to Liverpool Legend

Ian St John

On 1 March 2021, Liverpool Football Club lost one of its most legendary and iconic footballers, the irrepressible and truly magnificent Ian St John. The Saint's character and attitude represented everything good about the Shankly era, and it was everything Liverpool needed today, as they plotted a road back to Europe. This is his story.

We're at Easter Road, Edinburgh. It's mid-August and the year is 1959. A young, fresh-faced lad named Ian St John, 21 years of age, standing barely 5ft 7in in his boots and weighing 10st 4lb, is about to make Scottish football history … in the space of just 150 seconds, he blasts three goals past his opponents, Hibernian. It remains Scotland's fastest hat-trick.

The son of a steelworker, Alex, who died when Ian was just six years of age, St John had no ambition to follow his father into the industry. He loved sport, mainly football, but he was also a keen boxer. Despite his diminutive frame, St John could pack a punch as hard as rock, something many opponents discovered to their cost. However, his mother wasn't too keen on her boy pursuing a career in the ring, and Ian reluctantly took up an apprenticeship in engineering. He hated it.

Grabbing every opportunity he could to take to the pitch, the youngster turned out for various works' teams before joining his boyhood favourites, Motherwell, in 1956 as an apprentice. He was immediately loaned out to a feeder club named Douglas Water Thistle, and eventually signed a professional contract with The Well a year later.

Part of a cluster of talented young players managed by the legendary Scot Bobby Ancell, and known as the 'Ancell Babes', St John stood out. He was prolific in front of goal, scoring 105 goals in 144 appearances in all competitions. By 1961 he'd attracted the interest of Bill Shankly at Liverpool FC. Shanks fought tooth and nail to persuade the board at Anfield to pay a record £37,500 for the Scot, beating off competition from Newcastle.

Shankly told club moneyman Eric Sawyer that St John wasn't just a good striker, but the only striker in the game. The club couldn't afford not to buy him, he argued. His faith was immediately repaid when St John scored a hat-trick on his debut in the Liverpool Senior Cup Final against Everton. The Reds lost the game 4-3, but the Saint, as he would become known to countless Liverpudlians, had now established his reputation south of the border.

The capture of St John and fellow Scottish footballer Ron Yeats would prove to be pivotal in transforming Liverpool into a genuine force in English football. Ian even had a hand in the club's move to an all-red kit in 1964. Prior to this, Liverpool had played in red shirts, white shorts, and white socks topped with a red stripe. Shankly believed that the colour of the Liverpool shirt had a psychological impact on the opposition; he thought red spelled danger and power, and wanted to change the club's white shorts to match.

Summoning Yeats to his office, he asked the giant defender to model the new strip and immediately told him, 'Christ, lad, you look ten feet tall.' Liverpool then lined up against the Belgian champions, Anderlecht, wearing red shirts with matching shorts and white socks in the European Cup first-round, first-leg tie at Anfield on 25 November.

It was St John who later suggested that the socks should also match the rest of the strip, and so it came to pass that on 16 December 1964, in the second leg in Belgium, Liverpool wore all red for the first time.

It's almost impossible to overstate Ian St John's contribution to Liverpool's emergence from the second tier of English football and subsequent conquest of it. He made 40 league appearances during the club's promotion push in 1961/62, scoring 18 times. His 21 league goals powered Liverpool to the league title in 1964, and perhaps his greatest moment in a red shirt came in the 1965 FA Cup Final.

Liverpool had never won the cup. They'd failed to win a final on two occasions. In 1914 they succumbed to a single Burnley goal, and in 1950 they lost 2-0 to Arsenal. It was a running sore on the red half of Merseyside, and Evertonians, who'd seen their team triumph in the competition on two occasions, loved to pick at that particular scab.

Shankly said it was a 'disgrace' that a team like Liverpool had never won the cup, and he promised the board that the signing of St John would deliver the much-coveted trophy to Anfield.

Liverpool eventually reached another final, this time against Leeds, on 1 May 1965. With the game goalless at full time, the stage was set for St John to fulfil his manager's promise in spectacular style.

Liverpool went 1-0 up in the 93rd minute through Roger Hunt, before Billy Bremner levelled for United seven minutes later. Then, with just three minutes remaining, a delightful interplay between Tommy Smith and Ian Callaghan saw the latter race to the line and whip in a brilliant cross. In a moment replayed many times in the minds of all who were there, time seemed to stand still as St John rose to head home the winner and finally bring the FA Cup to Anfield.

Shankly loved St John and the feeling was mutual. The pair had almost a father-son relationship for much of the player's time at the club. His admiration for his boss is evident in interviews he gave to cameras years later, with one featured on LFCTV appearing to move him to tears. However, his time at Liverpool would end in sadness and a hint of bitterness towards his manager and mentor.

He'd always known that one day his playing career would end, he knew he couldn't go on forever at Anfield. But he'd always believed that his strong bond with Shankly would ensure that, when that time came, the boss would handle it the right way. An excerpt from his autobiography speaks of his profound disappointment at the way his boss managed his transition away from being a guaranteed first-team regular and describes how he learned that he'd been dropped from the team for a game against Newcastle in the lobby at St James' Park before the match:

> The great legend of the northeast, Jackie Milburn, who had become a football writer, was handed copies of the team sheet by a club official, and we amiably shared the latest gossip.
>
> As Milburn ran his eyes down the teams, I said I had to get back to the dressing room to change.
>
> Then he looked up sharply and said a few words that might have been, for the impact they had, imprinted on my brain with a branding iron – 'Bonnie lad, you're not playing.'

The news hit St John like a thunderbolt, and he couldn't believe he'd found out he'd been omitted from the team in this way. He was heartbroken and the sense of disappointment would live with him for a long time. In his book *The Saint*, he wrote movingly:

> To this day, I cannot shake the belief that, at the end, Shankly had let me down.

I was terribly disappointed he didn't handle it better. He should have taken me to one side, even in the hotel in Newcastle on the eve of the match. He could have said any of a hundred things. Anything would have been better than the blow administered by Jackie Milburn.

Neither Shankly nor I could change the realities of football, or the ageing process, but he could have shown a little courtesy. He could have taken away some of the rawness of the pain.

Shankly was a complex character. He was capable of great kindness and compassion towards his players, but he had a single-minded approach that acted like venom. It propelled him and his team to glory, but it often carried a sting in the tail.

It's sad that St John, after forging such a close relationship with his boss, would feel the full weight of the great man's ruthless streak. However, there's no doubting his boss's continued admiration for him. In 1975, Shankly gave an interview to a young Brian Reade, later of the *Daily Mirror*, and had this to say of St John:

My first great buy. Clever, canny, bags of skill, made things happen.

Liked a scrap too. Jesus, did he like a scrap. I sometimes wanted to tie his fists behind his back.

Great player though. Gave you everything on the pitch. Mind you, a lazy bugger at training. He hated it. Always trying to pull one on us. But what a player.

What a player indeed. Ian St John made 26 league appearances in the 1969/70 season, scoring five times. In his final campaign, he ran out just once, in an FA Cup fourth-round tie against Swansea. The Reds won 3-0 and, of course, he scored.

The Saint left Liverpool in 1971 and enjoyed spells at South African side Hellenic, Coventry City and Tranmere Rovers. He later managed Motherwell, his boyhood club, and Portsmouth. He was even be tipped by some as a possible replacement for Shankly after the Scot's retirement. However, it was a career in television that would introduce Ian St John to a whole new generation of football supporters, including me. St John went on to anchor the hugely popular and iconic *Saint & Greavsie* show on ITV from 1985 to 1992, alongside the legendary Jimmy Greaves.

It is, however, for his achievements in a red shirt that he'll be most fondly remembered by Liverpool supporters.

Ian St John left Liverpool in a better place than he found it, and took with him two league titles and an FA Cup winner's medal. He left Kopites with countless happy memories and would rank 21st in a supporters' poll of 'The 100 Players Who Shook the Kop'.

He died on 1 March 2021, aged 82, but in the minds of a generation of Liverpool supporters, he lives on.

Premier League Redemption
Reds Down Villa with First Home Win in Three Months

A peculiar feature of the Klopp era is the fact that we have at times endured runs of bad form, as well as performances so terrible that they utterly bewildered us, and yet, for the most part, the majority of us have managed to maintain the same sense of trust and belief that was there from day one.

After all, this was a man who'd led his team to Champions League Final heartache in Kyiv only to promise on the very next morning that he would not only return in another final the next year, but that he'd win it. Of course, he delivered on those promises. He'd repeat the same feat after losing out on the league title to Manchester City by a single point in 2019. If Jürgen told me I lived on Mars, I'd believe him.

Klopp had delivered the holy grail of a first league title in 30 years, and in doing so he'd banked an enormous amount of credit. I endured our collapse in the 2020/21 season, along with the jibes from rival supporters, because I genuinely believed that in Jürgen we had a manager who'd eventually find a way to turn things around. I also couldn't think of anyone else I trusted more to handle the 'crisis' than him.

As it turned out, my faith in the boss, and that of the rest of us for that matter, was well placed. He and his players would figure it out, and they eventually managed to climb out of the hole they'd dug for themselves on 10 April 2021, when Aston Villa arrived at Anfield.

The backdrop to this game would be the country's continuing slow climb out of the pandemic, and new vaccines were emerging with reassuring regularity. Although football was still being played behind closed doors, hopes that we'd eventually return to our seats were raised as ever-increasing numbers of people got the jab. The rollout across the UK would continue despite protests from the anti-vax lobby, and almost 28 million had received at least one dose of the vaccine by the end of March 2021.

Liverpool now sat in fifth place in the league table, some 22 points off the league leaders Manchester City, but crucially they were just two points off fourth place and the promise of Champions League football the following season. Targets had been revised down and we'd all adjusted our expectations accordingly. No longer were the Reds fighting to retain their crown. Instead, the more modest aim of ensuring our place at Europe's top table had become the distant rallying cry.

Naturally, confidence was fragile and no longer could Jürgen or the players rely on home advantage. Anfield was no longer a fortress. The 'This is Anfield' sign, so often a potent tool that lifted our own players and intimidated the opposition, had never been so, well, impotent.

Liverpool and Anfield had lost some of their power, I believe, thanks to the absence of us, the supporters. That meant the team would have to fight their way back to form and restore their reputation the hard way.

One player who'd have fancied his chances of prolonging Liverpool's home woes was Ollie Watkins. The Villa man had scored a hat-trick in the 7-2 drubbing of Liverpool earlier in the season. He must have been dreaming of a similar outcome when just two minutes before half-time he fired a shot that seemed to go through Alisson Becker.

Villa had gone 1-0 up and ominously Liverpool for their part were staring down the barrel of a seventh straight defeat at Anfield. I'm not sure what the next level up from crisis is – is it catastrophe? – whatever it is, if we didn't find some so-far-hidden depths of resolve, we would hit it.

To their credit, the Reds did keep going, and probably should have been level through Bobby Firmino, only for his close-range effort to be ruled out after another interminable VAR check eventually found someone in an offside position. That player was apparently Diogo Jota. Had Liverpool not eventually turned the game around, the resultant fume would have been epic, this was a ridiculous decision.

Fortunately for us, Liverpool did manage to level through a familiar hero. And not even Stockley Park could find anything wrong when Mohamed Salah headed the ball home after Villa's keeper, Emiliano Martínez, could only divert an Andy Robertson cross into the Egyptian's path. Amazingly, Salah had just scored Liverpool's first goal at home from open play since 27 December; it was his 28th of the season in all competitions. The sense of relief was enormous. Imagine the scenes on a full Kop as that ball went in, followed by the anxious wait for VAR to ruin the moment completely.

Villa's Trezeguet came close to breaking hearts and prolonging Liverpool's Anfield agony, when his effort struck the upright, but Liverpool would have one more moment to win the game. Another feature of the Klopp era is the late winner. They're like a drug, but the stress and withdrawal associated with waiting for them is sometimes hard to bear.

The anticipated moment duly arrived one minute into added time. With Liverpool pushing forward to find the elusive winner that could end their purgatory, Villa made a hash of clearing the danger and, from the edge of the box, Trent Alexander-Arnold curled in a wonderful effort to clinch the three points. Oh, how we'd have celebrated on the Kop had we been allowed in. Covid stole so much from us.

Liverpool had been more than worthy winners, racking up 23 shots in a game that contained yet another controversial VAR decision. The Reds had climbed into fourth place and fragile shoots of hope were returning.

There were just seven games remaining in a league campaign that had promised much but crumbled at the crucial moment. If Jürgen's men could salvage Champions League football from the ruins of this season with so little time left, it would go down as one of the German's greatest achievements.

That was our hope. However, as is so often the case with Liverpool, the path to salvation was far from smooth.

Reds Exit Europe and Late Pain Against Leeds and Newcastle

Top Four in Doubt

Throughout April 2021 the news was dominated by the build-up of troops on the border between Russia and Ukraine. The Kremlin's frequent denials that an invasion was imminent did little to reassure and it felt like the second hand on the so-called 'Doomsday Clock' was edging ever closer to midnight.

The death of Prince Philip also took over television for a while. With the commendable exception of Channel 4, all other terrestrial channels turned over their entire schedules to coverage of the royal death, a move which led to the BBC receiving almost 110,000 complaints, a record for the broadcaster.

The winner of the 173rd Grand National, held on 10 April, was Minella Times, ridden by Rachael Blackmore, the first female jockey to win the world-famous steeplechase. The race had been cancelled in 2020 due to the pandemic, and this year it was run entirely behind closed doors for the first time in its history. Four days later Liverpool welcomed Real Madrid to Anfield for their Champions League quarter-final, second-leg clash. With Liverpool 3-1 down from the first leg, they were in desperate need of the sort of atmosphere served up to Barcelona in 2019. Sadly, they had to soldier on without us, our banners and our songs. It would prove to be too much of a tall order, and the Spanish outfit prevailed.

The *Liverpool Daily Post* headline spoke volumes: 'Reds miss the Kop, miss sitters … and miss out.' The Reds, in particular Mohamed Salah, had squandered a series of clear-cut chances, but in the end the tie ended goalless, and with it the dreams of another European final that could have elevated a troubling season evaporated.

Attentions turned to the league and the quest to cement a place in the top four for a place in next season's Champions League. It had now gone from the minimum requirement at the beginning of the season to the only show in town. The next two obstacles in Liverpool's path were a trip to Elland Road to take on Leeds United on 19 April, then the visit of Newcastle United to Anfield on 24 April.

Neither match filled me with confidence. The run-up to the Leeds game was dominated by the news that six of the Premier

League's biggest clubs had announced their intention to join a so-called European Super League, including Liverpool Football Club. The news took journalists, players and management, in fact all of us, completely by surprise. The justifiable outrage of the Premier League's remaining clubs and their supporters was justified, but the backlash faced by Klopp and his players wasn't. They'd played no part in the decision and were quick to indicate their personal opposition to the move. Both Klopp and club captain Jordan Henderson were clear that they didn't back the scheme.

Social media and press and broadcast media were littered with reports of dire threats of retribution and demands to kick the six clubs out of the Premier League, European competition and presumably the planet. Once again, from a purely Liverpool perspective, this felt like yet another self-inflicted wound on the part of the owners. Coming at such a pivotal moment in the season, with the Reds vying for the top four, and seemingly motivated by greed as opposed to sporting integrity or any consideration of the impact on supporters or the game itself, it could not be more damaging. I and all Reds like me were left reeling.

The proposed competition would set up an elite closed shop with no possibility of relegation, and it threatened to wipe out more than a century of Liverpool history, trashing our legacy and throwing away the game we all love into the bargain. The move ensured the Liverpool team bus received the most hostile of welcomes as it arrived at Elland Road. It also meant the result, a 1-1 draw that had the potential to derail the Reds' quest for the top four, was greeted with glee by the nation's headline writers: 'SUPER LEAGUE HELD BY SUPER LEEDS' screamed the *Daily Mail.* Other back pages claimed that UEFA planned to ban all six clubs from European competition.

Aside from a handful of cyber warriors, desperate for Liverpool to become the footballing equivalent of a monarchy that's guaranteed success irrespective of merit, the vast majority of Liverpool supporters, including the Spirit of Shankly and other groups, were fundamentally opposed to the idea. For most of us this meant trading everything we held dear for little more than a handful of magic beans.

Despite the outside noise, Liverpool started the game well against Leeds and took the lead through Sadio Mané on the half-hour mark.

However, they failed to build on that and soon fell into a by now familiar lethargy that Leeds were eventually able to punish. In the 87th minute Diego Llorente duly levelled, and, in an instant, our fragile momentum vanished.

Five days later Liverpool welcomed Newcastle United, and there was a distinct air of déjà vu to the whole encounter. The Reds had now slumped to sixth place. Once again they took the lead in the first half. Mohamed Salah scored inside three minutes, only for another late, late goal by the opposition to infuriate.

The manner of Newcastle's equaliser was particularly frustrating. Liverpool had led for almost the entirety of the game before it moved into five minutes of stoppage time. The visitors saw an equaliser ruled out after a VAR check, but instead of heeding the warning signs, shutting up shop and seeing the game out and leaving with the three points, Liverpool's defence simply imploded. Newcastle substitute Callum Wilson saw his added-time strike cancelled out after VAR ruled that he'd handled. However, relief was short-lived, as in the fifth minute of added time another substitute, Joe Willock, levelled the scores, and this time there was no VAR reprieve.

Two games and two infuriating draws meant Jürgen and the lads were up against it. If they were to make the top four, it was time for them to use the outside ferment to create a siege mentality for the Reds to recapture that old never-say-die attitude that we'd once come to take for granted. Magically, gloriously, they would do just that, and, and, as we'll see, salvation would come from the most unlikely of sources.

Reds Hit by 'Friendly Fire'
FSG Decides to Join 'European Super League'
With a place at Europe's top table hanging in the balance, Liverpool's owners, Fenway Sports Group (FSG), inexplicably pushed the self-destruct button. Whether John W. Henry's decision on Sunday, 18 April to join a European Super League was motivated by greed or by a desire not to see the club left behind by its rivals, it was a move comprehensively rejected by the fanbase and most of the football world. The scheme would end in ignominious collapse days later, after a huge a wave of protest.

Liverpool announced their decision to leave the ill-judged scheme after interventions from Liverpool Supporters' Union, Spirit of Shankly and a tense transatlantic video call between high-ranking members of FSG, including Henry himself, the club's local leadership, who had apparently been caught off guard by the move, local MP Ian Byrne and the then chair of Spirit of Shankly, Joe Blott.

I caught up with Joe recently to discuss that meeting. He was adamant that the key to helping FSG understand the error of their ways was combining the outside noise with a calm rational approach that offered solutions along with a dose of reality. The outcome placed both the club and its supporters on a trajectory towards ever-closer collaboration, and eventually the establishment of the Supporters' Committee. Joe told me:

> There were no fists thumping tables. There was no need for that. The protests and uproar generally had focused minds. Ian Byrne [MP for Liverpool West Derby constituency] was excellent in that respect. He laid out the supporters' position and the way forward for the ownership.
>
> Ironically, engagement with the club had been at an all-time high before the announcement, and it caught everyone off guard.
>
> We knew and we argued that change had to come, and if Liverpool were to repair the damage, they had to put supporters at the forefront of decision-making.

Joe explained that everyone's goal was to get back on track as soon as possible, and it was supporters who had a plan to ensure such a 'mistake' could never happen again. Just three days later, on 21 April, a chastened John W. Henry used an online video to apologise and announce that the club had now abandoned its plans to join the so-called European Super League.

In a state of utter bewilderment at the damage this had done to the club, and worried about what the future may hold for the game, I penned an open letter to Henry, which was published by *This is Anfield* and is reprinted here:

Dear John,

Apologising when you've made a mistake takes courage and I know it can be difficult. So, in this respect your video apology to Liverpool's players, our manager and supporters is welcome. Who among us hasn't made mistakes? This though should be a first step and not an end in itself. It should inform future behaviour.

Sadly, though, we've been here before. After the £77 ticket hike, the attempt to trademark the Liver bird, and the word Liverpool when used in a football context, and the furlough controversy, you and your organisation issued apologies, backtracked and promised to do better. Yet here we are again.

Each of these issues have a common thread and are about squeezing as much money from the club as possible. They also reveal a staggering lack of insight into the ethos and philosophy of the club you own and its supporters.

More worryingly perhaps is the fact that your involvement in the failed breakaway Super League suggests that not only do you not understand your own club, but you don't get English and European football either. There isn't a single supporter of any club, not one player or manager who, if you had asked them, wouldn't have told you to swerve this whole idea.

Anyone who has grown up supporting their team from the terraces understands that what makes football special is that success is earned, and the possibility of failure makes victory all the sweeter.

The plan you were involved with would have transformed the game we love into a sterile, meaningless affair devoid of passion. Countless people have fought hard to build this club. We have spent small fortunes in the context of our income to drive it on to success.

Over a period of almost 130 years, on the pitch, in the stands and in the dugout men and women have worn the shirt, sung their songs, and a dynasty of truly great managers have won 19 league titles, and amassed six European Cups. Your reckless actions risked trashing all of that, and for what? More money?

Any Liverpool supporter could have told you that no amount of money could ever compensate for the loss of such a legacy, if only you had asked. Instead, we have faced days of uncertainty and unnecessary angst.

To give you an indication of how hard the last 72 hours have been for many of us, consider this. I have been supporting this club for five decades now. I have lived in and near to Anfield my whole life. This club is a part of who I am, and my moods are as aligned to its fortunes as the tides of the Mersey are to the moon. So, being locked out of the stadium I have genuinely come to call home for 12 months has been hard to bear.

One thing that has kept me going throughout lockdown has been my hope, that one day I would take my place on the Kop again. The day I renewed my season ticket was a milestone along the road to normality. Then, on Sunday, it felt like the rug had been pulled from under our feet. Many of us began to wonder if we would even be in the Premier League or Champions League next season. After waiting 30 years for a league title, would we now be stripped of it because of the actions of distant owners. It's no exaggeration to say I was heartbroken.

Now it's over. Just like that. You issue your apology, and you move on. Until the next time.

I am left wondering, just what were you thinking? Either you knew exactly how we would react and chose to carry on regardless, thinking you could ride out the storm. Or, you simply hadn't learned from your past experiences. Only you know which, and to be honest I can't decide which explanation is worse.

The real question though is, where do we go from here? My gut told me to join the chorus suggesting that your ownership is untenable and regardless of the challenges it would create, putting the club up for sale is the only viable option.

However, everything I have witnessed in football since 1992 tells me that we may only be swapping one set of profit-hungry owners for another. As fans, we once more find ourselves between the devil and the deep blue sea. This cannot continue for long before the bond we all feel with this club is broken forever.

I am willing to acknowledge your achievements since 2010. The Main Stand redevelopment, the training base at Kirkby, the plans for Anfield Road, bringing in Jürgen and amassing this incredible squad who have achieved so much, could all be worthy legacies of your ownership. Sadly, future generations will have to weigh these against the embarrassment and anger caused by your various misadventures, the latest of which has severely damaged our reputation and tarnished our achievements.

In your apology, you again mention that you have the club's interest at heart. I'm reminded of an open letter you sent to Spirit of Shankly in 2012, in which you concluded:

'Finally, I can say with authority that our ownership is not about profit. Contrary to popular opinion, owners rarely get involved in sports in order to generate cash. They generally get involved with a club in order to compete and work for the benefit of their club. It's often difficult. In our case we work every day in order to generate revenues to improve the club.

'We have only one driving ambition at Liverpool and that is the quest to win the Premier League playing the kind of football our supporters want to see. *That will only occur if we do absolutely the right things to build the club in a way that makes sense for supporters, for us and for those who will follow us.*

'We will deliver what every long-term supporter of Liverpool Football Club aches for.'

Noble sentiments indeed, and I acknowledge the club has now won the Premier League. However, I would draw your attention to the sentence in italics. Because, within those words may lie your salvation. If you genuinely want to build the club in a way that makes sense for the supporters and you, then there is a way for FSG to build a more positive legacy.

You must become part of the change that is needed in football. You need to lead and not be bounced into the right thing by protest and sanction. That means supporting and delivering greater supporter involvement at board level.

Involving fans representatives more will ensure similar mistakes won't happen in the future.

You also need to be more proactive on ticket prices, support supporters who travel to matches and advocate for them in negotiations with broadcasters over scheduling. While I don't speak for Spirit of Shankly or Spion Kop 1906, they do speak for me. I believe that if you engage directly with them in good faith, they will help you to lead, and maybe there will be a way back for you and FSG.

Maybe, Liverpool FC can become a beacon of supporter engagement with fans at the heart of the club's decision-making. What a truly historic legacy that would be.

Of course, this is a letter written more in hope than expectation. In truth, like many fellow supporters, I'm not convinced my words will resonate with you. Prove me wrong.

Man Utd 2-4 Liverpool

Supporters Party on Anfield Road as Reds Humble
Manchester United

On 13 May 13 2021, with talk of a future of hybrid working for British workers, Indian variants of the pandemic and precarious plans to end lockdown that seemed as foolhardy as they were desperately desired, Liverpool finally travelled to Old Trafford for their rearranged game with Manchester United.

The game should have taken place almost two weeks earlier, on 2 May; however, following a significant protest by around 200 United fans against the continued ownership of the club by the Glazer family, both clubs, the police, the Premier League and the local council took the decision to postpone the game, in an unprecedented move.

Two police officers were reportedly injured in the disturbances sparked initially by United's decision to join the so-called European Super League, but grievances were far broader than that. Demonstrators made their way into the stadium and on to the pitch, with staff and stewards having to lock themselves into rooms.

A second demonstration had taken place at the Lowry Hotel, where United players were staying in preparation for the match. United were sitting in second place in the league table, and a defeat to Klopp's men would mean their rivals City would be crowned champions for the third time in four years.

A statement released by United read: 'Our fans are passionate about Manchester United, and we completely acknowledge the right to free expression and peaceful protest. However, we regret the disruption to the team and actions which put other fans, staff, and the police in danger ...'

Naturally, reaction to the postponement from Liverpool supporters was mixed. While most had common cause with United fans' opposition to the way football was being run, distant owners concerned only with profit and who were loading their clubs with debt, others reacted in a more partisan way. The situation wasn't helped by the fact that some United fans sang anti-Liverpool songs during a protest that was supposedly against the governance of their club.

I wasn't alone in having mixed feelings. I knew that, despite some of the lumpen behaviour on show, there were serious grievances being aired, concerns about the way our football clubs are being taken away from us. I found myself in complete solidarity with a statement from the Manchester United Supporters Trust (MUST), who described the incident as 'the culmination of 16 years since the Glazer family's acquisition of the club'.

It continued:

On the back of the indefensible ESL proposals, and an 'apology' from the Glazers which we do not accept, we need to give fans a meaningful share in the ownership of United and a meaningful voice in how it is run.

The government now needs to act. That has to mean a process which results in fans having the opportunity to buy shares in their club – and, more to the point, no single private shareholder holding a majority ownership of our football clubs which allows them to abuse that ownership.

The government needs to reflect the views of ordinary people who see that now is the time to reclaim the people's game.

Those were words I simply couldn't disagree with, and although others struggled with partisanship and an understandable anger at protestors targeting Liverpool during the demonstrations, I wanted to stand with the decent United supporters struggling to reclaim the club they love from the grasping hands of profiteers and charlatans.

The online reaction was equally conflicted, with even some United fans condemning the scenes. Football feels like it's at a crossroads, now more than ever. If supporters of all clubs don't somehow find a way to put tribalism aside for all but 90 minutes of a game, then we may allow our clubs to be stolen from under our noses.

The rearranged fixture took place 11 days later, after lockdown restriction in Liverpool had been eased. That meant I was free to join supporters and creators of fan content, including *This is Anfield*, and Redmen TV, among others. The streets around Hotel Anfield were deserted as a group of us walked around the ground, revelling in the fact that we could. It was an emotional experience, and a few of us had a lump in our throats as we trod the pavements behind the Main Stand. Coming together with other supporters, experiencing the emotion at close quarters is what the game is all about. It's a communal experience, or it's nothing but a ghost of itself. We did a few interviews and chatted before heading back into the tent behind Hotel Anfield to watch the game.

By now I was deep into researching and writing *Untouchables: Anfield's Band of Brothers* with the founder of the Liverpool FC Historical Group, Kieran Smith. Writing about a team of a century earlier had become a mammoth task, complicated by the fact that Covid restrictions had meant the two of us had never met in person. We'd conducted the whole collaboration via video call, email and Facebook Messenger. We wouldn't see each other face to face until after the book was published, at an author event at Pritchards Bookshop in Crosby, Liverpool.

Although challenging, writing the book had almost been a salvation. Without that opportunity to completely immerse myself into something so all-consuming, I'm not sure how I'd have coped. However, that had meant that I had cut myself off from the family at times. An existence in which I was either living inside my own head for half the time and struggling with reality for the rest of it had been exhausting. The opportunity to give release to some of that while watching the Reds with a group of mates felt irresistible and thrilling.

In the run-up to the game, Liverpool had got back on track with a 2-0 home victory over Southampton and were still in with a shout of a top-four finish, now our 'holy grail'. That game was won thanks to another Mohamed Salah goal and a debut strike by Thiago Alcantara.

In the City, the news was dominated for a few days by the election for the first time in Liverpool's history of a black mayor, Joanne Anderson. Regardless of how any of us felt about the way in which the city was being run, or how the Labour Party had chosen their candidate, there was no denying that this was a momentous step in Liverpool's history.

There was also some noise about the Liverpool owners' pursuit of investment, with RedBird Capital touted as not only putting some money into the club, but possibly one day taking over the reins from FSG. I couldn't help but feel that this institution I'd grown up with, which once felt like it belonged to me and everyone who went to the game, was now being hocked around like any old commodity to the highest bidder, and without me or anyone who really cares about the club being involved.

Nostalgia and myths aside, we never had a meaningful stake in the ownership of our club, nor when I was growing up were we ever consulted on decisions about it; however, the perceived gap between us and the suits running Liverpool FC, in terms of what was important, our ethos and reason for existing, was far narrower. The problem facing us and supporters of all clubs was what we were going to do about that.

The Reds were still in sixth place, and if they were to clinch Champions League football, they would need a perfect finish to the season. That meant beating United, followed by victories over West Bromwich Albion, Burnley and Crystal Palace. Given Liverpool's indifferent form this season, it didn't feel like the easiest of runs.

The atmosphere at Hotel Anfield was raucous before the game, and with each passing moment and incident it ramped up until, by the final whistle, it could best be described as utter pandemonium. United almost cut across all of that with a Bruno Fernandes opener in the tenth minute. The tent fell silent for a second, but only for a second.

We were nowhere near the action but somehow we'd decided that we were the remote away end, and the noise was cranked up another level. As the beer flowed and tables creaked under the weight of supporters leading the chants, bar staff weaved in and out of the throng searching for empties, and I lost all sense of time.

A little over half an hour had gone by when Diogo Jota stuck the ball past Dean Henderson. The crowd inside the tent went berserk and erupted in an explosion of beer, which rained down on us as pints went flying. We were jumping up and down and going crazy, hugging each other and complete strangers. It was all so familiar, but I'd almost forgotten what it was like.

If I've gone halfway close to painting you a picture of the scenes that greeted Liverpool's equaliser, it's going to be impossible to do justice to what happened when Bobby Firmino put us in front, after three minutes of first-half stoppage time. 'Si Señor' echoed around the fabric walls and roof, and suddenly everything felt possible again.

We were miles away from the game, but somehow connected, feeding off its energy, and maybe, just maybe, we were having an influence. Nah, that's ridiculous. But if I tell you that's how it felt, you get a sense of the magic of those moments. This was as close as it was possible to get to being at the game without actually being there.

Two minutes after the half-time break, Bobby sent us to dreamland, notching his second and the Reds' third. We were on our way to another famous Old Trafford victory, but as is so often the case, we'd have to suffer a little to get there.

Marcus Rashford, a player you want to dislike because of the badge on his shirt, but you can't completely because he's a sound fella, had other ideas. In the 68th minute he grabbed one back for United. The tension in the tent was thick and the beer in our bellies felt a little heavier. The songs continued but they were more like prayers now. I felt that sick tension as the clock ticked down and just wanted the whistle to go – 75 minutes, 80 minutes, 85. It felt like the longest time.

Then normal time was up, so we just had to hang on a little longer. The tension was so hard to handle, until Mohamed Salah netted Liverpool's fourth. The resultant release of pent-up frustration and angst that gripped us the moment Rashford got United's second, although it had really been there for a year, sent the room into ecstasy. Arms flailed and fists punched the air. People hugged and danced, throwing their drinks into the air. The game was won, United were beaten, well beaten on their home turf, with their own fans outside protesting, while we celebrated and dreamed of better days.

As I wandered down Anfield Road, heading home but wanting to milk the night for all it was worth, I thought the season couldn't get any more magical than that. It couldn't, could it?

West Brom 1-2 Liverpool

Alisson Becker is from Heaven, as Reds Chase Down Holy Grail of Champions League Football

I've written before that in football there are moments that transcend the game itself. They have power and live on in the memory, regardless of the outcome of any fixture or season. They uplift and become eternal, whether a trophy is eventually won or not.

Think Neil Mellor's wonder strike against Arsenal all those years ago, Dejan Lovren's winner against Dortmund in those fledgling years of the Klopp era. Match-winning goals scored in a season or a competition in which the big prizes would elude us, but elevated to almost mythic status, nonetheless. To that ever-growing list of magical moments we can now add Alisson Becker's added-time winner against Sam Allardyce's West Brom at The Hawthorns on 16 May 2021.

The day before the game, Leicester had won the FA Cup with a 1-0 win over Chelsea at Wembley. The game had been played in front of 21,000 supporters. Slowly, sometimes painfully so, rightly or wrongly in terms of the pace, we were edging back to normality, to the post-Covid era. The game at West Brom, however, would be played behind closed doors, with nothing but the shouts of the players, barks of Klopp and the noise of Allardyce's relentless chewing filling the air.

This was a game Liverpool had to win if they had any hopes of breaking into the top four places. The win over United had seen them climb one place to fifth. A win would edge them even closer to the promise of another season of Champions League football. The two teams ahead of Liverpool in the race were the FA Cup finalists Chelsea and Leicester, who would face each other again in their next league game. Liverpool would travel to Burnley. The stakes were high and there was no room for error. Only a win against the Baggies would do.

Again, as is so often the case when it comes to Liverpool, we decided to abandon the easy route and took the most difficult route possible. With just 15 minutes on the clock, West Brom took the lead through Hal Robson-Kanu, who hadn't started a game of football since 2017. Could he not have waited?

The Reds restored parity 18 minutes later when Mohamed Salah – who was locked in an all-or-nothing battle with Harry Kane for the Golden Boot – provided a clinical finish. The strike brought him level with the Englishman.

Liverpool pressed for the winner, and it should have come sooner than it did and in far less dramatic circumstances. Bobby Firmino crashed a shot off the woodwork and Sadio Mané had a goal ruled out for offside, plus the Reds wasted a host of chances.

West Brom were stubborn and dug in, determined to wreck Liverpool's ambitions. There's no rule against a team playing football this way; there's more than one way to win or draw a game. Having said that, I really do pity the supporters of any team managed by 'Big Sam'. The footballing equivalent of a concrete bollard, the Midlanders' only ambition in that second half was to defend for their lives, hoof the ball up the pitch and hope to steal the three points. It's an art form perfected by none other than Jose Mourinho, so who am I to judge? And, of course, no opposition team is obliged to surrender to Liverpool's whims, no matter how much I think they really should. We'd just have to come up with some hitherto untried and untested method of grabbing the win, some strange sorcery that would bemuse and bewitch the enemy and hand the spoils of battle to us.

You know how overblown and far-fetched that last paragraph seems, yeah? Well, it's not a patch on what happened. Liverpool were all out of time, but in the 95th minute they won a corner. The Reds' bench ushered forward their goalkeeper, Alisson Becker.

It was a 'Hail Mary' for sure. So many teams try this tactic in desperation, but it almost never pays off. For Becker, struggling with grief at the loss of his father back in Brazil, the moment would be etched with emotions few of us could fathom.

'Here comes Alisson …' was a post by *The Athletic*'s Liverpool correspondent James Pearce on Twitter, now known as X. It's still pinned to the top of his timeline, such is the portentous nature of that tweet, as it was known then.

Trent Alexander-Arnold sent in the corner, and in the video replays we've all watched time and again – often accompanied by the *Titanic* soundtrack or some no less stirring music from the film *Rocky* it must be said – the ball seems to hang in the air for an age as the Reds' keeper rises to meet it. The ball then cannons off his head and past a despairing Sam Johnstone in the Baggies' goal.

There's complete disbelief among the watching press and media, and in the dugout the watching Liverpool bench erupts in a frenzy of disbelieving celebration. On the pitch, Alisson, holding his hands aloft, his eyes fixed on the skies in silent prayer to his father, is engulfed by his team-mates. It meant everything to him, and them. And behind the stunned expression of joy and of incredulity, there was solidarity.

The goal had put the Reds a single point and a place behind Chelsea, and three off third-placed Leicester with two games remaining.

Nothing, not VAR, not Sam Allardyce's whining at full time, could ever take this moment from us. If I could bottle it up and breathe it in every now and then, I would. I'll make do with it living in my heart, though, and rent-free in the minds of rival supporters everywhere.

Speaking to Sky Sports, an understandably emotional Alisson Becker fought back the tears:

> I just tried to run into a good place and be there to try and help my players, to bring a defender, but no one followed me, and I am lucky and blessed, sometimes things you can't explain.
>
> You can't explain a lot of things in my life, the only reason is God and he put his hand on my head today and I'm feeling very blessed.

Paying tribute to his father, who had drowned aged 57 back in February, Alisson continued:

> I'm too emotional, this last month for everything that has happened with me and my family, but football is my life, I played since I can remember with my father. I hope he was here to see it, I'm sure he is celebrating with God at his side.

His manager could scarcely believe what he'd seen:

It's an unbelievable header, I've never seen anything like that, good technique. I wasn't sure what I was seeing.

We are really close and know exactly what it means to him, it's outstanding, really touching. It's only football but it means the world to us.

This was the first time in the history of Liverpool Football Club that a goalkeeper had scored a competitive goal. That it should happen in such circumstances, with the Reds chasing what had seemed impossible only a couple of games ago, when almost all hope was gone, was unbelievable. When the men paid to score goals had struggled so much, and the man who eventually did score was so devout and suffering so much personal pain … well, it was almost enough to make me question my atheism.

Football can do that to you. In a world that's becoming increasingly cynical and difficult to survive with any sense of idealism intact, moments like these elevate us and take on a special significance that few other experiences can match. This is what the suits who run the game try to monetise but to us it's real, visceral and necessary.

We can't live by bread alone. We need Alisson Becker moments. Alisson Becker is from heaven.

Liverpool 2-0 Crystal Palace

Klopp Performs a Miracle as Reds Secure Third Place and Champions League

So, on 23 May 2021, the Premier League season reached its inevitable conclusion. Liverpool hosted Crystal Palace in front of 10,000 lucky supporters, the biggest gate at Anfield since football had entered the deep freeze over a year earlier. They did so in the knowledge that a win would guarantee them Champions League Football for another season.

To do so would be a remarkable achievement, given how far the team had fallen from the heady days of the previous May. Liverpool had arrived at this moment courtesy of a 3-0 victory over Burnley at Turf Moor on Wednesday, 19 May. That win had lifted them into fourth place on goal difference, with 66 points, thanks to Leicester's defeat at the hands of Chelsea, who had now moved into third spot.

In the news, in the UK the total number of Covid vaccines administered had reached 50 million, and in the Eurovision Song Contest the total number of points awarded to the UK's entry was nil. The song was called 'Embers', and as those of the 2020/21 season were about to flicker out, Liverpool would ensure the campaign finished with a flourish.

The Burnley game, contested behind closed doors, was won thanks to two goals either side of half-time, which put the Reds in the driving seat before victory was sealed with an 88th-minute strike by Alex Oxlade-Chamberlain. Now on to the next match, and a lucky 10,000 fans would get to roar the team on at an expectant Anfield.

As with previous games involving a reduced capacity, ticketing was decided by ballot. Sadly, what the football gods had given me for the Wolves game back in December, they'd taken away for the visit of Palace in May. Fair's fair, I couldn't complain, and felt the club was right to spread the love in this way. However, not being in the ground for the last game made me burn with jealousy.

Liverpool had gone unbeaten for nine games by the time Roy Hodgson's Palace turned up in L4. A win in the final match would make it eight wins in ten, with two draws. Those had come against Leeds United and Newcastle United, both from late sucker-punch goals. Had we failed to finish in the Champions League spots because of those two epic collapses, it would have haunted me forever.

Despite what was riding on this game, Liverpool failed to produce the necessary quick start. It was Palace who were the brighter of the teams, forcing Alisson Becker into two smart saves just minutes into the game. Both Wilfried Zaha and Andros Townsend were giving the Reds defence nightmares and the Kop palpitations as play got underway.

For Liverpool, young defender Rhys Williams headed wide from close range, before Sadio Mané settled the nerves with the Reds' opener from an Andy Robertson corner on 36 minutes. Crystal Palace must have been sick to death of the sight of Sadio, as this was the eighth consecutive game in which he'd scored against them. He was only the second player in Premier League history to complete this feat against the same opponent.

In the second half Liverpool racked up the chances, dominating for large spells. They enjoyed 69 per cent of possession, managing 19 shots (five of them on target) and won 14 corners. However, the longer the game went on, the more the nerves jangled. The Reds had embarrassed Hodgson's Palace with a 7-0 thrashing earlier in the season, but could he yet have the last laugh, stealing Liverpool's fairy-tale ending and flipping a metaphorical bird at his Scouse detractors?

It didn't bear thinking about. Fortunately, there would be no need, as Sadio Mané was once again the hero. Rounding off a lightning-quick counter-attack, the striker placed the ball in the net with 16 minutes remaining. Victory was sealed, and although those watching may not have realised it, so to had third – not fourth – place.

Chelsea had slumped to a 2-1 defeat at the hands of Aston Villa, and Leicester had been crushed 4-2 at home by Spurs, despite leading at one point. It was a remarkable achievement by a Reds team written off as dead and buried only weeks earlier.

Former Manchester United player Gary Neville found it almost impossible to believe, screaming, 'Have they finished third? How did that happen?' in a pitch that possibly only dogs could hear, into Sky TV cameras. Roy Keane was left eating his ill-advised and completely partisan words about Klopp's men being 'bad champions' earlier in the season. When will they ever learn?

Indeed, had the Reds managed to hang on in those two games against Leeds and Newcastle just weeks earlier, they'd have leapfrogged Manchester United and stolen second place. Anyway, I'm just torturing myself now. If wishes were horses and all that. Nevertheless, Liverpool had won five straight games to clinch 69 points seemingly from nowhere. It was quite the rehabilitation for a team declared on the critical list for so much of the season.

Klopp could barely hide his pride at his players' achievements. It had been an arduous and exhausting season, riddled with VAR controversy and injuries to key players. He declared the season's conclusion to be his 'greatest achievement', explaining that the Reds had been 'nowhere men five weeks ago'.

They had, of course, but was it his greatest achievement? I'm not so sure, but he'd pulled off a spectacular turnaround and secured our club a place at Europe's top table for yet another season. For that he deserved enormous praise. For what was about to follow in the season ahead, he'd forever cement his place in the hearts of everyone connected with the club.

We didn't realise it and no pundit would predict it, but we were all about to embark on a thrill-ride of a season that promised the earth and all its riches. We'd eventually make do with pots of silver and a host of memories. Some were the greatest of them all, remembered fondly forever, while others will be recalled for very different reasons – and through all of that, we'd have Jürgen Klopp leading the charge.

As the curtain closed on the 2020/21 season, that's all any of us needed.

A New Beginning and the Battles Still to Fight

Liverpool FC May–October 2021

Game-Changing Breakthrough in Battle for Supporter Representation

Liverpool Supporters Show the Way

The 2021/22 season would set new standards in the history of Liverpool Football Club, both on and off the pitch. On 16 June 2021, before a ball had even been kicked, a historic poll by members of the Liverpool Supporters Trust, Spirit of Shankly, saw 99.44 per cent vote in favour of plans for greater supporter participation in decision-making at Anfield. An astonishing 68.39 per cent of members took part in the ballot, which asked them to vote on proposals agreed between the Trust and representatives of the Liverpool board, including CEO Billy Hogan. Spirit of Shankly had recommended acceptance of the plans, which included the following:

- The establishment of a Supporters Board, which would be written into the club's regulations, making it a legally binding agreement. SOS would be head of this board.

- A formal recognition agreement between SOS and LFC, which would be written into the club's constitution so that if/when the ownership changed, this contract would remain in place.

- Collaboration between SOS and FSG on the government's fan-led review to improve the future of the game.

- Club owners FSG to meet any costs as a result of the European Super League, not the club.

- A representative of the Supporters Board to meet annually with Liverpool's board of directors to consult on issues pertinent to fans. Outside of this, if an agreed consultation matter was to be discussed at an LFC board meeting, the chair of the Supporters Board would be present.

- Supporters Board representatives to have a term of two years and be chosen as the result of a democratic vote.

- The proposals would constitute the Supporters Board led by SOS as a recognised legal body and ensure that the Liverpool board would be contractually obliged to consult with supporters' representatives.

A period of consultation with members followed, involving virtual meetings at which attendees could see the proposals in detail and ask questions. This meeting was then put online so that those unable to attend could watch, along with a published Q&A on the Spirit of Shankly website. Supporters were then invited to vote to either accept or reject the proposals.

Expressing his delight at the result, the then Spirit of Shankly chair, Joe Blott, said, 'Firstly I want to thank everyone who took the time to vote in our recent ballot. An incredible 99.44 per cent of our members voted in favour of our proposal and the turnout was 68.39 per cent.'

These numbers demonstrated the thirst for greater engagement in the club's affairs – no doubt given a boost by the recent failed attempts by the ownership to join a European Super League without consulting the supporters. However, much work remained before supporters could enjoy a legally binding say in how their club was run, something the head of the Supporters Trust was keen to acknowledge. However, the vote had put the group in a powerful position, as Blott explained:

Thanks to supporters giving us such a firm mandate, we are now empowered to step up our work with the club's board of directors and our engagement with representatives of other supporters' groups. Our vision of improved supporter engagement, enshrined in the club's articles of association and contractually binding between all parties is now a step closer.

The vote represented something of a watershed moment for Spirit of Shankly, who had up to this point racked up more than a decade of campaigning for supporters' rights. Their work spanned two ownerships, having started under the catastrophic and ultimately doomed reign of Hicks and Gillett.

The establishment of the board wouldn't follow for more than a year, taking place on 17 August 2022, with its signing into the club's articles of association. This followed months of negotiations and meetings with legals teams and members of Liverpool Football Club's hierarchy, with each side striving to compromise on an ultimate agreement.

Papers I've seen suggest that, although that process was cordial and professional, neither the club nor the Supporters' Committee found the process easy-going, and several sticking points had to be overcome before any agreement was signed. The main ones centred around issues that the Supporters Trust regarded as 'existential'. These included requirements that the owners would no longer have the power to enter or form a breakaway league or competition, move away from Anfield or agree a 'groundshare', without the consent of the supporters. While agreement was reached on these matters, the method by which consent was secured was a subject of great debate and negotiation.

These discussions go to the heart of what a supporters' board is. Should it be a conduit for passing information from the club to its followers or should it have meaningful engagement in which the supporters have a say in how the club is run. Furthermore, discussions among the senior leadership of Spirit of Shankly went to the very nature of how the new board would operate, drawing parallels with the way that trade unions and companies manage collective bargaining rights.

This passage from a consultation document illustrates the way that the supporters' union envisaged the relationship in those early discussions:

> To use existing union practices in employment as example, a company recognises a union for collective bargaining purposes. It is for the union to then represent its workforce. It does so through membership. Now not all employees may want to join the union so those employees cannot vote on for example, a pay rise or changes to terms and conditions, but they will still receive the benefits. The onus is on the union/unions to engage with non-members and seek their views and in turn, get them to join to increase its representative base.
>
> For the employer, there may well be a need on occasion to write to all its employees to tell them of proposed changes but this is not negotiation, this is information sharing – the negotiation rests with the recognised union.

This became Spirit of Shankly's red line, and agreement wasn't achieved easily. This is perhaps understandable, given that such a recognition of the Supporters Trust/Union challenged the way all football clubs at the top of English football had been run for more than a century. It's to the credit of both sides that agreement was eventually reached.

I caught up with the head of the negotiating team, Joe Blott, as the club and Spirit of Shankly got set to announce their historic agreement. I was keen to get a sense of how the club's failed attempt to join a so-called European Super League had been something of a watershed moment for supporter engagement.

For Blott, the whole debacle had felt like an aberration that had taken everyone by surprise. It left me increasingly of the view that John W. Henry's claim that the decision had been his only was, in fact, true. Blott explained:

> The relationship we had before all of this had been good. We'd been having talks and engaging with the club on various issues in the weeks before they announced they would be joining the European Super League, so the news came as a huge surprise.
>
> We felt there were any number of opportunities for them to discuss it with us – if they had, we'd have told them it was a huge mistake and that supporters would never support the idea.

The fallout after that disastrous decision doubtless played a part in convincing the club's senior leadership that if they were to avoid such an unforced error in the future, involving a group of well-organised supporters before taking decisions that have an existential impact on the club would be the right way to go.

Blott reflected further on the early days of those discussions and what motivated them to make a stand on certain matters:

> We view the club as belonging to the fans and the community. We needed a way to ensure that the club had a legal obligation to consult and seek consent on issues that directly affect the future of the club and impact on supporters and the community.

Many of us have used the phrase 'supporters on the board' as a rallying cry, demanding the right of fan representation at the highest level. However, for Spirit of Shankly there was a growing realisation that such a proposition was fraught with difficulties, according to Blott:

FSG is such a complex organisation with many investors and interests. There was a real risk that supporter representatives sitting on a board like that would potentially have their voice diluted. There's also the issue of independence and influence.

Board members are mutually accountable for decisions made after a majority vote, which raised the unwelcome prospect of any supporter representative being forced to defend board decisions they didn't agree with and hadn't voted for. Says Blott:

> Imagine having to go into the 12th Man pub after a board meeting and finding yourself explaining why the club has just decided to sell Mo Salah. I don't want to do that, and no supporter should.

Instead, he felt what had eventually been secured safeguarded supporter independence and ensured that there was a newly created Supporters' Board, which was genuinely representative of the fanbase, made up of 16 democratically elected members. With Spirit of Shankly formally recognised as the club's official Supporters Trust, they'd hold ten seats, with the remainder going to representatives of the Liverpool Disabled Supporters Association, Kop Outs, Spion Kop 1906, the Official Liverpool Supporters' Committee, Liverpool Women Supporters Committee and representatives of faith and ethnic groups.

Crucially, the agreement would be written into the club's articles of association, something that Blott argued would future-proof the relationship between supporters and the club, preventing future owners from ripping up the agreement:

> The deal now obliges the club to meet with the supporters board regularly. We will have monthly meetings with the local FSG board members, and we will have an annual meeting with the full FSG/LFC management board.
>
> The agreement gives us early access to accounts, strategic plans or anything that affects our football club or the local community.

It also allows us to lead on strategic issues, rather than waiting for the club to engage with us, we can initiate on issues that matter to supporters.

As a result of the latter point, the Supporters' Board has been proactive in leading the club's response to issues such as tragedy chanting in recent times.

Impressively, the deal agreed with the club went further than those proposed by the then government's own 'Fan-Led Review', putting Liverpool supporters and the club at the vanguard of supporter engagement. Tory MP Tracey Crouch has been leading this review into the future of English football, and proposals were published just days before Spirit of Shankly put their proposals for a supporters' board to their own AGM. Analysis of the government report – yet to be implemented – reveals recommendations for a 'golden share', fan veto and the introduction of shadow boards to give fans more power over decision-making on specific issues. Spirit of Shankly and Liverpool FC were clearly ahead of the curve.

The club formally announced the agreement with a statement on its official website. It included the following passage:

> The new engagement process will be enshrined in the club's Articles of Association and a legally binding Memorandum of Understanding between the club and the Official Liverpool Supporters Trust will be entered into, thereby ensuring supporters input on fan issues via structured dialogue.

Thanking supporters' groups for their engagement, Liverpool CEO Billy Hogan outlined the journey the club and Spirit of Shankly had been on for several years:

> The idea for the Supporters Board came from an understanding and recognition that there was a lack of engagement with supporters on some important fan-facing issues and that was something we wanted to address. We had the ability to engage directly with a number of our different supporter groups, and we started with our official Supporters Trust, Spirit of Shankly.

There has been a tremendous amount of engagement with our fans and supporters across the last several years, particularly the work that went into Kyiv and Madrid, a lot of engagement around the Club World Cup, and issues such as equality, diversity and inclusion, ticketing issues and our sanctions process.

There is a lot of engagement, but it was clear that we needed to address our levels of dialogue and put a process in place that was more formal. This has been a healthy process with a lot of engagement, and ultimately, we're really proud of where we've ended up. We think the Supporters Board concept is a really good one and it allows us to engage in a really meaningful way.

I do just want to say a huge thank you to all the different groups that we've engaged with to get to this point.

Perhaps symbolising how the new Supporters Board was now deeply entwined in the club's structure, the club website also carried a statement by Joe Blott:

We've been working really hard as a union to work alongside the club, to hold the club to account but at the same time to work in harmony to try and get the best for supporters.

The Supporters Board will be led by democracy, with an invitation to affiliate groups, not individuals, so when you work on the Supporters Board, you're operating at a level of speaking on behalf of supporters, not just yourself.

The key differences now the Supporters Board is in action will firstly be strategy, because we as a fan organisation can now take issues to the club, the opportunity to be strategic.

Here we also have a broader aspect of fan representation, anybody can have a voice and be part of one of these affiliate groups.

The club also wants to retain elements of the separate working groups, such as the ticketing working group, equal opportunities, and it's important that they can pick up day-to-day issues that will feed into and inform the Supporters Board strategy, which then informs the engagement with the club.

Another feature of the agreement is that it will be formally written into the club's articles of association, which future-proofs the relationship between supporters as it would form part of any transfer of undertaking to new owners.

Signifying relief that such a difficult process had now delivered real change, Blott signalled his optimism for the future, one that put past difficulties behind us:

We've come such a long way from the challenges of the past, and it was critically important to make sure the supporter voice is heard.

We know that fan representation is critically important to maintaining football. I think what we have now is a real synergy and organisational approach that ensures stronger representation and greater engagement.

Reaction to the Supporters Board was swift and almost universally positive, despite the mutterings and keyboard tapping on social media. Les Lawson, chair of the Merseyside Branch of the Official Liverpool Supporters Club, an affiliate of the new Supporters Board, spoke of his delight at the announcement and was keen to reinforce the message of unity between different groups:

Spirit of Shankly deserve rich praise for all the work they have done to reach this agreement that will transform fan engagement. As an affiliate of SOS, along with Liverpool Disabled Supporters Association (LDSA), Kop Outs, Spion Kop 1906 and LFC Women Supporters Club, we will continue to have input and work together as this groundbreaking launch moves forward. This is great news for all Liverpool supporters.

Another affiliate, Spion Kop 1906, is a group of supporters who organise flags and banner displays on the Kop during matchdays. They've also been among the most vocal critics of the earlier Super League debacle, leading a protest in April 2021 that saw all flags and banners removed from the famous stand in opposition to the move.

Emphasising that it's early days, the group has welcomed the creation of the Supporters Board and is pleased to have been a part of the process that brought about this landmark agreement. In a statement, Spion Kop 1906 said:

> We are delighted to be working with Spirit of Shankly and other supporters groups on this, to ensure that fans' views are represented when strategic decisions are made. We're happy to be involved in the process and it's good that all affiliates are working together.

Equally, the Liverpool Women Supporters Club has played a key role in scrutinising the whole process of negotiation and offering constructive feedback each time the Spirit of Shankly negotiating team feed back on progress. They also see the opportunity to join the newly created board as a positive step that will strengthen their voice. Jo Goodall, the chair of the Women's Supporters Club, said:

> We are really pleased to see that the club are listening to fans and are delighted that Spirit of Shankly have welcomed us with open arms. While we do have an open dialogue with the club already, being a part of the SOS Supporters Board gives us additional support and strengthens our engagement to ensure that our views will be listened to and that the women's team will be treated fairly and considered in all future plans.

Ted Morris, the chair of the Liverpool Disabled Supporters Association, feels that the new arrangement will help put the needs of disabled supporters at the heart of decision-making at the club. He also believes that the move will help ensure a brighter future for a whole new generation of disabled supporters, telling me:

> This is a major step forward for our disabled supporters. To know that our fellow supporter groups and Liverpool FC placed such significance in including the LDSA from the very outset of these discussions showed that they take disability seriously and care about their disabled supporters.

We believe that our junior disabled supporters should be able to enjoy the same rite of passage supporting LFC as non-disabled supporters, we believe that this is a significant step in making that a reality.

Similarly, Kop Outs, a group that campaigns on behalf of Liverpool's LGBTQ+ supporters, also sees this as a hugely significant step in ensuring that all sections of the fanbase are represented and that their voice is heard. Founder member Paul Amann told me:

Kop Outs are pleased to be part of these developments. This helps ensure that the needs of LGBTQ+ fans are heard from the beginning. That equality is central to the new board's design and ethos.

This board builds on our work with our allies and realises the ambitions to work with others to keep our club inclusive and accountable.

The importance of the move has not been lost on the city's representatives in parliament and others. Dan Carden, the Labour MP for Walton, whose constituency hosts both of the city's historic football clubs, had previously penned a letter to Liverpool FC's owners back in April.

Written on behalf of all 18 Merseyside MPs, the letter expressed objections to the club's involvement in the Super League and called on FSG to immediately withdraw from it.

Considering the progress made by both the club and its supporters' groups, Carden posted the following via his social media account: 'The new Supporters Board, backed by Spirit of Shankly, is a very positive step in the right direction.' He would later tell me of his hope that this was just the beginning for football in general, and he encouraged other clubs to follow suit:

The European Super League debacle was the end of a long road of commercialisation that is tearing football away from the working-class communities that built it. It showed that we need a reset.

The groundbreaking agreement between LFC and fan groups to introduce a new Supporters Board is very positive and a credit to the supporters who never stopped pushing for greater democratic participation.

I hope to see more clubs taking steps to give supporters a real say in how clubs are run. The Fan-Led Review of Football Governance presents an opportunity to safeguard the future of English football in the interests of those who follow and love the game that must not be missed.

Ian Byrne MP, co-founder of Fans Supporting Foodbanks, a member of the Spirit of Shankly Committee and MP for the parliamentary constituency of West Derby in Liverpool, agrees that the new governance structure at Anfield is of national significance. He was also keen to put on record his gratitude to the local representatives of FSG, who he believes showed a genuine commitment to move on from the mistakes of the past:

I feel this is a game-changer for both Liverpool supporters and supporter engagement nationally. The framework created in this agreement can be utilised by any football club and supporter representatives.

It begins to rebalance the scales of power to the supporter base and it's a proud day for all the affiliates involved in this agreement. I would also thank the local element of FSG for the good faith and genuine desire for change after the ESL debacle. It's an opportunity supporters must now grasp and ensure our influence and voices are never ignored again.

Adding his voice to the chorus of approval, former Shadow Chancellor and Liverpool supporter John McDonnell MP also posted the following on social media: 'Well done to Spirit of Shankly and all involved in securing this breakthrough agreement.'

The national Football Supporters' Association, which was consulted as part of the government's 'Fan-Led Review' of the governance of the game, posted the following in response to the announcement: 'The significance of this agreement cannot be underestimated. We can only hope that it leads to wider change for all supporters of the game.'

Hillsborough Trials Collapse

The Establishment Prolongs Families' and Survivors' Pain

It's my sincere wish that one day I'll write a chapter in this Odyssey that describes how justice has finally been done for those who suffered the most terrible loss and indignities during and after the Hillsborough Stadium disaster. In fact, I hope that one day there will be no need to write about the tragedy, because the families of the fallen and the survivors of the terrible day will have finally been granted a closure of sorts and be able to fully live all the days they have left.

For that to happen, we'd need the truth to be known to all, to feel confidence that such an injustice could never happen to anyone else again, for tragedy chants to vanish from our terraces and, finally, we'd need the establishment to stop resisting all attempts to achieve the above. For so many, Hillsborough is a wound they refuse to allow to heal.

On 4 June 2021, Saunders Law, a legal firm representing 219 of 601 claimants seeking justice for the orchestrated cover-up that occurred following the Hillsborough Stadium disaster in 1989, released a statement on behalf of their clients. In it they revealed that both South Yorkshire and West Midlands Police forces had formally acknowledged that a cover-up took place following the tragedy that cost the lives of 96 supporters, and, as a result, compensation would be paid to those who had suffered psychiatric distress as a result. It represented a significant step in the 30-year campaign for justice, as the statement suggests:

> Through this civil claim for misfeasance in a public office 601 victims sought justice and accountability for the deliberate, orchestrated and thoroughly dishonest police cover-up that suppressed the truth about the responsibility of the police and blamed the football supporters for the horrific events that unfolded at the Hillsborough Stadium on 15 April 1989. 96 Liverpool supporters were unlawfully killed as a result of the police failings that day, and countless others suffered physical and psychological harm.

The distress and heartache caused by the loss of life, and the injuries caused to those who survived, were made significantly worse by the lies told and the cover-up that followed. As a result of the cover-up, that was maintained for nearly 30 years, the victims, both the bereaved and the survivors, and their families and loved ones, suffered additional psychiatric injury. No amount of money can compensate them for the ordeal they have suffered but this settlement acknowledges both the cover-up and its impact upon each of the victims.

South Yorkshire Police issued their own statement, saying:

We offer an unreserved apology to those affected by the Hillsborough disaster and its aftermath. Serious errors and mistakes were made by SY Police, both on 15 April 1989 and during the subsequent investigations.

Those actions on the day [...] tragically led to lives being lost and many being injured. The force's subsequent failings also caused huge distress, suffering and pain, both to the victims and their families. This is something South Yorkshire Police profoundly regrets.

Finally, it seemed, the truth had been acknowledged by those culpable, and some form of compensation agreed. However, the fact that the authorities could have successfully contorted and suppressed the truth for so long, inflicting pain and misery on people already damaged by the tragedy, is in itself astonishing and should be deeply worrying to us all. As Saunders Law points out:

It took until 2012 and the publication of the report of the Hillsborough Independent Panel for the lid to finally be lifted on the depth and extent of the cover-up. The findings of the Panel formed the basis for an apology to the victims and families by the then Chief Constable of South Yorkshire Police, David Crompton. On 12 September 2012 he accepted that there had been a high-level dishonest cover-up by South Yorkshire Police officers, and that the police failed the victims and families and lost control.

After the publication of the Hillsborough Independent Panel report, Prime Minister David Cameron reaffirmed the existence of a cover-up, telling the House of Commons:

> The families have long believed that some of the authorities attempted to create a completely unjust account of events that sought to blame the fans for what happened [...] the families were right.

In quashing the original verdicts of accidental death, the Lord Chief Justice spoke of a tenacious campaign to blame the fans, which he described as false.

Despite this, the families and survivors would once more have to disprove attempts to shift accountability and avoid justice at fresh inquests conducted in Warrington between 2014 and 2016. Fortunately, the jury rejected these lies once more. The inquests ruled that those who perished at Hillsborough had been unlawfully killed.

Tragically, though, subsequent prosecutions failed, leaving those who have battled for so long for truth and justice heartbroken. To add to their pain, in the aftermath of failed prosecutions, Jonathan Goldberg QC repeated claims that supporters were somehow responsible to listeners of a BBC Radio show hosted by Adrian Chiles. Goldberg later apologised for any offence caused, and the BBC and Chiles issued apologies for not challenging his claims on air. For many, though, the damage had already been done.

That nobody has been held to account for both the unlawful killing of 96 people at a football match or the cover-up that followed is an injustice of monumental proportions. It should be unacceptable to every citizen of this country. However, the continued smears and attempts to rewrite history are a chilling warning to all who have been wronged by the state and who seek justice. The victims of the Grenfell fire may be starting out on the same journey as the families of the 96.

Lawyers representing families and survivors of the Hillsborough disasters expressed their hopes that, in light of the acknowledged cover-up, there would now be an end to all attempts to distort the truth:

> We trust that this settlement will put an end to any fresh attempts to rewrite the record and wrongly claim that there

was no cover-up. In so commenting, we contrast the dignity of the bereaved families and the supporters, with the conduct of those who still seek to peddle the discredited lies of the past.

However, not 24 hours after the historic settlement, Chris Daw QC, writing in *The Spectator*, claimed that there 'was no cover up', and suggested that we should 'start to view tragedies as opportunities for truth, reconciliation and learning'. He continued:

> If we cease clamouring for prosecutions at all costs and focus instead on making sure these tragedies do not happen again, the world will be a much better place. Vengeance helps nobody.

It's hard to know where to start with this, aside from screaming, 'When will this ever end?'

Once more we're forced to defend basic truths that have long since been established. It's exhausting and I suspect it's part of a deliberate strategy aimed at wearing down campaigners and forever muddying the waters for future generations. This won't work on Merseyside or with the families of those affected, who live all across the land. However, tragically, it could work with the public at large. That's deeply worrying and it's why articles like this must continue to be challenged.

The final paragraph of Daw's piece is the most sickening of all because it's disguised as an appeal to reason. However, it's little more than a thinly veiled attempt to portray the fight for justice as a quest for 'vengeance'. In it, the QC, who claims to be a Liverpool supporter, calls for a new spirit of truth, reconciliation and learning in the aftermath of disasters. In doing so, Daw is describing a future utopia that's so utterly unrecognisable to those who have battled for decades to find truth, while being denied any hope of reconciliation and seeing scant evidence of any meaningful learning along the way, that he cannot be taken seriously.

If we're to have a culture of learning – and I believe that would be a fitting legacy of the tragedy – then that can only happen when institutions and officials are compelled by law to tell the truth. Victims and their families must be provided with the same support and representation as the authorities who are accused of wrongdoing. In short, we need a 'Hillsborough Law' to be enacted.

I firmly believe, and I always have, that if in 1989 the authorities and institutions had held up their hands at the earliest opportunity, acknowledged their failings, apologised and arranged for prompt physical, psychiatric and financial support for the victims and their families, then those harmed would by now be in a better place. There would be no sense of betrayal, anger and injustice, and the grieving and recovery process would have taken its natural course.

Instead, these same people have been forced to put healing on hold in order to fight for the truth, for decades. Their pain and distress have been greatly exacerbated by the denial of the facts and of justice. To then accuse these same damaged souls of 'pursuing old men', and of 'vengeance', as Chris Daw does, is cruel and shameful. Reconciliation is only possible when the truth is told as quickly as possible, and when there is accountability. This doesn't always mean punishment, but when the wrongdoing is criminal, it should.

We've ultimately been denied justice after Hillsborough. Attempts to blur the truth and shift blame have continued unabated for decades. Even now they continue, despite the overwhelming weight of evidence that supporters played no part in the disaster and that there was an orchestrated cover-up. It remains a national scandal and a wound that sections of the establishment won't allow to heal.

If there's to be any positive legacy from the events of 1989, it has to come in the form of a Hillsborough Law and an end to the rewriting of history. But deeper than that, the British people need to think more critically. Too often in the last 32 years we've battled not just officialdom but public opinion too.

The country hasn't always marched at our side. I hope all those who doubted the campaign will now reflect on that and realise that if they tolerate this, then it could well be them or their loved ones fighting a lonely battle for justice one day. Is that a forlorn hope? Maybe it is, but in the end that's all we have.

Klopp Takes a Stand Against Homophobia

In the run-up to the game against Chelsea at Anfield on 28 August 2021, concerns among Liverpool's LGBTQ+ fans about homophobic chanting on the Kop led to a historic meeting between their representative, Paul Amann, and Jürgen Klopp. For years, Reds' supporters have berated Chelsea with chants of 'Chelsea rent boys!' In truth, many supporters didn't realise this was a homophobic slur and have since resolved not to sing it any more. It's considered so because it uses the phrase 'rent boy' as an insult, and many gay fans feel uncomfortable and ostracised upon hearing it. A smaller group of fans refuse to accept it's a problem, and an even tinier minority simply don't care, arguing that Chelsea fans sing about poverty and Hillsborough, so why shouldn't they return fire.

In the week before the game, I spoke to Paul Amann, the founding member of Kop Outs, an organisation that has campaigned to end discrimination in football for many years, to discuss the issue. Paul has been a Liverpool supporter since childhood. Born to mixed-race parents, his father was a lifelong Red who came to the UK from Trinidad, and his mother was born in Exeter. Paul has always felt that the Reds are in his blood. He jumped at the opportunity to move to the city to begin his studies at university and has since set up home here. Indeed, you'd struggle to find a more committed and passionate Liverpudlian.

'I chose to live in Liverpool, and I chose to support this club,' said Paul, who had recently spoken to Jürgen Klopp at the club's training base at Kirkby about the issue. The Anfield boss received praise in many quarters for taking the issue seriously, signalling his unequivocal support to the LGBTQ+ community and calling for the song to be stricken from the Anfield song book, stating, 'I don't want to hear it. From now on, it is not our song.'

For Paul and many others, Jürgen's words were hugely significant and a sign that the club is showing real leadership in this area. In particular, Jordan Henderson's commitment to wearing rainbow laces and his high-profile engagement with LGBTQ+ supporters on social media coupled with the club's wholehearted support for Virtual Pride are all seen as signs that Liverpool FC are doing much more than paying lip service to the issue.

Of course, events would cast Henderson's apparent commitment to advancing equality and diversity in a new light. His decision to leave the club and play his football in Saudi Arabia in the summer of 2023 would draw huge criticism from swathes of supporters. Perhaps those who felt it was an overreaction, reading Paul's words here, will realise why so many felt that decision represented a betrayal.

Homophobia, like racism in sport, is a societal issue. It causes real pain, psychological damage, and it excludes people from many aspects of community life that others enjoy and take for granted. It also results in a sense of isolation and exclusion. In addition, LGBTQ+ people experience physical violence and hate crimes in the same way that ethnic minority groups do. Tragically, the city of Liverpool has experienced a series of horrific attacks on young gay men, which illustrates graphically that normalising abuse of the LGBTQ+ community in the name of 'banter' is something we shouldn't tolerate as a fanbase.

Paul calls on straight supporters to stand in solidarity with the lesbian, gay and transgender community:

> We've had kids lying battered on the streets of our city just for being gay. It's unacceptable and we all have a role to play in stopping this. The time for being a bystander is over. We need more than words. If you see someone being abused for their sexuality or any other protected characteristic, stand up and challenge it. Tell them it's unacceptable, educate your mates. If it's unsafe for you to do that, then do call the police.

Paul accepts that one club or even football as a game can't solve the problem alone. Instead, it's about all parts of society doing their bit to tackle the issue. If we all do what we can, we have more chance of success, and that starts with all Reds being prepared to listen and show solidarity with fellow fans who are asking for their help.

There are, of course, those who claim the song is just 'banter' and simply aimed at winding up the opposition. Others claim the song isn't homophobic, but a reference to the club selling out in the Abramovich era. To be clear, this is *not* true. The song predates the arrival of the Russian oligarch by many years. It's clearly an attempt to use 'rent boy', a pejorative term for a male prostitute who exclusively services men, as an insult. If you're simultaneously arguing that the song is only meant to 'wind up' the opposition, while arguing it's not derogatory, then you're on shaky ground.

The fact is that using being gay, lesbian or transgender to insult or 'wind up' others does contribute to normalising discrimination against these communities. As a fanbase that prides itself on being inclusive and welcoming to all, this should be unacceptable. However, what frustrates the LGBTQ+ community is that even if you accept that it's sung to get under the skin of the opposition, it doesn't work, and it's counterproductive.

'The players it's aimed at don't even hear it, and, if they do, they don't care,' says Paul. 'Instead, you're only really harming your own fans by singing the song.'

Others have pointed to the abuse Liverpool fans receive over Hillsborough, Heysel and the songs sung about Scousers living in poverty as justification for responding in kind. Kop Outs accept that these songs are also unacceptable. For them, the point isn't to meet one wrong with another; instead, we should be looking to rise above it and challenge all forms of discriminatory behaviour, as Paul explains:

I have wholeheartedly championed the rights of other groups and fought against racism and given my support to the Hillsborough Justice Campaign, Fans Supporting Foodbanks and observe the city's boycott of the S*n.

For me, the ethos of the club, its fans and the city is about solidarity, unity is strength and an injury to one is an injury to all. When I'm at Anfield, I feel I am part of a community that is welcoming and united. It's a warm and positive atmosphere. But when I hear vile chants like the 'rent boys' one aimed at Chelsea players, it's like having a bucket of cold water thrown over you. You feel like an outsider, not welcome.

I will continue to argue the songs sung about our city and the Hillsborough disaster are wrong, and I am proud to live in Liverpool and support this club. But the 'rent boys' chant is wrong too. All we are asking for is the same solidarity we have shown others over the years.

Paul was elected to the Liverpool Supporters' Committee as the LGBTQ+ rep a decade ago. He's the only member of that body to be re-elected and is immensely proud of the service he has provided to the club and its supporters, which includes educating staff and employees alike about LGBTQ+ issues. Paul is also a lifelong trade unionist and has spent his life campaigning for the rights of others and against all forms of discrimination.

For all of that, though, Paul has no problem with singing songs that wind the opposition up and get under their skin. He just feels that the way to do that is to use the legendary wit and humour the Kop has become famous for. He feels we shouldn't need to scrape the barrel, and says Liverpool supporters are too creative for that. 'We have such an amazing range of inventive songs,' said Paul. 'We don't need this one.'

Kop Outs will be at Anfield for the visit of Chelsea on Saturday. Their members and supporters are excited about the new season, just like you are. They'll be there to roar the Reds on, just like you will be. And win, lose or draw, they'll be back again for the next game, just like you. Why would anyone want to make these supporters feel excluded or out in the cold? 'Unity is Strength', the banner on the Kop declares. It would be great if we could show that this is more than just words.

A New Season Beckons
Winds of Change Blow Through Anfield

As we'll learn, Liverpool would start the 2021/22 season in fine form, and there were signs that both the club and its supporters were starting to shake off the traumas of the past two years. However, pre-season friendlies against the likes of Wacker Innsbruck, VfB Stuttgart, FSV Mains, Hertha BSC, Athletic Club Bilbao and Osasuna, which yielded two victories, three draws and a defeat, gave little clue as to how the season would progress.

Indeed, the game against Athletic Club, with the stadium just a third full, finished with Andrew Robertson as the campaign's first serious casualty, leading to concerns that we might be in for another campaign beset with injuries. Off the pitch, the club had introduced new technology that was slowing progress through turnstiles and generating huge queues prior to kick-off. Allocating supporters with designated time slots to arrive didn't go down well.

There had been progress in terms of retaining players, with contract talks ongoing for Adrián, Kelleher, Trent, Alisson and Salah

– contract negotiations that would prove the saga of the summer. And we were all saddened to see Gini Wijnaldum go, in an ill-fated move to Paris Saint-Germain on a free transfer. However, Fabinho, Trent, Robertson, Van Dijk and Alisson would all sign new deals. Liverpool were also busy raising money through sales, generating around £33m from offloading fringe players and hoping to receive a further £40–£50m by moving on the likes of Neco Williams, Divock Origi and Xherdan Shaqiri.

On 26 July, the city of Liverpool and its people were heartbroken to hear that Andrew Devine had become the 97th victim of the Hillsborough disaster. Andrew, aged 55, had suffered life-changing injuries at the game played in 1989. His family released a statement via the club's official website. It included the following lines:

Our collective devastation is overwhelming but so too is the realisation that we were blessed to have had Andrew with us for 32 years. We welcome the conclusion of the coroner, Mr Andre Rebello, made today at Liverpool Coroner's Court, that Andrew was unlawfully killed, making him the 97th fatality of the tragic events that occurred on April 15, 1989.

Andrew had continued to attend games at Anfield, despite the challenges he faced and, in its response, Liverpool Football Club comment that: '[…] in doing so he defied expectations that he would not survive for six months after the tragedy. The thoughts of everyone at the club are with Andrew's family and his carers.' His courageous struggle is yet another tale of resilience and heartbreak associated with that terrible day in 1989.

Pre-season saw the club move forward on several fronts. Contract extensions aside, the first team moved to Kirkby, bringing together the first team and its youth players. Ongoing discussions were underway about the future of Melwood, which would ultimately see it become the permanent base for Liverpool's Women's team, preserving its legacy and providing world-class facilities for the club's female players.

On the transfer front, Ozan Kabak's loan spell was at an end, and Ben Davies left the club without kicking a first-team ball. The Reds added Ibrahima Konaté for £36m, and despite him being linked with

Liverpool every summer since the day he was born, Kylian Mbappé did not arrive at Anfield, again.

The news continued to be filled with tales of government scandal and incompetence that felt eerily reminiscent of the kind of bawdy *Carry On* movies I watched as a kid. However, the news that former Reds legend, Terry McDermott had joined the ever-growing list of former footballers struggling with dementia was heartbreaking. McDermott, speaking to the club's official website, said:

> I've got to get on with it and I will. It's the way I've been brought up. Nothing has come to me easily. I'm not frightened of taking it on and also, as we've seen, there are a lot of former players in a worse state than me.
>
> Battling is second nature. The worst thing was, until my condition was diagnosed you don't know what's going on. The number of ex-players being diagnosed with dementia or Alzheimer's is frightening.
>
> I've been looking forward to going down to Anfield and seeing the lads, people I have known for years and having a good craic with them. Thankfully there are games coming up regularly now which I can go to.

The news was terrible. However, Terry's reaction to it was typical of the man.

Across the park, Rafa Benítez's decision to become Everton's new manager would spark rage among the Blues and hilarity on the red half of the city. Many Everton fans can barely tolerate the fact that Santa Claus wears a red suit, or that traffic cones are red. The social media backlash when former manager Ronald Koeman posted a picture of his Christmas tree, replete with red baubles, forced the Dutchman to take it down and replace it with one suitably decked in blue. Imagine then the fury that greeted the Goodison hierarchy's decision to appoint a former Liverpool manager, the architect of one of the Reds' greatest nights, Istanbul – which just happened to be every Evertonians worst nightmare – to the job of manager of Everton Football Club.

While most Liverpool supporters were bemused by a decision so obviously doomed to failure, very few felt any real animosity towards him. He had, after all, left Liverpool over a decade earlier and had managed other teams in England, Spain and Italy since. At least he'd get to spend time in his palace on the Wirral now. That luxurious abode would hilariously become a target for a squad of 'guerilla Blues' angered that Rafa was now their leader, except they somehow missed their target. As a result, a bemused family of Wirral residents awoke one morning to see a bed sheet strewn across their bushes, with the words 'WE KNOW WHERE YOU LIVE' scrawled across it in blue emulsion. It was obviously aimed at intimidating Benítez, who nevertheless would rest easy in his bed, safe in the knowledge that the mob had no idea where he lived.

Benítez's tenure would be hamstrung from the beginning, with the majority of the Everton board opposed to his appointment, a hostile fanbase and the club's perilous financial position setting him on an unavoidable road to ruin. The money paid to him and his staff by way of compensation after his inevitable sacking would do little to ease that.

Meanwhile, Liverpool's vast social media following provided great entertainment with their now annual mass rant about what they perceived as Liverpool's – or FSG's, to be more accurate – lack of spending. The subsequent departure of transfer guru Michael Edwards from Liverpool fuelled their ire and convinced them it was evidence of the owners' lack of ambition.

When it comes to FSG, I'm ambivalent. I'd agree that, in terms of the transfer market, they could afford to be a little more generous when it comes to player acquisitions, and they could stand to take a few more risks. I've also been more than happy to protest their actions when I felt they conflicted with the interests of supporters or the club. However, overall, I'm happy that they don't spend like drunken sailors on shore leave, as other owners have. And I'm realistic enough to know that any ownership would need to be held to account, and their primary motive will always be profit over supporters. But for those who live out their lives in cyberspace – and some who don't – our current owners can do no right.

The summer of 2021 saw this reach almost comedic levels when several accounts started posting virtual flyers for protests aimed at driving the owners out, which involved supporters marching from the Arkles pub to Anfield Road – not a long march, to be fair. Such a demonstration would have been particularly challenging, though, given that, at the time, Anfield Road was a building site due to the expansion of that end of the ground, funded by the club's owners. Inevitably, though, I was assured by one post originating far from Anfield that 'there is going to be a huge FSG Out demonstration in Liverpool', and that 'things are going to change'. Nothing materialised.

The reality is that although few match-going Reds would describe themselves as 'FSG in', they don't spend any time demanding that they leave. We are, of course, sceptical of any ownership model, and keen to hold them to account. However, those of us who lived through the Hicks and Gillett era fully understand how bad things can really get. And believe me, under FSG we're nowhere near those levels. If they ever stoop that low, I'll be sure to jump on that bandwagon. Until then, better the devil you know.

For the media and punditry class, with few commendable exceptions, Liverpool were deemed a complete write-off for the season ahead. Gabriel Agbonlahor declared that Liverpool's bench was like a tenth-placed team's, while Gary Neville worried about Klopp's mental health, declaring 'something's not right with him'. The 21 pundits asked by the BBC for their season's predictions didn't give Liverpool a chance of top four, let alone the title. By the season's conclusion, they'd be forced to acknowledge that Klopp's Reds were a team on the cusp of brilliance.

So, as silly season ended, it was starting to feel like Covid was fading from view. Of course, it wasn't, but it suited us all to at least try to move past the trauma and embrace a new season. Soon stadiums would be full again. It was an exhilarating prospect, so with season ticket renewed, I couldn't wait for it to all kick off.

Klopp's Rejuvenated Warriors Roar into New Season

It was a new-look Jürgen Klopp that led his men to Carrow Road for the season opener against Norwich City on 14 August 2021. Sans trademark spectacles, following corrective eye surgery, the boss had lost none of his passion and desire. Neither had the away end, who after a year's enforced absence sang their hearts out.

An almost constant refrain of 'Si Señor', an ode to Roberto Firmino, was just one of the highlights of the game, in which the Reds triumphed 3-0, despite the absence of Andy Robertson. Liverpool blew away the Canaries thanks to strikes by their front three: Jota, Firmino and Salah.

The Egyptian's agent, locked in contract negotiations with Liverpool's hierarchy, clearly felt his hand had been strengthened because of his client's two assists and a goal, and immediately took to social media to post: 'I hope they were watching.' It was a move that angered many supporters and handed ammunition to those claiming that the club was dragging its heels due to financial issues. The club, meanwhile, briefed the media that talks had opened to make Salah the highest earner in the club's history. They had, and they did.

Liverpool followed up the win with a 2-0 victory at home to Sean Dyche's Burnley a week later. The game marked the first capacity attendance at Anfield since the country entered lockdown 529 days earlier, with an attendance of 52,591. And, in an emotional moment, Jordan Henderson laid a wreath at the front of the Kop, in memory of all those who had lost their lives in the pandemic. Goals from Jota and Mané sealed the points. Jürgen Klopp, clearly delighted with the day's proceedings, revelled once more in football played in front of a crowd, declaring that 'all our dreams were fulfilled'.

A video released online on the eve of the game featured Jürgen Klopp and had many of us in tears. 'You cannot believe, and you will never understand how much I've missed you. Football is a nice game without you. But with you it's the best game in the world,' the manager said.

For me, it was difficult to keep emotions in check before, during and after the game. In truth, I remember little about it, only how it felt, how the stadium looked and sounded, and how relieved we all were that the seats around us were filled with the same familiar faces. We'd all made it through and couldn't have been happier to once again take our places at Anfield.

The Reds got to the end of August with a creditable draw away to Chelsea at Stamford Bridge on 29 August. A Mohamed Salah penalty on the stroke of half-time clinched a point after Kai Havertz had put Chelsea in front. Just three days later, Liverpool announced that Jordan

Henderson had signed a new contract, with the player promising to 'end his career at Anfield'.

Manchester City had flown into the new campaign with three wins from three, scoring 11 and conceding just one. It was said that Pep Guardiola had been inspired to change his side's formation and tactics after watching a flock of wild geese flying over the club's training facilities. As metaphors go, it wasn't a bad one, I suppose, but when I think of Pep and City's approach to football, it reminds me less of wildfowl and more of expensive jets. They get you to your destination faster, and the aircraft don't shit on your car.

Key to Pep's genius would be the purchase of bench decoration Jack Grealish for £100m, bringing the five-year spend to £1bn, which allegedly is the Financial Fair Play equivalent of shitting on everyone else's car.

Five wins and a draw saw Liverpool comfortably through September, advancing in both the league, the League Cup and in Europe. A 3-0 win over Leeds United at Elland Road was marred only by a horrific injury to Harvey Elliott, who had started the season in scintillating form. His link-up play with Salah had us all dreaming of the possibilities. He'd face a lengthy lay-off, and the injury would derail his astonishing progress. Klopp vowed to wait for him, words that no doubt sustained the youngster throughout his extensive rehab.

Club captain Jordan Henderson reflected on what Elliott offered to the game, with a glowing assessment of the player's contribution, saying:

> Harvey's a special player. He's been fantastic last season when he was on loan at Blackburn and then he's come back in great shape for pre-season and done really well, so he deserved his start today and I thought he took it.
>
> I thought he was outstanding, his work rate, but also obviously the stuff he can do on the ball, the final passes. Overall, I thought he was outstanding.

As the Reds headed into October, they found themselves top of the league, leading Manchester City by a single point. By mid-October Liverpool had seen off AC Milan, Porto and Atlético Madrid in their

Champions League group-stage matches and had advanced further in the League Cup, with another 3-0 win over Norwich City.

In the Premier League, Mohamed Salah lit up two games, against Manchester City at Anfield, and Watford at Vicarage Road. The first saw him dazzle the Manchester City defence with a display of close ball control that had the home crowd mesmerised. Their oohs and aahs were audible around the ground as the Egyptian, bathed in sunshine, danced past a succession of challenges to put the ball in the back of the net to put the Reds 2-1 in front. From where I sat, it was difficult to fully appreciate his brilliance, even though we could see how unlikely a goal was when he picked up the ball, and how he seemingly glided past the opposition as if they were training-ground dummies. As the ball hit the net the resultant exultation engulfed all four ends of the ground, while all City's players and supporters could do was stand and watch in stunned silence. Footage of the goal was played on repeat on Liverpool's in-house channel and was lapped up by Reds all over the world. The only fly in the ointment was City's equaliser.

It was a moment of sublime Salah genius never to be repeated, or was it? Lightning doesn't strike twice, but Mohamed Salah does. Almost two weeks later, Liverpool travelled to Vicarage Road to take on Claudio Ranieri's Watford. It ended with a complete rout of The Hornets. The Reds ran out 5-0 winners, thanks to goals from Sadio Mané, Roberto Firmino (3) and, of course, Mohamed Salah.

I felt some sympathy for Bobby, who had scored a hat-trick and assisted in another, but there was no getting away from the world-class play of the Egyptian King. Once again he tormented the opposition with a goal that was almost a carbon copy of his masterclass against City, and the away end was equally as beguiled. It was a performance that would see Salah lauded – with some justification – as the world's best, and it meant Liverpool needed to do everything in their power to keep him at Anfield.

For his part, Mo would leave us all in no doubt not only of his brilliance, but of his desire to stay. In an interview with the foreign press, he would declare, 'I want to stay until the end of my career.' The ball was now firmly in Liverpool's court.

Manchester United 0-5 Liverpool

Reds All-Conquering Start Crowned by Old Trafford Demolition Job

On 24 October 2021, Liverpool travelled to Old Trafford and delivered a message to their greatest enemy. Number one in the UK singles chart was a song by Adele that contained the line 'Go easy on me', and it would have been difficult to find a more fitting lyric for the way the United board must have been feeling before kick-off.

This was a victory so comprehensive that it left United's players, their manager, Ole Gunnar Solskjær, their army of TV pundits and, of course, their supporters with nowhere to hide. To score five goals without reply against Manchester United is a rare joy, and to do so in their own backyard is a result for the ages. However, the thrashing of the old enemy would be just one of a catalogue of high points in a season that was so far threatening to defy all expectations. It was a victory that the BBC's Phil McNulty said 'emphasised the vast gulf between the sides in brutal fashion'.

Liverpool raced out of the traps from the off, cutting the home side to pieces at will. It took just five minutes for them to take the lead after Mohamed Salah, who would go on to bag a hat-trick in a game so one-sided it bordered on embarrassing, sent Naby Keïta clean through on goal. The Guinean composed himself well and slotted the ball past a helpless David de Gea. The faces on the supporters in the Stretford End, a dazzling portrait of dejection and utter misery, were a joy to behold as the Liverpool players celebrated in front of them. In the away end it was pandemonium as the travelling Kop smelled blood. United's defence had been useless and were ruthlessly exposed.

A trip to Old Trafford is rarely easy. You'd take any kind of win, and even a draw – given the history of the two clubs – isn't a terrible result. You never dream of coasting. Yet as the Liverpool supporters watched on with glee throughout that incredible first half, that's exactly what the Reds did.

Just nine minutes later, Diogo Jota doubled Liverpool's lead, sliding on to an inch-perfect assist from Trent Alexander-Arnold, who was enjoying so much freedom against a United midfield that had gone completely AWOL and a back line that looked terrified every time he went near them.

121

Liverpool were now toying with their victims and looked like they could score at will. We'd have accepted a 2-0 half-time lead, but Salah had other ideas. His first came when Keïta returned the favour and teed him up beautifully to smash the ball into the roof of the net. By now the Stretford End was silent, save for the occasional expletive and furious gesture towards their own players. They could barely muster a song, while the away end mocked with chants of 'Ole's at the wheel'.

Salah had now scored in ten consecutive games. However, he wasn't about to take his foot off the gas. On the stroke of half-time, the Egyptian took a Jota pass in his stride and beat De Gea with ease. It was 4-0 with 45 minutes to go, and Solskjær suffered the gauntlet of United fans as he headed for the tunnel. In truth, there was barely anyone left, as the stands began to empty, with United fans choosing an early exit to spare themselves any further humiliation.

Everything the United manager did exploded in his face. His decision to remove Mason Greenwood and replace him with Paul Pogba failed to make a jot of difference, as Salah charged down a sublime Jordan Henderson through ball and dispatched it with aplomb, completing his hat-trick on 50 minutes.

United's misery was complete when Pogba saw red for a horrible tackle on Keïta, who would see no further action, having been stretchered off. Much to my and the entire away end's disappointment, Liverpool elected not to rub salt in the Stretford End's gaping wounds and saw the game out without further incident.

By now there were so many empty seats, we'd have been forgiven to thinking we had re-entered lockdown. Solskjær later declared that his team 'won't give up' after the rout at the hands of Liverpool, but judging by the sound of his players' voices echoing around an empty cavernous Old Trafford, their fans already had. This was the first time a United team had conceded five without reply at home since 1955, during the Matt Busby era. It was their worst defeat to Liverpool since 1925.

The reaction of the media was as damning of United's performance as it was effusive in its praise of Liverpool's brilliance. Writing in the *Daily Mail*, Martin Samuel was blown away by Liverpool's demolition of their old rivals:

Quite simply, Liverpool took Manchester United apart. Not just with their football, but their wit, their game management and intelligence […] In the build-up it was possible to imagine this as a looming battle royale. Liverpool are the better team, but Manchester United always raise their game for this match; just as Liverpool did in the days when they were underdogs.

It could be one of those epic, toe-to-toe encounters, both teams at it, like the old days. That illusion was quickly dispelled.

David Hytner of *The Guardian* spoke of the Reds' utter dominance:

Liverpool were excellent. Again. They remain unbeaten this season and the statistics show that they have scored a minimum of three goals in every away match, with Salah's hat-trick continuing his club-record scoring run.

It is now an astonishing 10 matches on the spin in which he has found the net. But, as strange as it sounds, Liverpool did not have to locate their highest gears. They almost strolled to victory.

Freddie Keighley, writing in *The Mirror*, focused on Keïta's performance, capped by a goal and an assist:

With Thiago and Fabinho ruled out of the trip to Old Trafford through injury, Keita maintained his spot in the starting XI and took a matter of minutes to reaffirm the many qualities he offers Liverpool.

Operating as the most-advanced of the midfield trio, the 26-year-old put the Reds ahead with a calm finish from Mohamed Salah's through ball.

Eight minutes later, he set up Trent Alexander-Arnold to assist Diogo Jota and later grabbed an assist himself for Salah's first goal.

Having endured a goalless 2020/21 season, Keita has already scored three times this campaign and regardless of supposed defensive vulnerabilities, his contributions on the front foot are vital for Liverpool.

According to *The Telegraph*'s Jason Burt, only Manchester City and Chelsea stood in the way of a second Liverpool title in three years. There was also a note of sympathy for the United manager:

Liverpool, Manchester City and Chelsea, the three title contenders, are in a different league. United are eight points behind leaders Chelsea after just nine games – that is almost a point a game – and surely, already, the best they can hope for is fourth place.

Maybe that is good enough for the Glazers, but they should have looked at Solskjær's face as he walked off. He was shell-shocked. He was lost. He looked like a man drowning.

They were words that read like an epitaph for the United manager, and so it might. He'd survive less than a month, sacked on 21 November 2021.

For Liverpool it was a case of job done, and another marker on the road to recovery for a team who had been completely written off at the start of the campaign.

A dejected Solskjær faced the cameras at full time. There was nowhere for him to hide, and no excuses offered. 'It's not easy to say something, apart from it's the darkest day I've had leading these players,' he said, honestly. 'We weren't good enough individually or as a team. You can't give a team like Liverpool those chances and unfortunately, we did.'

The contrast with his opposite number could not be starker. Jürgen exuded pride and passion, as he told the waiting media:

Did I expect that? No. But what we did in the last third was absolutely insane. How we pressed them high, won balls, scored wonderful goals. I actually told the guys at half-time we need to play better!

The result is insane. It will take a while if it ever happens again. After the game I got told this has never happened before in the long history of LFC and this group wanted to make new chapters for this big history, and tonight was a new chapter.

But you have to understand these games right. We lost once against Aston Villa, 7-0, or 8-0, whatever, I forget these kinds of things very quickly, but it was high.

[...] I couldn't be happier, because it's just incredible being part of this team. Winning 5-0 is exceptional.

Somehow, exceptional didn't begin to describe it.

The Reds Go Gathering Cups in May

Liverpool FC October 2021–May 2022

Reds Bid Farewell to Ray Kennedy

Shankly's Last Gift to Liverpool

On 30 November 2021, Liverpool Football Club said farewell to the legendary Ray Kennedy. A key member of Bob Paisley's all-conquering teams of the 70s, he'll live forever in the hearts of generations of Kopites.

Born on 28 July 1951 in the North East, Ray Kennedy became a legend for both Arsenal and Liverpool. However, on Merseyside he forged a timeless bond with the army of supporters who stood on the Kop. Kennedy tasted success most players can only dream of, winning every honour possible at both Highbury and Anfield.

He was persuaded to join Liverpool, who were managed by Bill Shankly, in 1974. Arsenal manager Bertie Mee was about to sign Brian Kidd for Ray's position, and suggested that Kennedy should stay and fight for his place or take Liverpool up on their offer. He chose Anfield and Liverpool, only for the man who signed him to announce his own retirement on the same day Kennedy was unveiled as a Reds player. As welcomes go, it couldn't have been more dramatic.

Kennedy didn't have an easy start, and felt the supporters lacked confidence in him. Deployed as a striker for the Gunners, he struggled to compete with the likes of Kevin Keegan and John Toshack. However, when Paisley moved him out to the left side of midfield, everything changed for the player. It was a masterstroke that Kennedy fully appreciated:

> When I first arrived at Anfield I struggled with my form and don't think the fans rated me but as soon as Bob Paisley moved me to midfield that's when they started to appreciate me.

The departing Shankly gave his final signing the best of references at the press conference that shocked football, saying the following of the player:

> There is no doubt Kennedy will do a good job for Liverpool. He is big, brave and strong. His signing means that we now have the greatest strength in depth we have ever had.

It has been a momentous day, but his signing shows that I am not running away. Maybe it will be said that one of the last things I did at this club was to sign a great new player.

His words could not be more prophetic, as Kennedy would go on to play a key role not only in the delivery of silverware, but also in providing some of the greatest moments in the club's illustrious history. His pass that set up David Fairclough's historic strike against Saint-Étienne on route to their first European Cup in 1977 is now the stuff of legend.

During his time at Anfield, Kennedy formed many friendships and won the respect of his team-mates. But none were as strong as the bond he forged with local hero Jimmy Case. As Kennedy would later recall, the pair were something of a dangerous duo:

Fines, court appearances, jail ... we were bad for each other. We had a bit of fun, but we did it at the right time. At hotels, when we asked for the room key, the receptionist would dive under the desk and say: 'Not you two!' Everyone has a pal, but Jim and I went deeper than that. If something went wrong, one of us sorted it out. It was a good friendship.

His friend would be equally effusive when discussing both their friendship and the qualities that Ray possessed:

Tactically Ray was in a different league. He had a delicate touch; a sweet left foot and his movement was phenomenal. I used to cover much more ground and tackle more and he'd cover less ground but use his head more.

We worked well together. His best point has to be his timing. I'd have the ball; I'd look up and he was gone. A perfectly timed run, ghosting in from the left, losing his marker. I'd put in the simplest of balls and bang! One nil.

Kennedy scored many important goals for the Reds, but perhaps his most significant was the one he managed against Bayern Munich in the semi-final of the European Cup in 1981. Munich had fought out a goalless draw at Anfield in the first leg, and with the Reds struggling with injuries and then the loss of Kenny Dalglish early in the return, hopes of progress were looking bleak. With the game heading into its 83rd minute, Kennedy picked up a David Johnson pass and hit a powerful right-footed shot into the net, clinching a priceless away goal and seeing the Reds through to their third European Cup Final in five years.

Ray was diagnosed with Parkinson's disease in November 1986 but always felt the signs were there during his playing career. In his autobiography, he reflected on his feelings of exhaustion in the dressing room after a game. And how his team-mates would be full of energy, while he'd be slumped in the corner. He'd always managed to give everything for 90 minutes, but his developing illness allowed him only that, and his recovery time was longer than his peers.

In an interview with Tony Barrett, Ray spoke emotionally and affectionately of his relationship with the Liverpool supporters. Speaking of the support he'd received from them during his long illness, he said:

> The Liverpool fans have always been very special, and I always knew that, but I suppose I didn't realise just how special – now I do.
>
> I really appreciate how much they have done for me, and it is hard for me to put into words just how much I appreciate it.
>
> It is great they remember me and for people to give so generously [to the Ray of Hope Charity set up by Liverpool supporter Karl Coppack] to try and help me is tremendous. Absolutely tremendous [...] I will always be Liverpool through and through.

Ray Kennedy won it all in football. At Arsenal he won the Fairs Cup, league title and FA Cup. For Liverpool he made 393 appearances between 1974 and 1982, scoring 72 goals. He carried away five First Division titles, three European Cups, one UEFA Cup, one League Cup, a European Super Cup, and four Charity Shields.

Mohamed Salah Masterpiece Leaves Rafa on the Brink

We've arrived at 1 December 2021, and as Liverpool prepared themselves for the short trek across a frosty Stanley Park, the city was still dealing with the aftermath of an apparent terrorist attack, after a taxicab was engulfed in a fireball outside the Liverpool Women's Hospital. Everton were a team in freefall under Rafa Benítez, having lost their previous seven games, while Liverpool had won five, drawn one and lost one. A defeat for the Blues would plunge them closer to a relegation dogfight and possibly seal their boss's fate.

The Reds were continuing to defy expectations, making a mockery of their showing of the previous season. They'd advanced to the fifth round of the League Cup with a victory over Preston North End, and triumphs over Atlético and Porto in Europe had put them in pole position in their Champions League group; and, of course, Liverpool were second in the Premier League.

We'd been here before, though, only to implode at exactly this stage of the season. I couldn't bring myself to even dream of the sort of season we ended up having, and despite Everton's terrible form, I could never take a game against the Blues for granted. There's a strange sort of logic that takes you over before a derby day, and it's more about the law of averages than the quality of the opposition. My rational self was telling me that Everton didn't stand a chance, but the side of me ensconced in the city and only too aware of how unbearable the blue half could be, if they won, gnawed away at my confidence, reminding me that they're due a win, you know.

If you haven't grown up cheek by jowl with Evertonians, this probably sounds ridiculous. Chances are you don't pay the Blues that much attention, and you most likely seldom come across one in your daily life. You're more likely to run into an Arsenal, Chelsea or United fan, so why spend too much time worrying about a defeat to Everton. For me, though, the consequences of a slip-up in the Merseyside derby don't bear thinking about.

In truth, my anxiety wasn't totally without justification. Liverpool had won just one game in their previous nine visits to Goodison Park. The risk of a sucker-punch could never be completely ruled out, no matter what sort of form both teams were in.

For our neighbours, the fear was real and logical. They were on their worst run of form for 22 years and facing a ruthless Liverpool attack featuring possibly the world's greatest marksman. They were anticipating a mauling of historic proportions, and that's exactly what they got. My in-laws were left crying about the result for weeks.

Writing for *Royal Blue Mersey*, Tom Mallows had the following to say:

> It was the total humiliation that all Evertonians feared, with a double from Mohamed Salah plus strikes from Jordan Henderson and Diogo Jota completing the victory, while the Liverpool supporters chanting Benitez's name – just as we all predicted when he made the controversial move to Goodison in the summer – topped off the embarrassment.

It was a passage that so perfectly summed up the psyche of both sets of supporters in the run-up to and the aftermath of such games. Losing to any other opponent can be painful in its own way, but defeat at the hands of your nearest rivals is associated with embarrassment that lasts for weeks if not months, and you're forced to live with your tormentors throughout all of that.

Having watched Liverpool put four past Arsenal and Southampton in their previous two league outings, Evertonians had feared the worst. However, being prepared for defeat made it no less difficult for them to take. The defeat to Liverpool ramped up their relegation fears, which now became ever-present. For Liverpool fans it would ensure a very merry Christmas on the Mersey.

Liverpool tore into Everton, whose defence simply couldn't cope with the ferocity of the Reds' attack. Klopp's men were two up in 19 minutes thanks to goals from Henderson and Salah. Demarai Gray gave the Gwladys Street hope in the 38th minute, latching on to a Richarlison through ball and slotting it past Alisson, but as David Moyes once said, 'It's the hope that kills you.'

In the 64th minute, Seamus Coleman dawdled when trying to control the ball close to his 18-yard box and was immediately pounced upon by a hungry Mo Salah, who picked the Irishman's pocket, raced clear and beat Pickford with ease.

Next it was the turn of Diogo Jota to twist the knife and send what was left of the home crowd into fits of apoplexy. Latching on to an Andrew Robertson pass, the Portuguese glided past Allan and launched a shot high over the advancing Jordan Pickford and into the roof of the net. The humiliation was complete and, as the Goodison faithful stared down the barrel of another relegation battle and launched yet another protest at their club, their manager and everyone else, Liverpool's eyes were firmly fixed on the top end of the table.

This was Everton's worst defeat at home in 39 years and they were now eight games without a win. Benítez's confidence that they 'would improve soon' seemed to be pulled from a place somewhere south that never sees the sunshine. Little wonder that the 'Rafa's at the wheel' chants got a joyous airing.

The Reds were now the leading scorers in Europe's top five leagues with 43 goals. Although they were third in the league, two points behind leaders Chelsea, the display against Everton gave us all belief that we could close that gap over the coming weeks.

Demands for 'Hillsborough Law'

TV Drama, Anne, *Lays Bare Injustices that Must Never Happen Again*

On 7 January 2022, bereaved families, former prime ministers and a host of high-profile public figures came together in an unprecedented joint call for a major rebalancing of the justice system to prevent others from experiencing the same injustices experienced by the Hillsborough families. The 'Hillsborough Law Now' event united powerful voices from across society and the political spectrum and came in the aftermath of Kevin Sampson's powerful drama *Anne*, broadcast on ITV. It told the story of Anne Williams's fight for justice for her son Kevin. It provoked a hugely emotional response across the nation.

Despite the horrific experiences endured by the families of those who lost their lives at Hillsborough and the countless survivors who still struggle daily with its aftermath, promises of change have failed to materialise. Therefore, there's no guarantee that a similar injustice could not befall others.

The event took place four years on from Bishop James Jones's review of the brutal experiences of the Hillsborough families at the hands of the system. Yet the government had still not provided a formal response.

Bishop Jones's powerful report – 'The Patronising Disposition of Unaccountable Power' – contains 25 recommendations, which together would form the basis of a comprehensive reform of the system. The most significant of these are:

- A charter for Families Bereaved Through Public Tragedy, which should be binding on all public bodies.

- A statutory duty of candour on all police officers – and other identified public servants – which applies during all forms of public inquiry and criminal investigation.

- Proper participation of bereaved families at inquests, through publicly funded legal representation and an end to limitless legal spending by public bodies. There is a case for parity of legal funding to create a level playing field in courtrooms.

- A Public Advocate to act for families of the deceased after major incidents.

In the years that followed the report we saw the collapse of Hillsborough trials, which meant that, despite a coroner's verdict ruling that the 97 victims of the 1989 disaster were unlawfully killed, nobody has been held to account for their deaths.

The 'Hillsborough Law Now' event, held in Manchester and symbolically co-hosted by Mayor of Greater Manchester Andy Burnham and Mayor of Liverpool City Region Steve Rotheram, was yet another step on a very long road. There would need to be many more. Burnham, whose speech at the 25th Hillsborough anniversary memorial held at Anfield was interrupted by cries of 'justice', said:

> The appalling treatment of the Hillsborough families at the hands of the legal system shames our nation. But it is sadly not unique.
>
> From Peterloo 200 years ago to Grenfell today, ordinary bereaved families continue to be treated in a cruel and dismissive way by a justice system which favours the powerful and the connected. It is a pattern that keeps on repeating itself and it is time to break it.

We need to level up the scales of justice in favour of bereaved families so that the truth is established at the first time of asking. We must spare families the secondary trauma that is often inflicted by cruel treatment at the hands of the system.

Truth, justice and accountability will not flourish without a fundamental rebalancing of our legal, coronial and judicial systems. Out of respect for the Hillsborough families, we call on the Government to commit to that by bringing forward a Hillsborough Law – now.

Steve Rotheram, a Liverpool supporter who was at Hillsborough on that fateful day in 1989 and has previously spoken of how he swapped his Leppings Lane end ticket for a stand seat just 15 minutes before kick-off, said:

What happened at Hillsborough in 1989 and the cover-up that followed is a national disgrace. It is a testament to the courage and determination of the families and campaigners that the truth was finally uncovered after decades of battling against the might of the state. That cannot be allowed to happen again.

The story of Hillsborough is not an outlier. There are countless other injustices that follow the same pattern. It is time that we broke that cycle and put integrity back at the heart of our justice system.

This is an issue that should be well above petty party politics. Levelling up cannot only be about big spending announcements and shiny infrastructure projects. It should also be about righting long-term, structural injustices. And there are few bigger than this. Levelling the scales of justice is the very essence of levelling up.

We need a Hillsborough Law now to ensure that ordinary people have a fair chance at getting the justice they deserve.

The event was successful in galvanising football, with many clubs throwing their weight behind the campaign. The first of them was Brighton & Hove Albion. In a powerful statement, published on the club's official website, the Seagulls declared they were proud to stand in solidarity with all those affected by the Hillsborough disaster, and Liverpool Football Club:

> Brighton & Hove Albion are proud to add their support to the campaign to launch a Hillsborough Law to provide transparency to bereaved families and rebalance the scales of justice in the UK.
>
> The new law, proposed in 2017 by the Hillsborough families and survivors, and championed by the Mayors of Liverpool and Manchester, Steve Rotheram and Andy Burnham, seeks to compel all public officials to be truthful at inquiries into public tragedies.
>
> It also aims to ensure bereaved families have access to adequate public funding to support their quest for answers.
>
> We stand in solidarity with all the families who lost their loved ones at Hillsborough on 15 April 1989, or as a result of the tragic events; the survivors and Liverpool Football Club – who have carried themselves with such dignity for almost 33 years in the search for truth and justice – and call for a Hillsborough Law Now.

The statement finished with the words 'Justice for the 97'. The club also published their message of support in their matchday programme ahead of their home game against Crystal Palace.

Ian Byrne, MP for Liverpool West Derby Constituency, was keen to express his gratitude to Brighton:

> This is a brilliant show of solidarity from Brighton, a football club that understands the meaning of the word and has shown it once again with its support for a Hillsborough Law. We now need every club and their supporters to back the call and make it impossible for this Government to ignore it.

Responding to the move, Joe Blott, chair of Spirit of Shankly, who had been at Hillsborough in both the 1988 and 1989 FA Cup semi-finals, had this to say:

I can't speak on behalf of the bereaved or their family members left haunted, alone and often vilified for over 30 years, they do that brilliantly with composure and humility, but I can tell you one small story that has lived with me this whole time.

Being at the stadium was numbing but you also felt powerless, because you could see what was happening but the police, the FA and stewards were adamant that once the pitch was cleared the game would continue.

We asked if we could get on to the pitch to help; we were told in no uncertain terms to 'stay where you are'.

As we watched fans carry fellow supporters on advertising hoardings, we knew that something terrible had happened. Eventually, the game was called off and we left the ground to the rumours of the numbers of dead and injured.

About 10 miles from Sheffield we found a telephone box, and we rang home. My mum answered the phone and simply shouted, 'Joe's alive.' She'd been watching the disaster unfold on TV, and was far more aware than me, even though I'd been at the match.

That's when it hit me, I was alive but clearly others weren't. Others weren't ringing their mum. Their mum wasn't getting that call.

This is why the Hillsborough Law is so important. It took the families of the bereaved 30 years to effectively receive that phone call. In any civil society that is not right, for the victims and relatives of any disaster.

On behalf of Spirit of Shankly and myself, thank you to all at Brighton & Hove Albion FC for your compassion, values and leadership in supporting this campaign.

Hillsborough is just one in a long line of historic injustices suffered by many at the hands of the British state. Contributions were also heard at the event from families of 22,000 UK service personnel who suffered deadly radiation poisoning after the Second World War, as a result of their exposure to nuclear weapons testing. Many of them had been involved in a generational, 70-year campaign for truth and justice.

Others spoke of Orgreave, the Manchester Arena bombing, Grenfell, the campaign of the Covid bereaved, and all identified similarities in the way the state responds to such cases.

Steve Kelly, whose brother Mick died at the disaster in Sheffield in 1989, argued that society can no longer afford not to support the proposed new law. Recalling how many times he has heard the phrase 'haven't they had enough?' in reference to him and fellow justice campaigners, Steve believes that the lessons of other disasters showed that all of us are vulnerable and none of us would want to spend decades fighting for justice if we were caught up in tragedy.

In my heart it's difficult to reconcile the idea that we live in a 'civilised society' with the need to have a legal requirement to tell the truth in the aftermath of a civic disaster, but that's where we continue to find ourselves. Campaigners have proposed that a Hillsborough Law would provide a level playing field for the victims of such tragedies, ensuring that they're properly supported by a Public Advocate, given the best legal representation and it would legally bind public bodies and individuals to a 'duty of candour'. As this book nears publication, no such law has been implemented. However, following the Labour Party's election victory in July 2024, a commitment to implement such a law has now been included in the King's Speech.

To be clear, this proposed law isn't about reopening inquiries into Hillsborough. It's about protecting future generations from the kind of harm the families of the 97 and the survivors have suffered over 35 years, and, as such, it would be a fitting legacy for the victims of all disasters.

Neither is this a Liverpool issue; in truth, it never was. It's about social justice and basic human fairness – and all of us should feel we have a common interest in that. We all owe it to ourselves and each other to support this campaign, whoever we support or wherever we live.

Sadly, the shirt on your back, the badge on your chest or the town where you live is not enough to protect you from injustice and cover-ups. However, a Hillsborough Law would.

Relentless Reds Go Toe to Toe with City
More Silverware Beckons

With Britain battered by Storm Arwen in December 2021, thousands of homes were without power as football continued in time-honoured fashion. Liverpool swept through their schedule, blowing away Wolves, AC Milan, Aston Villa and Newcastle, before running aground at Tottenham, where a frustrating draw threatened to ruin their festive cheer.

A dramatic late goal by Divock Origi at Molineux on 4 December broke Wolves' stubborn resolve and sent Liverpool to the top of the table, at least temporarily. At Villa a Mohamed Salah penalty was enough, and Klopp's charges then came from behind at home to Newcastle to win 3-1. A Trent Alexander-Arnold rocket settled a nervous affair with just three minutes left on the clock and the Reds nervously held on to a 2-1 lead. The way in which the Scouser rolled up his sleeves, said, 'I've had enough of this,' and just sparked out Newcastle with a strike that sent all of us wild with relief and joy was the stuff of *Boys' Own* tales. It was a great way to settle a scrap, and the player's knee slide, arms folded across his chest in front of an adoring Kop, smacked of the best form of arrogance.

In Europe, Liverpool dispatched AC Milan 2-1 at the San Siro, ensuring that they'd won six out of six games in the group phase of the Champions League, topping their group comfortably. With the Christmas period about to reach its tinsel-topped, belt-busting peak, the Reds looked forward to a trip to the capital and the Tottenham Hotspur Stadium.

In London, referee Paul Tierney gave a rocket boost to his apparent feud with Jürgen Klopp and Liverpool. In a game in which Liverpool came from behind to lead, before Son Heung-min levelled for Spurs in the 74th minute, the Londoners should have been down to ten men after a horror tackle by England's Harry Kane on Andrew Robertson earlier in the match.

Just five minutes before Son's equaliser, the Scotsman saw red for a foul on Emerson Royal. The injustice drove Klopp into a frenzy of rage and led to accusations of a vendetta by Paul Tierney against Klopp personally, and of favouritism towards Harry Kane.

Tierney had endured a shocking game, denying Jota a clear penalty, and Klopp raced on to the pitch at full time to confront him. The draw saw the Reds lose ground in the title race. Fortunately, better luck awaited with the visit of Leicester City to Anfield for a League Cup fifth-round clash just three days later.

A heavily rotated Liverpool team, featuring the youngsters – Caoimhín Kelleher in goal, Neco Williams, Conor Bradley, Billy Koumetio and Tyler Morton – fell 3-1 behind within 33 minutes. Goals by Jamie Vardy (2) and James Maddison saw the visitors head into half-time in the most comfortable of positions.

As expected, Klopp turned to some experienced players in the second half to recover the situation. However, with ten minutes to go, he brought on Owen Beck in place of the Greek international Kostas Tsimikas at left-back. Diogo Jota had already reduced the deficit on 68 minutes, but with the game heading into the fifth minute of stoppage time, the Foxes looked to have done enough to secure passage to the semi-final. Up stepped Takumi Minamino, with a rocket that almost burst the net in front of the Kop, ensuring an almost volcanic celebration. It was a goal that felt especially sweet, given that the Leicester supporters packed into the Anfield Road end had spent much of the game singing about poverty on Merseyside.

All of us who attend Anfield regularly are used to such shouts. However, I've seldom heard them sung by so many nor as loudly as that night. Grown adults and children were joining in and the display was as sickening as it was depressing. I wrote the following for *This is Anfield* after the game:

> Those singing them [poverty-mocking chants] will doubtless be filled with a smug sense of self-satisfaction, believing that they've somehow injured us with their 'wit' or scored some great 'banter points'. They'll laugh and congratulate themselves on successfully baiting the Scousers.
>
> Then, tragically, most of them will return home to uncertain employment, no employment, insecure housing, walking past foodbanks and homeless people as they go. And all the while they'll be blissfully unaware that to the people who continue to create these problems – the Tories – they are little more than useful idiots.

The last line was a reference to how the real architects of social injustice on Merseyside, and indeed Leicester, which has 25,000 children living in poverty, would be delighted to realise that rather than feeling a sense of mutual anger at such inequality in both cities, those suffering would choose to mock others perceived to be less fortunate than them, rather than blame the government.

The Reds won the resultant penalty shoot-out 5-4, with Diogo Jota scoring the winning spot kick. He clearly enjoyed his finish, racing along the touchline in front of the visiting fans, cupping his hands to his ears and appearing to hurl an expletive at them. It was richly deserved.

The Reds faced Leicester again at the King Power Stadium on 28 December. There they lost further ground in the title race, falling to a 1-0 defeat. The result was particularly frustrating as Mohamed Salah missed a penalty and a chance to put Liverpool ahead in the 15th minute.

Further frustration awaited at Stamford Bridge on 2 January 2022 when Liverpool threw away a two-goal lead in the first half. Goals by Sadio Mané and Mohamed Salah were cancelled out before the interval, thanks to strikes by Mateo Kovačić and Christian Pulisic, whose leveller came on the stroke of half-time. The Reds saw out the game and took away a point, but the result saw them fall to third place.

Liverpool advanced to the fourth round of the FA Cup with a comfortable 4-1 home victory over Shrewsbury Town. The Liverpool crowd had shown the visitors great respect during the game, a point acknowledged by their goalkeeper, Marko Maroši, on social media. So it was particularly infuriating to see footage of their fans marching in packs through the city centre, singing 'Fuck the 96'. Their actions were roundly condemned by their club.

Liverpool made it to the League Cup Final after a two-legged semi-final ended 2-0 on aggregate to the Reds. The tie saw an Arsenal player sent off in each game, but there was no denying Liverpool's superiority at the Emirates. Two goals from Diogo Jota booked Liverpool's place at Wembley.

Either side of the second leg, the Reds recorded victories over Brentford and Crystal Palace. And while Everton were looking for a new manager after the sacking of Rafa Benítez, Liverpool were looking to close the gap on City with the £49m acquisition of Luis Díaz.

January had begun with the warmest New Year's Day on record, and things continued to heat up for the UK government with news emerging of lockdown parties in Downing Street while the rest of the country faced restrictions. As the prime minister struggled to justify his place in the UK's highest office, Liverpool finished the month in second place, with their sights trained squarely on top spot, and a cup final to come.

The Reds' progress in the league, coupled with their dominance in Europe and advancement in both domestic cups, meant that, for the first time, I and many others began to entertain thoughts of a historic quadruple. Although I'd never have uttered it publicly, I was beginning to sense that I may be watching the greatest team in the club's history.

The unusually warm January soon gave way to a February dominated by Storms Dudley and Eunice, which saw the country battered by 100mph gales, and snow. Liverpool, meanwhile, blew past Cardiff City in the fourth round of the FA Cup in a game marked by the return of Harvey Elliott after a long spell on the sidelines through injury. The youngster crowned his return with a goal in a 3-1 win.

The Reds then breezed past Leicester City at Anfield in the Premier League thanks to a Diogo Jota masterclass. In an attempt to atone for the shocking behaviour of their supporters earlier, the Foxes Trust made a donation to the North Liverpool Foodbank.

Klopp's men then endured brutal weather conditions to see off Burnley at Turf Moor, with Liverpool elevating the art of catching teams offside with their 'high line', something television pundits struggled to appreciate, preferring the 'Liverpool taking big risks' narrative. The reality was that the Reds would win more offside calls than any other team in the league, and with the knowledge that any that slipped through the net would be picked up by VAR, it would be a calculated risk that was paying huge dividends.

On 16 February, Liverpool suffered through 75 minutes of their Champions League last-16 first-leg tie with Inter Milan at a freezing-cold San Siro, before clinically dispatching the Italians. Mo Salah became the first player to score in eight consecutive European games, as the Reds all but booked their place in the quarter-finals. They'd later lose 1-0 at Anfield, but win 2-1 on aggregate.

With trains cancelled and threat to life warnings issued across the UK, Manchester City's plane was forced to land in Liverpool instead of Manchester after their game in Portugal against Sporting Lisbon in the same competition. Such was the damage caused by the storms that the army was placed on standby to deal with the crisis.

Of course, all of that paled by comparison with the news that Goodison favourite Richarlison angered by Liverpool fans making fun of Everton on social media, didn't want Liverpool to do well in Europe. How on earth were we ever to recover from that bombshell.

As the League Cup Final drew ever closer, Diogo Jota, who had sustained a knee injury in the victory over Inter Milan at the San Siro, was facing a race against time to be fit for the trip to Wembley. He missed the 3-1 win over Norwich City, played on 19 February at Anfield. Goals from Sadio Mané, Mohamed Salah and a debut strike from Luis Díaz secured the points.

Internationally, tensions were at an all-time high with a constant build-up of Russian troops on the Ukrainian border, and gallows humour in the Cabbage Hall pub before and after the game saw us muse that after nearly being robbed of a league title by a global pandemic, we may be about to have a possible quadruple stolen by the Third World War. I'd now progressed from dreaming about it to joking about it in the pub, out of earshot of rivals.

The crisis in Eastern Europe meant that Russian oligarchs living in the UK – many of them, such as Usmanov and Abramovich, funding English football teams – were now facing sanctions. The consequences of Putin's eventual invasion of Ukraine would, of course, be far-reaching. In English football it would also imperil the futures of Chelsea and Everton.

Liverpool gave supporters at Anfield, who were preparing for the journey south for the League Cup Final, the perfect send-off. The Reds demolished Marcelo Bielsa's Leeds United 6-0 to close the gap on City, prompting Pep Guardiola to refer to Klopp's men as a 'pain in the arse'. For us, it was a case of long may that continue.

Kelleher the Hero and Kepa's a Zero
Reds Have Last Laugh in League Cup Final Shoot-out
The day began with a hellish journey by car, and an arrival at Wembley just minutes before kick-off, thanks to a back-seat driver who, when it comes to satellite navigation, was more of a doubter than a believer, and it ended with the most remarkable penalty shoot-out I've ever seen.

One that had more in common with 'Russian roulette' than football, leaving the Reds stand-in keeper, Caoimhín Kelleher, to fire the fatal shot as far as Chelsea were concerned.

Thomas Tuchel had started the game with the solid Édouard Mendy in goal. The Senegal international had enjoyed a great game, but with the 30 minutes of extra time ending goalless, the German coach opted to substitute his keeper for the man he believed was a penalty-saving specialist. Who knew how Mendy felt after keeping his side in the final for 120 minutes, only to be replaced by Kepa Arrizabalaga, but to me and countless Reds at Wembley it was a move that screamed gamble. Like loading the bullet into the chamber and giving it a great big spin. It was a move that had worked earlier for Chelsea in the European Super Cup Final, but here in the capital it would backfire spectacularly. On such decisions managers live and die.

This was an incredible final, possibly the greatest 0-0 the competition had ever seen. The teams had gone toe to toe for 120 minutes, exchanging blows like two heavyweights, neither of them able to land a knockout punch. That, of course, due in no small part to VAR.

Chelsea saw three goals ruled out for offside and squandered a host of chances. Liverpool also had the ball in the net, only to see it overturned. And as I chewed through fingernails and struggled to dampen down the stress, Klopp's men took the fight to Chelsea, dominating possession.

Liverpool could have had the game won before it entered that energy-draining last 30 minutes. Jöel Matip had a goal ruled out when VAR ruled that Virgil van Dijk had been in an offside position and interfering with the Chelsea substitute Reece James as Trent Alexander-Arnold's free kick dropped in the box. As the ball hit the net, the Liverpool end was ablaze with pyro, and smoke drifted across the pitch as the goal went to an inevitable review. The tension was unbearable and the announcement that it had been disallowed was greeted with a deafening chorus of boos from our end of the ground. It felt harsh at the time and, after seeing it back on TV later, I still can't see how they managed to rule the goal out.

For Chelsea, who had the ball in the net three times, only to see their efforts ruled out, the result would have been hard to bear.

Kai Havertz's two overturned goals looked clearly offside, at least to the lad behind me who called each one before VAR. However, he was equivocal about Lukaku's finish in the 109th minute. I wasn't. I thought it was definitely onside and felt sick. Thankfully, eventually, VAR ruled the strike out.

Lukaku had taken a pass from Trevoh Chalobah in his stride, cut inside and rammed the ball past Kelleher. It was a hammer blow and the Chelsea end filled with smoke and light. However, it was now their turn to have their celebrations cut short by the vagaries of lines and slow-motion replays.

Penalties it was then. It was simply impossible to get a handle on my nerves as the shoot-out began. Each time a Liverpool player approached the spot, I felt sick; every time a Chelsea opponent scored, my heart sank. I've seen – some at home and many in person – so many finals settled in this way now. I can tell you it's worse when you're in the stadium. The consequences of defeat are infinitely magnified when you're present. The journey home can take on nightmarish proportions when you've seen your dreams ended by a single kick of the ball in the mother of all lotteries.

In an ideal world, the agony is ended after both teams have had their regulation five spot kicks. However, this rally went on for what seemed an eternity. One by one, each player put the ball in the goal, and with each rattle of the net the tension increased its grip on all of us. Then, with every outfield player having done their bit, it was down to the keepers.

Would Tuchel's gamble pay off or would he and Kepa be left looking like mugs. If the Chelsea men were shouldering the weight of the world, Kelleher was a man lifted by the faith of his manager and a wave of belief from the stands. Chelsea's specialist had failed to save any of Liverpool's 11 spot kicks, and he was about to fail spectacularly, comically and joyously from the spot. His opposite number had finished so emphatically; his penalty had all the panache of a seasoned striker.

This was the only moment in the game where I was able to banish doubt and allow belief to take hold. I gazed out over our end, a sea of red concentration, with some seemingly in prayer, to God, to Shankly, or maybe to both. Way off – it seemed – in the Chelsea end, a few store-bought flags waved in forlorn hope. The sense of inevitability hung so heavy in the air, it seemed to overpower the Chelsea keeper, whose manager had only minutes earlier placed the hopes and dreams of the club and its supporters entirely on his narrow shoulders.

It would be too heavy for him to bear. As the ball sailed high over the bar he fell to his knees, burying his head in his hands. All around him Liverpool players danced, punching the air in wild celebration. The end designated for the Liverpool following descended into glowing red pandemonium, a sea of limbs, a cacophony of sound and smoke. The Chelsea supporters made for the exit.

Kelleher leapt skywards, his face a picture of sheer joy. His manager had placed great faith in him, and he'd repaid the boss in spades. The Liverpool end was a fury of delirium that threatened to engulf us all. Then the stadium PA system acted like a defibrillator, shocking the army of fans to dance to their own beat of the rhythm as Dua Lipa declared that 'one kiss is all it takes'. In an instant, the swaying and cavorting crowd picked up the tune, joining in with each verse, as the players danced on the turf.

It was magical and glorious, and I felt elated. Klopp had delivered a domestic trophy at last, and it felt so sweet. All that remained was for us to see the Liverpool captain, Jordan Henderson, lift the trophy as confetti cascaded down all around him. And, once again, send one half of the stadium into wild celebration.

As I weaved my way through the throng to my car ride home, I reflected on how many deride the League Cup. In so-called modern football, the holy grail has become money, and the means to play the sport's equivalent of Top Trumps in the transfer market. For teams with ambition, that has translated into sacrificing domestic cups for the heady heights of a top-four finish.

How have we allowed this to happen to our game, how have we demeaned days like this, trading the glory and glee for the promise of Europe's magic beans in the season to come. I want them both, of course, but football is about trophies.

To my relief, the journey home would be far smoother with our navigator asleep and the sat nav leading the way. These were the days my friend, and I never wanted this one to end.

The Promise of Immortality

Liverpool FC March–May 2022

March of the Reds

Klopp's Men Chase Down City

With spring well and truly underway, it was hard to escape the sense that we were witnessing something magical. On 2 March, Liverpool welcomed Norwich City to Anfield for an FA Cup fifth-round tie. Again, rotation was the order of the day, and nobody moaned. We'd now reached the stage where trust in Jürgen Klopp was such that I believed that no matter who he picked, they'd be good enough to do the job. And so it proved to be.

The boss chose to rest several key players for the match, but the likes of Takumi Minamino and Divock Origi had banked significant credit in cup competition and the Reds had shown themselves capable of finding solutions, even when they suffered setbacks. Confidence was high.

The Reds stormed into a two-goal lead thanks to a Takumi Minamino double, then survived an unlikely consolation goal from Norwich City's Lukas Rupp in the 76th minute. According to the press, the victory and, in particular the performance of Liverpool's Minamino, were fuelling dreams of an unprecedented quadruple. What I'd only been prepared to entertain in my wildest dreams or in bar talk was now being openly and credibly discussed by neutrals and football writers.

Liverpool followed up that victory with a comfortable home win over West Ham to keep them in the title race, despite City's dubious 1-0 win over Everton. The Blues had been denied a clear-cut penalty after a VAR review failed to spot the most obvious of handballs. I'm not usually a believer in conspiracy theories, nor do I usually subscribe to the notion that match officials have it in for my club, but decisions like that make it difficult to hold on to my faith in the game.

In the news, barristers had gone on strike, meaning that there was almost no section of British society not in dispute with the government. Meanwhile, the police were issuing fines to Downing Street staff for breaches of Covid lockdown rules. Among those fined were Prime Minister Boris Johnson. Where's a good barrister when you need one.

On 16 March the Reds travelled to the Emirates to take on Arsenal after successfully negotiating their two-legged tie against Inter, despite that 1-0 defeat at Anfield. They'd then taken care of Brighton at the

Amex, winning 2-0. Prior to the game against Arsenal, City had played out a goalless draw with Crystal Palace, meaning a win over the Gunners would move the Reds to within a point of the leaders, having played the same number of games. City's dropped points prompted Bernardo Silva to launch a Twitter rant in which he branded Liverpool supporters as 'pathetic'. It was nice to see us occupying so much space in his head.

Two second-half goals by Diogo Jota and Roberto Firmino against Arsenal secured the points for Liverpool. It was the Reds' ninth win in succession. Jürgen Klopp expressed delight at the result and his excitement about the levels being produced by his team, telling BBC Sport:

> Coming here and winning against Arsenal is already special, but winning the game like it was – more special. We started really well then it became an open game. We wanted to improve in the second half.
>
> I'm very excited about the team and the situation we are in but that does not change everything. We just need to keep going. We really want to enjoy the situation we are in by winning football matches.

Liverpool then travelled to the City Ground for an FA Cup sixth-round tie with Nottingham Forest. It was an emotional encounter, given that the last time the teams met in the competition was in 1989, in the ill-fated semi-final in Sheffield. A delegation of Forest fans presented a wreath in memory of the 97 at the game, but some supporters let themselves down with chants of 'always the victim'. Liverpool had the last laugh, though, winning 1-0 thanks to Jota's goal. Liverpool were now into the FA Cup semi-final at Wembley, and the stage was set for a memorable encounter with Manchester City and a chance to rub salt in Bernardo Silva's wounds.

Liverpool had won 12 out of 13 games, which were coming thick and fast now, with one arriving every 3.3 days. Jürgen Klopp was managing his squad magnificently, with his substitutes developing a knack of changing games. Elsewhere, Everton were in freefall and financial peril after Alisher Usmanov, the alleged money behind their owner, Moshiri, was sanctioned by the UK government. Meanwhile, Chelsea FC was put up for sale after owner Roman Abramovich faced similar punishment.

The sense that Liverpool could reach another two finals was growing, while Salah's contract saga rumbled on. Meanwhile, the development of Anfield continued at pace, with the expansion of the Anfield Road stand ongoing.

On 24 March, the City of Liverpool awarded the 97 victims of the Hillsborough disaster the Freedom of the City. It was also announced that every school on Merseyside would include a Hillsborough day in its curriculum. The move was a powerful vindication of the work carried out by the 'Real Truth Project' led by Ian Byrne MP.

As March came to an end, the Reds prepared for a momentous April, which would see two titanic clashes with Manchester City. One of those, of course, would come in the FA Cup semi-final. Before that, Liverpool struggled to a 2-0 victory over Watford at Anfield, needing a Fabinho penalty in the 89th minute of the game to seal a nervy victory.

In the Champions League, Liverpool managed a 6-4 aggregate victory over Benfica, who had stunned Anfield after fighting back from a 3-1 deficit to draw 3-3. They were denied a win thanks to a goal disallowed by VAR. A certain Darwin Núñez caught the eye in that epic battle, scoring the Portuguese side's equaliser and generally giving Liverpool's back line a nightmare evening.

Sandwiched between those two memorable games was a dress rehearsal for Wembley. On 10 April, Liverpool travelled to the Etihad to take on Manchester City. They desperately needed a win to gain an advantage in the title race, but Guardiola's men refused to budge. The home side dominated the first half and went into the interval 2-1 up thanks to goals by Kevin De Bruyne and Gabriel Jesus, either side of a Diogo Jota strike. The press and media were in raptures as the two giants went toe to toe, trading blows like a couple of punch-drunk boxers. A minute into the second period, Sadio Mané, celebrating his 30th birthday, lapped up a Mohamed Salah assist and levelled the game for Liverpool.

Both sides pressed for the winner, and Sterling had the ball in the net, only to see it ruled out. In the dying seconds, Riyad Mahrez squandered a glorious chance to win the game. A defeat for the Reds would have been disastrous, but undeserved. Equally, a draw didn't feel good enough. Guardiola left the stadium the happier of the two managers. There was just a point in it, with seven games to go.

Klopp claimed that both teams were operating on a different level to the rest. Few would disagree. Now all eyes turned to Wembley and the semi-final. Little did we know as we headed home from the Etihad, but when it comes to next-level football, we hadn't seen anything yet. An epic Wembley encounter with Guardiola's men beckoned in the semi-final of the FA Cup. We'll get to that later, but first let's deal with a much older foe, Manchester United.

Liverpool 4-0 Man United

Reds Untouchable as Anfield Blitz Sends Klopp to the Top

On 19 April, Liverpool geared up for the visit of Manchester United, for whom memories of their 5-0 drubbing at the hands of the Reds at Old Trafford were no doubt still raw. They'd have arrived at Anfield expecting little, and they got less.

The game was close to the centenary of the date that Liverpool's all-conquering 1920s team clinched the first of consecutive league titles, in 1922. I'd commissioned a banner from Peter Carney to commemorate the achievement and proudly displayed it at the front of the Kop before the game and in Block 109 during it. The banner was a homage to one created by the club to celebrate their first league title in 16 years, arguably the first banner ever to adorn Anfield.

Before the game I was privileged to meet Chris Peers, the great-grandson of one of those players, Don McKinlay. The sun was shining, but Anfield was buffeted by a strong wind and the banner billowed in front of the Kop as we posed for pictures under the floodlights.

The backdrop to the match brought the tragic news that Cristiano Ronaldo's baby son had sadly died on the eve of the game, and a minute's applause was planned by supporters in the seventh minute. The timing reflected the player's shirt number. It felt especially poignant, coming so soon after Liverpool had gone ahead in the fifth minute. In commentary for Sky Sports, Gary Neville described the tribute as 'a massive touch of class by the Liverpool supporters'. Sadly, though, United supporters were condemned by both clubs for their tragedy chanting during the game, in reference to the Hillsborough Stadium disaster.

Klopp had called for Liverpool's players to treat the win as the most important three points of their lives, and the four goals scored sent them to the top of the table. With one trophy already in the bag, Liverpool in the semi-finals of the Champions League and the final of the FA Cup after defeating Manchester City, dreams of securing another three were becoming irresistible. The idea that the Reds could win a historic quadruple was now being openly discussed in the media as a realistic possibility. It felt like momentum was building and that the Reds could become the greatest top-flight team in the history of English football. Untouchable.

Their display against United was nothing short of magnificent, and the gulf in class between the two clubs was now the greatest it had been in my lifetime. An aggregate 9-0 win against the Red Devils would have been unthinkable, even during the glory days of the 70s and 80s.

The mood on the Kop during and after the game was more suited to a festival than a football match, and each goal was greeted with a mixture of joy and amusement. It was hard not to revel in the *schadenfreude*. United's demise was as glorious for us as it was agonising for them.

After Díaz opened the scoring, Liverpool simply ran riot. Next up was Mohamed Salah, who was amazingly on a run of eight games without a goal. The Egyptian grabbed Liverpool's second following a brilliant assist by Sadio Mané. Red supporters had never lost faith in him, and our sense of delight at the end of his dry spell was evident as we bellowed out the player's song at full volume. The noise was reverberating around the ground as all four sides joined in. As Salah kissed the turf, he could be in no doubt that at Anfield he enjoys a connection with the people that he could find nowhere else.

I've always loved football played in midweek, with the floodlights burning and the grass impossibly green under their glare. There's something about those evening kick-offs that sets them apart from a weekend match, and I drank it all in as the Reds continued to pummel the opposition. I roared them on at the expense of my vocal cords.

The second half brought more misery for United and sent their petulant support scurrying for the exit signs, and many of them would have been well on their way home by the final whistle. They had a lucky escape, as the sight of Sadio Mané's first-time strike from a Luis Díaz cross in the 69th minute, then Salah's second five minutes before the end would have made harrowing viewing for them.

For us it was a welcome demolition of a team who have on many occasions been a thorn in our sides, and a fanbase who had disgraced themselves during the game. The win meant that Klopp's men had become the first team to manage more than eight goals against Manchester United in a single season.

Writing for the BBC, Phil McNulty had this to say:

> United were on the rack from the first whistle and were swept away by wave after wave of Liverpool attacks, all conducted from midfield by the master orchestrator Thiago Alcantara.
>
> Urged on by an exultant Kop, Liverpool simply overwhelmed United as they were quicker, slicker and simply in a different class to their fallen rivals.

The win left Liverpool two points clear of Manchester City, who could regain their place at the top with a win over Brighton the following night. But for now the Kop would gleefully sing 'the Reds are top of the league' as they headed out of the ground and into the night.

Kopites So Glad as Jürgen Stays a Red
Klopp's Contract Joy as Liverpool Go Marching On

On 28 April 2022, with Liverpool supporters still basking in the afterglow of back-to-back 2-0 wins at Anfield, first in the Merseyside derby, then against Villarreal in the Champions League semi-final first leg, the club announced that Jürgen Klopp had signed a new contract that would tie him to Liverpool beyond the current deal that ran until 2024. It was the best news possible and added to the growing sense of optimism surrounding the club. A statement on Liverpool FC's official website read:

> Liverpool Football Club is delighted to announce Jürgen Klopp has signed a new contract to extend his commitment with the club.

The deal means the manager will remain at the helm of the Reds beyond the expiry of his previous deal, which was set to end in 2024.

Assistants Pepijn Lijnders and Peter Krawietz have also put pen to paper on new terms, mirroring those of Klopp and reaffirming their dedication to the project, which began with the German's appointment in October 2015.

Liverpool were still fighting on all fronts as the season moved into its final stages. The Reds were in second spot in the league, had already secured the League Cup, were looking forward to an FA Cup Final in May, and were just one game away from a Champions League Final in Paris. These were the best of times for the Reds, and Klopp had built one of the greatest teams in the club's history. The boss said about his contract extension:

There are so many words I could use to describe how I am feeling about this news [...] delighted, humbled, blessed, privileged and excited would be a start.

There is just so much to love about this place. I knew that before I came here, I got to know it even better after I arrived and now, I know it more than ever before.

Like any healthy relationship, it always has to be a two-way street; you have to be right for each other. The feeling we were absolutely right for each other is what brought me here in the first place and it's why I've extended previously.

Jürgen went on to talk about how energised he felt and singled out his relationship with club CEO Billy Hogan and its sporting director, Julian Ward, and developments at the club's training centre in Kirkby:

There is a freshness about us as a club still and this energises me. For as long as I have been here, our owners have been unbelievably committed and energetic about this club and it is clear that right now this applies to our future as much as I've ever known.

We are a club that is constantly moving in the right direction. We have a clear idea of what we want; we have a clear idea of how we try to achieve it. That's always a great position to start from.

He went on to explain the role his wife Ulla had played in helping him to reach the decision. Jürgen's all-or-nothing approach to management takes a heavy toll on him and leaves little time for family. He'd always said he'd take a break when his current deal ended and had promised his family that they'd travel together. Therefore, any decision to extend his deal would need the support of those closest to him. Ulla's calm insistence that she didn't see the family leaving Liverpool in two years gave the green light for Klopp to sign the extension on offer. Liverpool fans would brand her a 'Scouse Queen' for the role she'd played, and some would even take a banner bearing her image to Paris on 28 May.

Echoing the song sung in his honour, to the tune of The Beatles' 'I Feel Fine', Jürgen concluded his interview with the club's website by saying:

I didn't need too long to answer in truth [when the owners presented his new deal]. The answer was very simple, I'm in love with here and I feel fine!

FSG's Mike Gordon, who had flown in for the Champions League tie with Villarreal the night before, hailed the completion of the deal as a momentous step:

It's always hard to find the right words to adequately reflect Jürgen's importance and contribution to our club, but today's announcement really does speak for itself.

Speaking on behalf of my partners John [Henry] and Tom [Werner], as well as myself, Jürgen is the perfect figurehead for the modern Liverpool FC. This is especially true of what he stands for, on and off the pitch.

It also applies to the leader he is and the man he is. Because of our extraordinary playing squad, outstanding coaches, world-class football operations team and brilliant club staff, we are blessed with the most valuable resource an organisation could wish for: amazing people.

Everything Jürgen has said publicly about his future previously was reflected by his words privately to us. It was about him having the inclination and desire to keep going. In this respect, it is clear he is more energised than ever.

Klopp's win percentage was already higher than any of his predecessors, at a staggering 61.39 per cent, eclipsing his nearest challenger Kenny Dalglish, who had won 60.9 per cent of the games he'd managed. Now he had the opportunity to become one of the club's longest-serving managers, and this in modern football, with its demands for instant and continued success, and that spoke volumes about his ability, but also the respect he commanded on and off the pitch.

With renewed impetus and focus, the Reds would continue their charge both at home and in Europe. They finished the job against Villarreal, winning 3-2 in Spain, and recorded two wins and a draw as they geared up for the FA Cup Final clash with Chelsea.

City and Chelsea Outdone
Liverpool Win Wembley Double

Liverpool reached the final of the FA Cup courtesy of a 3-2 semi-final victory over Manchester City on 16 April. I'd travelled down for the semi-final but my attempts to get a ticket for the final failed in the ballot.

Due to chaos on the rail network, there were no trains available for the trip to the semi-final, and despite appeals to the FA to move the game to a stadium nearer to the north-west, including by Reds captain Jordan Henderson, the FA refused to listen. Instead, they agreed to provide 100 coaches for supporters. This was woefully inadequate. Fortunately, I managed to get a ride down there from a friend, and along with tens of thousands of Liverpool supporters we found a way to get to the capital. The game against City felt like a final, with the Liverpool fan parks around Wembley packed out from early on. There was, of course, plenty of room in the Manchester City equivalents, but they didn't look like fun at all. So we made our way into the stadium early.

Inside the ground, waves of Reds fans roared up an endless series of escalators that deposited them on to concourses. They were singing songs and dreaming of trophies in May as they went. We sang Jürgen's song all the way up and then in the impossibly long queues for beer. Inside the stadium bowl, I realised that our opponents had failed to sell out their ticket allocation. Immediately opposite me, vast swathes of seats lay empty, save for a giant banner, presumably purchased by City. It was draped over the plastic to hide the fact that their fans had stayed home.

Once more Pep's followers would be outnumbered and out-sung in the stands. However, the City fans who had turned up would make enough noise to disgrace themselves during a minute's silence in memory of the Hillsborough disaster in 1989. The game was being played close to the 33rd anniversary of the tragedy. My sense of frustration and anger made beating them even more important. I had a feeling our players felt the same. However, I didn't expect the three-goal blitz that would see Liverpool go into half-time 3-0 up.

Goals from Ibrahima Konaté and a brace from Sadio Mané did the damage. Mané's quick thinking embarrassed City keeper Zack Steffen, who took too long to clear the ball, and Sadio clipped it into the net. His second, and Liverpool's third, was a stunning volley from the edge of the box. We were in dreamland and could barely believe what we were seeing. As each goal went in, the sense of joy was mixed with incredulity. Could it really be this easy? Guardiola's team had given themselves a mountain to climb.

However, we'd need that three-goal cushion, as City mounted a late fightback to shred nerves. It ended 3-2. The result flattered them, and it would be the Reds making the journey back to the north-west dreaming of another day out in the capital.

With one cup in the bag and a second on the horizon it was impossible not to dream of an epic end to the season. The feeling of … well, okay, I'll say it … destiny, was palpable. As a football supporter, you sometimes get these feelings. I had them in the run-in to that incredible treble season under Gérard Houllier and on the way to Rafa's epic final at Istanbul. Those same flutterings had appeared in my gut. Could we actually pull off a clean sweep of all four trophies?

Awaiting the Reds in the final were Thomas Tuchel's Chelsea, no doubt looking for revenge for their penalty shoot-out heartache at the hands of Klopp's Liverpool in the League Cup Final. No chance, I thought; for us success was written in the stars.

As I failed to get a ticket, I'd have to watch the match on television. The teams served up another titanic struggle, with neither able to break the deadlock after 120 minutes of football. It was exhausting to watch, and as the players gathered around their managers to decide who would take the decisive spot kicks, it was difficult to tell which of Liverpool's players had enough in the tank to take a penalty in the most stressful circumstances possible.

This time, it seemed, we'd be spared any agony in the shoot-out. César Azpilicueta missed Chelsea's second kick, handing Sadio Mané the chance to win it for the Reds with their fifth penalty. I had zero doubt in him as he stepped up to take it, and the fluttering things in my gut told me the FA Cup was coming back to Anfield. As it happened those feelings were premature. Sadio missed his penalty, and the agony went on. After one more successful penalty each, up stepped Alisson Becker as our latest hero, saving from an inconsolable Mason Mount.

The stage was now set for Kostas Tsimikas to become the unlikeliest of heroes. Like fellow left-back Alan Kennedy had done in Rome in 1984, the Greek rose to the challenge before wheeling away in manic celebration. Few Liverpool supporters would have felt confident as the Greek Scouser stepped up to take his penalty, but he finished like a seasoned striker and was duly mobbed by his team-mates, as the bench emptied on to the pitch and raced towards him.

Liverpool had edged a pulsating final, with the effervescent Luis Díaz and tireless Andrew Robertson both striking the woodwork. The sight of Mohamed Salah being substituted with an injury in the first half and Virgil van Dijk leaving the pitch on 90 minutes and failing to return for extra time were the only worries in a game we absolutely deserved to win.

Rival supporters, drowning in bitterness, consoled themselves with the fact that Liverpool had won neither cup final in normal time. They'd needed penalties, so this wasn't a real double, they said. Maybe it should have an asterisk next to it, so that future generations will know just how chewed up and twisted Liverpool's rivals had become.

Chelsea had their chances, with Marcos Alonso hitting a shot against the post. He was also denied by a great save from Alisson. However, the loss meant that the Londoners had tasted cup final defeat to Liverpool twice in the same season, in the most devastating way possible.

The Reds had become cup kings, with their focus now on winning a historic quadruple. It's hard to put into words the incredible sense of pride we all felt. After suffering through a difficult 2020/21 campaign, the 'mentality monsters' were back in fine style. They'd earned their domestic double and, regardless of what was to come, this was a team with the potential to achieve greatness.

Klopp was magnanimous in victory, telling the BBC:

Outstanding, it was an incredible, intense game against Chelsea – they would have deserved it exactly the same way, like in the Carabao Cup. That's how small the margins are.

I couldn't be more proud of my boys, the shift they put in, how hard they fought, the early changes. I think Virgil is fine, but his muscle was hurt.

All of these things, missing good chances, overcoming good moments from Chelsea, then having really good moments ourselves …

Then in the penalty shoot-out, it was nerve-racking, my nails are gone but I really feel for Chelsea. For the second time, 120 minutes and you get nothing, that's too hard. But for us I'm pretty happy.

We are mentality monsters but there were mentality monsters in blue as well – it was one penalty. Chelsea played outstanding but in the end there must be one winner and that was us today.

A disconsolate Tuchel could barely hide his pain as he spoke to the media after the game:

Like in the last final, in the Carabao Cup, it's no regrets. I told the team I'm proud.

We were sure that we would be competitive and make life very difficult for Liverpool. We did it again. We struggled in the first 15 minutes but then we were excellent for the whole match.

We got to 0-0 against maybe the best attacking team in the world and we also created a lot of chances. We deserved it, as they deserved it as well, but again we lose on penalties.

We are very disappointed, of course. We are sad but at the same time proud. I was sure we would win today. I was sure before and I was sure during the match that momentum was on our side. I was sure until the very last minute but, unfortunately, I was not right. I have to digest it and keep on going. That's life in sports.

The Chelsea manager was in choppy waters. He'd gone under twice. His claim that Chelsea deserved the win was difficult to swallow, but he was allowed to clutch for those straws, I guess. The Reds would sail on.

A picture from the Kop. Liverpool's first game in front of supporters as the country emerged from the pandemic.

Fans queue for temperature checks as a lucky few attend the home game against Wolves.

Socially distanced supporters on the Kop ready to welcome the champions as they were set to face Wolves in December 2020.

A Covid steward ensures fans remain socially distanced, the Kop, Anfield, December 2020.

View of Liverpool playing Wolves from the Kop. Anfield is mostly empty aside from a lucky few thousand.

Commemorating the centenary of the 1920s team of 'Untouchables' who won back-to-back titles in 1922 and 1923, with the players descendants at the Cabbage Hall Pub, Anfield, 2022.

Unveiling the 'Untouchables' banner in front of the Kop prior to the game against Manchester United, Anfield, 2022

Manchester City fail to sell out their ticket allocation for the FA Cup semi-final at Wembley, so they send a banner instead.

Peter Simpson's family, Charlie Smith, Adam Simpson & Clare Cooney with her banner. at Wembley. Photo courtesy of Peter Simpson.

Joanna Durkan and mum, Bev, at Wembley for the 2024 League Cup Final. Photo courtesy of Joanna Durkan.

Ryan Dean, Jack Glover and Mike Holt at the Santiago Bernabeu 2022/23. Little did they know this would be Klopp's last Champions League away game. Photo courtesy of Mike Holt.

Hong Kong Reds showing their love for the boss. Photo courtesy of Yumiko Tamaru.

Penang Reds gather to show their support for the Reds. Photo courtesy of Mook San Lim.

Saying farewell to Bobby Firmino. Photo courtesy of Les Jackson.

Saying farewell to Bobby Firmino. Photo courtesy of Les Jackson.

Wembley League Cup Final 2024.

Keith Salmon and his son Charlie at Wembley. Photo courtesy of Keith Salmon.

Reds parade their FA and League Cup double. Photo courtesy of Emma Case and The Red Archive.

View of the continuing Anfield Road expansion from my seat on the Kop.

View of Anfield Road expansion from the Kop. Photo courtesy of Keith Williams.

A view of the new Anfield Road as it nears completion.

Supporters unveil an old standard from 1981 at Paris final in 2022. Photo by Becky Arntsen and courtesy of The Red Archive.

Reds fans at the Stade de France, Champions League Final, 2022. Photo by Becky Arntsen and courtesy of The Red Archive.

Carl Clemente and his son taking in the sights before the Champions League Final in Paris, 2022.

Massed ranks of Liverpool supporters fill fan park in Paris, 2022. Photo by Daniel Melia and courtesy of The Red Archive.

Liverpool fans celebrate ahead of the Champions League Final in Paris 2022. Photo by Daniel Melia and courtesy of The Red Archive.

A great big red party in Paris. Photo by Daniel Roe and courtesy of The Red Archive.

Statue in Paris park decked out with Liverpool banners. Photo by Donna Scully and courtesy of The Red Archive.

Paris 2022 street scene. Photo by Donna Scully and courtesy of The Red Archive.

The men in the van: me, Keith Williams and Billy O'Connor on our way to Paris in the back of Andy Knott's van.

A Liverpool supporter serenades fellow fans caught in a traffic jam at Dover ahead of Paris final with Madrid, 2022.

Me, Steven Scragg, Keith Williams, Billy O'Connor and Andy Knott enjoying the Paris sunshine with the Italian Norwich City supporters on their end-of-season tour.

Andy Knott, Billy O'Connor, Me, Keith Williams and Scraggy in Paris ahead of the Champions League Final, 2022.

Me and my son Joe in Paris ahead of the final against Madrid. Shortly after this picture was taken, we would part as he left for the stadium and the chaos that would follow.

The Final Push and a Tale of Two Cities

Liverpool FC May 2022

Liverpool 3-1 Wolves

Destiny Denied on Final Day

On 25 May 2022, Liverpool Football Club entered the final day of a league campaign still competing for a historic clean sweep of all four trophies on offer. In years to come, the history books will show that they ultimately fell short of that target. However, to judge this team solely by that barometer does them a disservice. As I took my seat at Anfield for that final showdown, with hope in my heart, I didn't doubt for one second the Herculean efforts that had got the boys this far. They would forever be heroes to me. Regardless of the outcome.

The Reds' victory over Southampton at St Mary's and City's draw with West Ham – they'd been two goals down – ensured that, as we filed through the turnstiles, our club lay just a single point behind the leaders. Should we win this game against Wolves and City fail to beat Steven Gerrard's Aston Villa, the Premier League trophy would be decked in red ribbons after the final whistle. Although we all pretended that we'd all resigned ourselves to City as champions, hope burned brightly in our hearts as the game got underway.

We'd watched the greatest team in the club's history all season, and what we needed now was the four trophies that would prove that beyond a reasonable doubt. The first two, a League and FA Cup double, were already in the bank. A third today would complete a domestic treble, and the might of Real Madrid stood in the way of the fourth in the Champions League.

With the sun blazing in the skies above, Anfield got set for another tumult of colour, noise and fury. The atmosphere fizzed during the warm-up and crackled as the teams came out. The Kop did its best to drive the lads on, although nerves made it a tetchy affair at times. There was so much at stake.

We'd suffered through a seemingly endless toe-to-toe punch-up with Manchester City, and neither of us had so far managed to floor the other. As the weeks went by in that run-in, the tension had at times been unbearable. You want to be in those title challenges every season, where every game matters, but it's tough on your psyche and on the heart. Now we'd reached the final battle – it all came down to this last 90 minutes.

Disaster struck just three minutes into the game when Pedro Neto scored for the visitors. It was like a lightning shock, and it momentarily stunned the Kop, before they found their voices once more, letting out an almighty roar as Liverpool got set to go again. This wasn't in the story; it wasn't meant to end like this. Under Klopp we'd come to expect only impossible victories or heroic failures, with nothing in between. It just didn't seem possible that the season could fizzle out with a dull defeat, or that the Reds could go down without a fight.

They would, of course, deliver at least that, but for long spells in the game it looked like the Reds would be the architects of their own downfall. Sadio Mané drew them level in the 24th minute to a huge outpouring of relief. Soon afterwards news was filtering through that Villa had gone ahead in their game against City. Was Steven Gerrard about to finally fulfil his dream of helping Liverpool to win a league title? It all seemed scripted.

Midway through the second half, with Liverpool struggling to find the goal that would ensure they at least did their part, a pocket of supporters on the Kop began to dance and cheer. Soon celebrations were breaking out in all areas of the ground at news that Aston Villa had gone 2-0 up. We were in dreamland, but the league title remained out of our grasp, with Wolves resistant and stubborn. By the time the Reds finally broke through their defence in the 84th minute, City had levelled their game. However, Salah's goal received a huge roar, as with just minutes remaining, we believed we'd done enough.

Tragically, the heartbreaking news that somehow City had not only already completed a comeback but had now gone in front at Villa Park arrived like a hammer blow, and when Andrew Robertson netted at the Kop end in the 89th minute, there were only muted celebrations. He'd later comment on how, in that moment, he knew the title had gone.

There was still time for someone to spark rumours of a Villa equaliser and my heart leapt. A guy in the seats in front of me turned and shouted to a friend, 'Check your phone. Is it 3-3?' He wore an expression that said, 'Don't fuck with me.' His mate shook his head and our dreams evaporated. 'Bastards!' shouted someone else.

That we'd come so close was a huge source of pride, of course. But there was no hiding the disappointment in the immediate afterglow of the game. The celebrations would have spanned days, had we managed to secure the domestic treble that day. And, although the city centre would still echo to the sound of our songs, thoughts had now turned to another titanic tussle in Paris, and the possibility of a magnificent seventh European Cup.

Few, if any, football supporters ever get the chance to contemplate such an ending to a season. How could we possibly be down about this? The Reds had done us proud.

A Tale of Two Cities
Liverpool's Epic Journey Ends in Horror but Home Comforts Ease the Pain

> *The contrast could not be starker, where Paris on Saturday was moody and hostile, L;verpool on Sunday was joyous and welcoming.*

For every steel cordon erected by the French authorities, the people of Liverpool created a vast wave of emotion and love. We'd turned up in our tens of thousands for a festival of football, the Parisian police turned up for a fight.

It began as such trips always do, with hope, excitement and laughter. In Liverpool on Sunday it would end the way it began, with love and camaraderie, but sandwiched in between that, the experience for thousands couldn't have been further removed.

The journey to Dover in the back of a van that had seen better days was as uncomfortable as it was comical, with our makeshift seats coming loose as every push of the brakes caused the screws holding them to the floor to pop out. Our driver, Andy Knott, had installed the old bus seats only days before, and the three of us in the rear of the vehicle had been only too glad to accept the ride.

It was a memorable drive down to Dover, filled with gridlocked roads, laughter and entertainment as we watched a Scouser with a guitar, standing on the roof of a van, singing Beatles tunes. One of them, 'The Ballad of John and Yoko', had seen its lyrics adapted:

> *Standing on the dock at Southampton*
> *Tryin' to get to Paris in France*
> *With Díaz in attack and Van Dijk at the back*
> *We can win it if you give us a chance*

> *Jürgen makes it look easy*
> *You know how hard it can be*
> *I said the Red men are going*
> *To win the Champions League*

However, all the jokes, the songs and the stories about getting there are now lost in anger and hurt.

Five of us went, only three had tickets, but all of us were desperate to be part of the story, to be around the action and to sample the atmosphere. The journey would be convoluted, in the back of a van to Dover, then a ferry to Dunkerque, followed by a train ride to Paris. Being a football supporter can be hard work. Getting to finals is like a full-time job, and in this day and age I'm wondering why it should be that way?

Why don't those who preside over the game and profit from it not cherish us? Why don't they move heaven and earth to make it easier for us to support our team and experience the game's greatest moments? Why is it so difficult and so expensive? Why are we still herded like cattle, corralled beneath underpasses in 22-degree heat without water for 90 minutes, then tear-gassed and beaten, our tickets robbed, and ultimately left outside the game we love?

Does any other industry treat its lifeblood this way? Are theatre-goers or spectators of any other sport handled with a disdain bordering on loathing in the way football supporters are? Long before the debacle in Saint-Denis we'd seen tickets hived off to corporate interests and sold on at extortionate rates. We arrived on the south coast of England to tales of planes and ferry cancellations, and supporters who had shelled out a few months' salary to get to the game now left high and dry. This doesn't happen unless the sport's governing body and the opportunist spivs who leech off it see us as little more than a cash cow.

Nevertheless, we keep coming back for more, because it's us who truly love the game for what it is. Football brings people together in a way few other sports can – people of all races, ethnicities, religions and cultures. It's filled with beautiful moments, passion, pain and pure euphoria. This is how I see the game. Those who own it and control it see gold, so much gold. I get the feeling they suffer us, barely tolerating our existence so long as we keep filling their coffers, but to the Paris police, the stewards at the Stade de France and it seems, to UEFA we're expendable.

'The fans arrived without tickets,' they said. 'They arrived late, and they forced their way in,' they said. Where have we heard that before? The speed at which these lies were parroted without question is both remarkable and depressing. The fact that so many rivals were willing to lap them up and repeat them was predictable and sad.

Within moments of the problems occurring outside the stadium, I was in a bar in Gare de Lyon, waiting to watch the match and receiving text messages about crushing at the turnstiles, fans climbing over fences and 'trouble' at the match. My blood turned cold; my son and three of the lads I'd travelled with were at the game.

We'd been in and around the fan park earlier that day, soaking up the sun, after walking along the Seine and having a beer near the Pont Alexandre III. We'd posed for pictures with a group of Italians from Bergamo. Incredibly, they were wearing Norwich City shirts and, to our amazement, they were a delegation from the Canaries' Italian supporters' club on their relegation party weekend. We laughed together and shook hands.

We mingled without incident with Madrid fans along the Champs-Élysées and marvelled together at the Arc de Triomphe, then on to Cours de Vincennes for the Boss do. The place was already rammed when we got there and our attempts to join the party were hampered by a ring of steel encircling the park, interspersed with armed police who looked more geared up for a riot than to protect the public attending what amounted to a festival.

Eventually, we were able to share a few beers in the sunshine. We watched the pyro, marvelled at the banners on show and drank in the atmosphere of yet another European final with the Reds. It was like a carnival – smiles, laughter and song everywhere. If the police had studied what we were really about that day, they couldn't possibly have seen us as a threat. We were there to support our team and enjoy their city. We'd later agree that had we properly taken in their demeanour that day, we probably could have predicted how they'd behave later.

The truth is, they policed the supporters they were expecting, not the people who actually turned up. Their expectations were fuelled by prejudice and bias, and a deep-seated mistrust of football fans. They got it horribly wrong, and their bias prevented them from changing tack when their plan went awry. Where have we seen that before? Those supporters of other clubs pedalling tired old tropes and stereotypes beware: you're only fuelling the same prejudice that led to these horrible scenes outside the ground. It could easily have been you, and somewhere down the line, it will be.

My friends and my son left us at around 4pm that afternoon. They'd be in the queue outside the stadium for several hours before the game. They did as they were told and they had genuine tickets. They had little idea what lay in wait for them.

A friend and I decided to enjoy Jamie Webster for an hour and then find a quieter environment to watch the game, meeting up with a couple of other mates in Gare de Lyon. When the text messages came through, I instinctively contacted my son: 'Did you get in, mate? Are you okay?' His reply almost broke my heart.

He's 26 and this was his second European final. He has experienced the joy of Madrid, countless European away days and has travelled to Wembley many times now. In Paris he spoke of seeing a young lad assaulted by police, and fans being tear-gassed. His ticket had been confiscated and he was told it was fake. It wasn't. He was with two other lads, one of whom actually made it into the ground. When he arrived at the seats, he was confronted by three French locals who had no tickets. But at least they were now safe, and I was glad of that. My three friends had made it into the ground, but had experienced horrendous treatment outside, kettled into a narrow underpass, tear-gassed and scared for their safety. They weren't late, they had tickets, they followed instructions, and they were only going to a bloody football match!

The result of the game was a bitter disappointment, but it's meaningless in the grand scheme of things. I've seen posts from mates and other fans saying they're finished with football. On the journey back, all of us said we'd never go to another final again. My son described the behaviour of police and stewards as 'bordering on callous'. All this at a football match, a sporting event in which our only crime is wanting to see our team in a major final.

The journey home was the polar opposite of our outbound adventure. None of us could get angry at the result. Instead, it was events off the field of play that consumed us. I'm grateful to the journalists and broadcasters who immediately told the truth, countering the lies fed to them by the police, the French government and UEFA. We didn't have that in 1989. But what lifted me most were the pictures and video from the parade in Liverpool.

What happened in Liverpool, after the events in Paris, was nothing short of a miracle. To see vast swathes of red lining the streets to welcome home a defeated team was like food for the soul, it was a great big hug, and it reminded me that there's really no place like Liverpool. If only the authorities and football's governing bodies could see us for who we really are.

This really was a tale of two cities. Where the Paris police and stewards had shown hostility and disdain, my hometown had shown love and loyalty. On Sunday the city of Liverpool successfully managed half a million people safely and without incident. By Monday morning its streets were clean and gleaming once more. Paris – and UEFA – would be left contemplating the aftermath of their incompetence and failure, and searching for lessons. Meanwhile, Liverpool was looking forward with renewed hope and energy.

Paris can learn so much from Liverpool.

The Long and Weary Road

Liverpool FC July–December 2022

The Egyptian King Continues His Reign
Reds Gear Up for the New Season

At the beginning of July 2022, Liverpool supporters rejoiced at the news that, after weeks of speculation, Mohamed Salah had put pen to paper on a new deal. The news was announced on the club's official website after the player's agent had provoked an angry response from Jamie Carragher for appearing to troll supporters on social media, when in fact he knew his client was about to sign a new contract. Carra would see the funny side.

To lose Mo would have been disastrous, but the eye-watering sums of money involved meant it was difficult to rationalise. In the end, we swallowed it because we accepted, reluctantly in my case, that this was the price of competing at the top end of the table.

We've had world-class players before, but not on Salah's level – and the alternative to giving him a new contract was not worth imagining. In the post-match haze, amid the euphoria associated with Liverpool's historic rout 5-0 of Manchester United at Old Trafford, one image had stood out above all the rest. On Instagram, a smiling Trent Alexander-Arnold posed with a grinning Mohamed Salah, and beneath the picture the Scouser had simply written: 'Best in the world.' His teammates knew it, his manager and the supporters knew it. Now it seems the whole world had finally caught up. In a rare moment of clarity and consensus, the jury of football opinion had returned a majority verdict, declaring Salah the best player on the planet.

Think about that for a moment; a player once ridiculously declared a 'one-season wonder', who cost Liverpool a mere £36m just four years earlier, and who most of us thought was just a decent winger who might improve the squad, is now without equal in the world of football. The Messi and Ronaldo hegemony is over, the kings are dead, long live the Egyptian King.

Liverpool had been here before in recent times. Players like Fernando Torres and Luis Suárez both arrived full of promise and reached stratospheric heights in a Liverpool shirt, only to leave for what they believed was greener grass. Anfield had been a stepping stone for them and, although we fumed and bemoaned the situation, deep down inside we could all understand it. Liverpool then were a million miles away from being able to satisfy their aspirations.

This was different. Since then, the changes around Anfield had been nothing short of seismic. The team built by Jürgen Klopp was no rung on a ladder, no stopgap on the way to greater things. Liverpool FC in 2022 were the ultimate destination for the world's best players. They boasted the best full-backs and centre-back in the game, and the best keeper. In Salah, they had a player who I believed would one day be regarded as the club's greatest ever. His numbers remain incredible, and each week he seemed to ascend to new heights of brilliance.

This in no way undermines the achievements of those who've gone before. It was no slight to Elisha Scott to declare Ray Clemence Liverpool's greatest keeper. Kenny's magnificence did not undermine Keegan's greatness, and it was no insult to Sir Roger to call Ian Rush the club's greatest striker. Neither did it demean the achievements of Steven Gerrard to state the bleeding obvious, that Salah has discovered new levels and he's currently completing them on his own.

All of this meant we must draw the inescapable conclusion, that the man is irreplaceable. There's no one in world football who can do what Mo does, and certainly nobody better. At 29 he was at his peak physically and in terms of ability. Salah still had years ahead of him at the highest level. And, get this, he wants to stay until his last ball is kicked. This was a situation few of us dreamed was possible just five years earlier. The best player in world football playing at Anfield and not wanting to go anywhere else.

The price of keeping Salah was a reported £350k per week – or, to put that into context, around £72.8 million over four years. Of course, in days of food poverty and social collapse, this is an obscene sum of money. In the context of the pandemic and its impact on club finances, it absolutely must have presented the Anfield hierarchy with a challenge, but one they simply had to meet, on both footballing and economic grounds. To replace Salah would have cost Liverpool anywhere between £150m and £200m, and realistically that wouldn't have guaranteed a like-for-like replacement.

Of course, a player signed to take Mo's place in the team would have also commanded a huge salary. Suddenly that £83.2 million didn't sound such a big deal. It may be an indictment of football's bloated bubble that we could make an argument for paying a footballer these sums, but here we were.

Where all this will end up is anyone's guess. How long before we're debating the merits of the first £1 million per week contract, and is any of this sustainable? I doubt it. However, the cold hard reality was that allowing Salah to leave potentially on a free transfer in 18 months' time would have been criminally negligent in footballing terms, and, amazingly, giving Salah what he wanted appeared to be the least expensive option.

Mohamed Salah was and still is a machine. Astonishingly, in 2022, despite the dizzying heights he'd already reached, he could climb higher. That must have been a frightening prospect for our opponents. Even more terrifying for us was the possibility of him hitting his best form while wearing the shirt of another team.

Jürgen's Reds See Off Pep's Blues
New Season Gets Underway

Picture it, the back page of the *Manchester Evening News*, a frustrated Erling Haaland, his sad expression with a damning headline scrawled across his face:

CITY GET THE COMMUNITY BLUES

It was 30 July 2022, and Liverpool had just outgunned Manchester City by three goals to one in the Community Shield. It was a match in which Haaland had squandered guilt-edged chances and Darwin Núñez, making his debut for Liverpool, had taken his, leaving one newspaper to declare that 'Nunez puts Haaland in the shade'.

It's hard to imagine that now, given how prolific the latter has been compared to the former. As I write, there are doubts as to whether Núñez will stay at Anfield for the post-Klopp era. I hope he does. I can understand why he frustrates, but I'm a big fan and I hope that Arne Slot can find that magic recipe that will unlock his obvious talents, turning him from wrecking ball to world-class striker. We'll see.

The 2022 Community Shield was switched to the Leicester City stadium, meaning it would see the lowest attendance since 23,988 turned out to see Manchester City beaten 1-0 by Burnley in 1973. Talk about omens. Despite the scarcity of tickets – I was unsuccessful in a ballot – Liverpool supporters still outnumbered their counterparts, as City fans continued to live up to their motto: 'We're not really here.'

In the news, Liz Truss was about to become the UK's prime minister after the resignation of Boris Johnson, and the country's rail network was paralysed by strike action as the transport minister did his best to look tough and blame the unions for – checks notes – representing their members' aspirations. Truss would establish herself as the most calamitous premier the country had ever seen, lasting about as long as a decaying lettuce and crashing the economy in the process.

Making their debuts for Liverpool at Leicester were Fábio Carvalho and Darwin Núñez. Haaland, a £51.2m signing from Borussia Dortmund, was making his bow for Manchester City.

Both Salah and Robertson went close in the early stages, hitting the side netting, before Trent Alexander-Arnold opened the scoring for Liverpool. The right-back picked up a pass from Mohamed Salah in the 21st minute before curling a delightful effort into the top corner of the goal. Replays showed it took the slightest of deflections but there was no doubting the quality of the strike, and nobody in red could care less.

The Liverpool end erupted in an ocean of crimson light, and smoke filled the stadium as supporters rejoiced in the Reds' opener by setting off flares. Prior to the game dire warnings had been issued about bringing pyrotechnics into the stadium. Specialist sniffer dogs would be deployed, the authorities said. Maybe they'd been on a break when those Liverpool fans smuggled in enough distress flares to equip an armada.

What City fans there had done was their best to embellish their manufactured rivalry with Liverpool by goading the Scouse defender, and Trent duly returned the favour by placing a finger on his lips as he celebrated in front of them. Their faces and reactions were a joy to behold – picture the zombies in *World War Z* – and Trent clearly enjoyed the moment.

Haaland had tested Adrián, deputising for Alisson in the Liverpool goal, while at the other end Darwin lost out in a one-on-one with City keeper Ederson. Liverpool held on to their lead until the 70th minute, when another City debutant, Julián Álvarez, pounced when Adrián could only parry a Phil Foden shot into his path. A lengthy VAR check failed to come to Liverpool's rescue. It was a blow, but against City not entirely unexpected.

The Reds kept going, though, and eight minutes from time Rúben Dias appeared to handle the ball in his own penalty area. VAR couldn't decide and sent referee Craig Pawson to the pitch-side monitor to review. The infringement was obvious, leading to the question of why Stockley Park couldn't have simply awarded the penalty. Perhaps they didn't want to rob Pawson of the opportunity to draw an invisible square in the air and ceremoniously point to the spot from a distance.

The Liverpool faithful erupted in celebration. From the moment the referee had been sent to the monitor, few doubted that he'd award the pen, but the sense of relief was palpable and nervous expectation took over. Salah, his future now settled after signing his new deal at Liverpool, puffed out his cheeks, arced his now familiar run and slotted his spot kick home. Cue another raucous celebration. The Reds were back in front.

It was left to Darwin to place a metaphorical cherry on top of the icing on the cake, stooping to head in an Andy Robertson ball from close range. His joy was plain for all to see and, as he wheeled off in celebration, the Liverpool supporters danced in the stands, roaring their approval as Darwin roared back. A new hero was born.

Liverpool were off and running and, with another piece of silverware in the bag, hopes were high for the season ahead. Hindsight would show that it wouldn't live up to those early raised expectations, but the Community Shield win over City was one of the campaign's special moments.

Liverpool 9-0 Bournemouth
Anfield Rocking as Cherries Roasted

In so many ways, the 2022/23 season was a struggle. Exhausted from the frustrating end to the previous season, the traumas of Paris and, frankly, the daily grind of life, I felt genuinely jaded, exhausted, and to some extent I'd lost that sense of magic that going to the game has provided me down the years.

There's something so soul-crushing about witnessing what in my view was the greatest Liverpool team of my lifetime denied league titles because of what looks to me to be financial doping. To come so agonisingly close to a domestic treble and to lose out on the final day by a single point felt so hard to bear. It still does. You may say I'm bitter, but I'm not the only one.

I had no problem with the Champions League result against Madrid. We weren't good enough in that game, and Ancelotti had us sussed out. Madrid deserved their win, in my view. But obviously the events around that game had cast a long shadow and it was hard to shake it off.

August had seen the country in the grip of a so-called 'cost-of-living crisis'. I always thought that phrasing to be a clever ploy, as calling it that almost makes it sound like some sort of natural phenomenon, rather than the man-made social and economic catastrophe it is. Everything was becoming more expensive, and while some people struggled to fund their match-going expenses, others had to decided whether to eat or heat their homes.

One of Jürgen's legacies is that he has taught us to revel in the moments. If a season is falling short of expectations, there will always be games, goals or moments that can elevate you and bring you joy. As a spoiled Liverpool fan who has grown used to seeing his team win trophies, I've developed certain expectations. When we fall short, it can feel like the world is ending. Well, not quite, but you see what I mean.

For the supporters of most other clubs, this is, of course, how they maintain interest over decades. If you're a Bournemouth fan, for instance, you don't start the season dreaming of a league or European title, you live for the moments the game brings you. I'd lost sight of that, and when the Cherries visited Anfield on 27 August 2022, I was there to witness one of those glorious moments that punctuated a mediocre season for us. Sadly, for Bournemouth, it would have the opposite effect.

August had begun with a heatwave, but Liverpool were hardly setting the world on fire. Draws with Fulham and Crystal Palace and a defeat to Manchester United at Old Trafford were symptomatic of Liverpool's failed quadruple hangover. The 3-1 Community Shield victory over Manchester City and the optimism generated by that now seemed a distant memory.

As I sat, gazing out over the sun-drenched pitch, the stadium just beginning to fill up, I didn't expect a rout. I just hoped we could reignite the campaign with a win. Such was the margin of victory,

Jürgen Klopp handed senior debuts to Stefan Bajcetic, Bobby Clark and Fábio Carvalho as substitutes, the latter grabbing his first goal for the club.

The Palace game, our first of the season at Anfield, had been a study in frustration. Liverpool had failed to hit the heights, gone a goal down in the first half, then saw new signing Darwin Núñez dismissed for an act of naive petulance, before Luis Díaz rescued a point moments later.

Liverpool had then travelled to Old Trafford to face a club in crisis, beset with supporter protests and with a manager and players fearing the worst. Most would have predicted a Liverpool win, and they'd have been wrong, as the Reds slumped to a 2-1 defeat.

So, as the referee got ready to sound his whistle and commence the game against Bournemouth, I just wanted a moment that at least gave me something to smile about for the rest of the week, something to allow me to dream of distant possibilities come May. I got nine.

The pre-match display on the Kop was as colourfully vivid as ever, and as 'You'll Never Walk Alone' rang out from all four sides of the ground, I thought it felt more like a prayer than an anthem. There are times when the place is a bear pit, rocking and rolling, tormenting the opposition and driving the home team to plunder every drop of energy they have left for the cause. Then there are other times when Anfield feels like a cathedral, solemn and fearful. For a little while, it felt like the latter for the visit of Bournemouth.

That didn't last long, though, as Liverpool ran through the gears, dispatching their opponents with seeming ease and making a mockery of their earlier trials. This was an occasion in which they inspired and lifted us. It has so often been the other way round.

Five of Liverpool's nine goals came in the first half. Jürgen had demanded that his players react to their sluggish starts so far, and they did so in fine style. With the Reds 16th in the table, another slip-up would have piled on the pressure and turned what could be argued was a blip into a full-blown crisis, such is the nature of modern football.

The Reds were two up inside six minutes through Díaz, who headed home a Firmino cross, and Harvey Elliott, whose partnership and interplay with Mo Salah promised much. His fierce drive struck the net and sent us all into raptures.

However, so fragile was our belief in the early days of that campaign that even a two-goal lead wasn't enough to light up the cigars, put our feet up and relax. Anfield, bathed in August sunshine, struggled to hit the heights, although a vocal few on the Kop did their best to rally the atmosphere.

Then Bobby Firmino was again the provider, then scorer, either side of the half-hour mark. The Brazilian set up a Trent Alexander-Arnold goal in the 28th minute before grabbing one for himself three minutes later. Then, on the cusp of half-time, Virgil van Dijk grabbed Liverpool's fifth, a blockbuster header from an Andy Robertson corner.

It was already a rout, and after the struggles in our early games it came as a welcome relief. 'Class Liverpool' came a voice to the side of me. I looked skywards, closed my eyes, fists clenched, and inside I was screaming for joy, revelling in the moment.

I expected the Reds to take their foot off the gas, preserve energy and simply see the game out in the second half. Not a bit of it. After the start to the season we'd endured, Jürgen Klopp demanded more, later declaring:

> We had to prove a point to ourselves. We were not happy with how we played so far this season, but we had good moments in those games.
>
> We just had to give the game a proper direction and that's why I loved the start today. Two wonderful goals, everything about them. We kept going, scoring different goals but with the same purpose to keep up the pressure. In the end it was the perfect football afternoon.

It certainly was. Liverpool flew out of the traps in the second half, when Trent forced defender Chris Mepham into an own goal. Firmino, Carvalho – on as a substitute for the brilliant Harvey Elliott – and Díaz rounded off the scoring, equalling a Premier League record and evoking memories, for me, of our 9-0 thrashing of Crystal Palace all those years ago, in 1989.

With the Kop baying for blood, chanting, 'We want ten,' Liverpool surged forward in search of history. They were even to be denied a penalty moments from time. Bournemouth manager Scott Parker cut a dejected figure in front of the cameras at full time. 'It was a humbling experience what has happened today,' he said. 'We need to make a decision [in the transfer market] and give these players a break. They are struggling for air.'

To be fair, he'd have had to sign football's equivalent of the Harlem Globetrotters, and even then his side would have struggled to live with Liverpool in that sort of mood.

Rangers Destroyed at Ibrox
Reds Continue Mixed Start to Campaign

On 12 October 2022, Liverpool travelled to Ibrox to take on Glasgow Rangers in the Champions League group phase. After suffering a surprise 4-1 defeat at an impressive Napoli in the group's opener, the Reds had got their campaign back on track with a 2-1 win at home to Ajax. In the double-header with Rangers, they had a comfortable 2-0 win at home but Ibrox promised a raucous and partisan atmosphere. Liverpool got that, and in the opening passages of play, it looked as if they were in for a difficult night.

Scott Arfield scored for the home side after 17 minutes and lit the blue touchpaper on an explosive reaction. As I feared the Reds would be blown away by it and fall to an embarrassing European defeat, they simply shrugged off the setback and set about taking their opponents apart.

In the run-up to the game, Liverpool had been in uninspiring form, recording just four victories in the 11 matches played since winning the Community Shield. The highlight included a last-minute winner from the boot of Fábio Carvalho, in a tense game against Newcastle United at Anfield. However, defeats to Arsenal and Napoli had felt damaging, as did frustrating draws against Everton and Brighton.

At Ibrox, a Mohamed Salah hat-trick, a Bobby Firmino brace, and goals from Darwin Núñez and Harvey Elliott ensured it was a painful night for Rangers and their followers. In the stands, Liverpool and Rangers fans were separated by stewards, as an army of local youths attempted to attack the visitors. The mad charge led to laughter and chants of 'what the fucking hell was that'.

Liverpool followed their success north of the border with a home victory over Manchester City, as Alisson once again turned defence into attack, launching a clearance into the path of Mo Salah, who outstripped City's defence and scored with aplomb. The game became fractious as Pep Guardiola was struck by coins thrown from the Main Stand, and City supporters launched into their now customary Hillsborough chants and set about trashing the concourse in the away end. Klopp saw red in the 86th minute, and an injury to Diogo Jota in stoppage time took the gloss off a fine win. He would be out until February 2023.

The Reds limped on in the league through October and November and, as they reached the season break for the World Cup in Qatar with a 3-1 win over Southampton, they sat in sixth place. However, Europe had provided their salvation, victories over Ajax and Napoli, ensuring they reached the knockout stage.

In the news, the UK government's disastrous 'mini budget' led to economic catastrophe and ended the tenures of Prime Minister Truss and her chancellor. Few felt any sympathy for the pair, as the pensions and personal finances of millions of people had been put in jeopardy.

In the League Cup, a heavily rotated Liverpool struggled to a goalless draw against Derby County and needed a penalty shoot-out to progress. Despite missing two of their spot kicks, the Reds won 3-2, setting up a huge game at the Etihad after the World Cup.

The break came at an unwelcome time, with the season reaching a crucial phase, and all we could do was hope that our international players returned unscathed.

Jürgen Klopp Awarded the Freedom of the City of Liverpool

On 2 November 2022, in recognition of his achievements in football and contribution to civic pride, Jürgen Klopp was awarded the Freedom of the City of Liverpool at a special ceremony in the town hall. It's an ancient title, the city's highest honour, conferred only on the city's most impactful citizens.

Klopp had overseen Liverpool's return to glory after arriving in 2015 to replace Brendan Rodgers, and at the time of his award had led the club to seven major honours, including our sixth Champions League trophy, in 2019 and the Premier League title the following year, ending a 30-year wait. He was nominated for the accolade back in July and received his Freedom of Liverpool scroll during a special ceremony in his honour. A beaming Klopp told the club's official website:

> It's great, I cannot really describe it. I was never in a similar situation in my life, to be one hundred per cent honest. It was a bit overwhelming tonight.
>
> I like traditions, I like these kinds of things, I just usually don't want to be in the middle of everything – but tonight I enjoyed it anyway. It was good, the speeches were nice, the video was nice, everything.
>
> The occasion is incredible, I love it in these wonderful rooms, being here – my first time in the Liverpool Town Hall. I was already really close with everything in Liverpool, but it brought me even closer tonight.

Jürgen had forged a special bond with Liverpool supporters and is to this day still adored by them. However, he and his wife Ulla also enjoy a fond connection with the city and the region as a whole. A point he was keen to emphasise:

> We love living here. We will not live forever here because at one point we will go back to Germany, whenever that will be, but it was always clear we will stay connected.
>
> And this makes it even more because we will take that, we will take care of it, we will take it to everywhere we go because it's just special. For a city we love so much, getting something like this really is big.

Jürgen also commented on how nobody could have forecast the success he'd go on to achieve at the club but was keen as always to emphasise the importance of the players and the people behind him. Surely the secret to Jürgen's enormous power as a human being is his ability to relate to people, to understand their value and contribution, and to help them maximise that. It's a rare talent that sets him apart.

In a sign that his energy levels were still at the maximum, Jürgen enthused:

But with some good decisions, hard work, fantastic players, incredible coaches, great support from owners and especially supporters, things can happen and that's what happened. But we have still a lot to do and that's what we will do. And I can't wait to keep going.

In an interview with the *Liverpool Echo*, Jürgen was asked whether this meant he was an honorary Scouser:

I cannot. It is not for me to say that, but I feel like that and over the years you realise that the Scouse people and us as a family have a lot of things in common. We care about similar things, have similar political views and we like to be very open, that's how it is. All people around me, my friends and family, see more of the city than I do, and I hear always that they enjoy it exactly because of that; because people are really open, nice, kind, and friendly. That's what I want to be as well.

Hillsborough campaigner Margaret Aspinall, whose son died aged 18 at Sheffield in 1989, felt Jürgen was more than worthy of the honour, telling the BBC:

I'm absolutely delighted. He's a great ambassador for our club and also our city. He's just a great manager, a great human being, a great personality and a great humanitarian.

Unfortunately, the demands of being a Liverpool manager meant that Jürgen never got to drive his sheep down the city's streets, as is now his right under the ancient title. Maybe one day, eh, Jürgen lad.

Merseyside Mourns the Death of David Johnson
The Red Who Won the Derby for Liverpool and Everton
Many players have represented both Liverpool and Everton throughout their long rivalry, but one of those, David Johnson, holds a particular distinction, having scored goals that won a Merseyside derby for both Liverpool and Everton. In doing so, he has cemented his place in the region's football folklore forever.

Johnson, courted by Shankly and eventually signed by Paisley, was a boyhood Red who won championships for Liverpool. His exploits in the game and for Liverpool would be overshadowed by the later emergence of Ian Rush, who went on to become one of the club's greatest-ever goalscorers.

Writing for *These Football Times*, author Steven Scragg said this of Johnson's virtues:

> A versatile striker, Johnson could be both bludgeoning and deft. Intelligent in his link-up play and dangerous with his back to goal, there were several skills that Johnson possessed that were adopted by his successor in the Liverpool number 9 shirt, a certain Ian Rush.

Born in Liverpool in 1951, Johnson first played for Everton, then had success at Bobby Robson's Ipswich, before moving to Anfield, then back to Everton. He was capped by England eight times. This is his remarkable story.

It's winter, November 1971, and Merseyside is once more in the grip of derby-day fever. Among the 56,500 people crammed into Goodison Park are the family of Everton striker David Johnson. They don't know which way to turn. They're devout Liverpool supporters, yet their loved one is lining up for the enemy. They wish him both pleasure and pain – it's an impossible dilemma.

In the dugout is Harry Catterick, who signed Johnson for Everton back in the January. He's determined to hang on to his prized asset. Sitting just yards away is Bill Shankly, who has been pestering his opposite number to sell Johnson to Liverpool for almost a year.

The object of their affection is facing the team he's adored since childhood and is determined to ruin their day. It's not personal, it's football. It's his first derby and no prisoners can be taken.

The teams trade blows until the 71st minute. Johnson finds himself in the box at the Gwladys Street End. The ball is flying through the air and he heads it towards goal. Ray Clemence dives and touches it on to the post, but the 20-year-old then volleys the ball in. Goodison explodes, his family are stunned, and the young lad they raised a Red is now an Everton hero.

The Blues triumph 1-0 and it's a magical derby debut for Johnson.

Fast-forward to the same setting in April 1978. Again over 50,000 Scousers are packed in, among them Johnson's family. This time their hero is wearing Red. Everton's manager is Gordon Lee. Liverpool's is Bob Paisley. He'd signed Johnson from Ipswich Town in 1976, where he'd played after leaving the Blues in 1972. The atmosphere is febrile. The Reds are reigning champions of England and Europe. In a month's time they'll conquer Europe once again. Everton are chasing the title but will fall painfully (for them) short.

In the 13th minute Johnson finds himself in that same place once more: in front of the baying tumult that's the Gwladys Street. Evertonians scream 'Judas' as he races on to a perfectly weighted Ray Kennedy pass. He charges towards goal, holding off a defender and slots the ball past the advancing George Wood. The Gwladys Street is spitting fury, and a coin is hurled at Johnson as he celebrates.

On Merseyside, you're either an ally or an enemy. There's no middle ground. His feats in the blue of Everton were forgotten in an instant. Johnson didn't care, his goal in red was far more precious than any scored in blue.

Nicknamed 'the Doc' by Terry McDermott due to his tendency to carry throat soothers and other medicines and potions in his bag, Johnson played 149 times for Liverpool, scoring 49 times. He won four league titles, two European Cups, a European Super Cup and a League Cup in a Reds career that spanned just six years.

He said, of his European Cup triumph in 1981, after the agony of missing out in 1978:

> It was the most satisfying night of my European career. It meant so much to be after being on the bench in 77 and on crutches in 78. This time I actually played, and for the whole 90 minutes too.

David Johnson died in November 2022, at the age of 71. He'll be remembered as a local lad who represented both Liverpool and Everton with distinction, a consummate professional who always gave his all. He was a winner and a champion who played under some of the greatest managers in the history of English football, and a proper Scouser.

Liverpool 2-0 Everton

Reds Deliver New Year Joy as 'Elf' Watches On

On Monday, 13 February, Liverpool ended a miserable run of form with a derby-day win over Everton. And the star of the Christmas movie *Elf*, Will Ferrell, was there to see it.

Club football had returned some magic to December, after Lionel Messi had finally added a World Cup winner's medal to his tally of trinkets, as Argentina saw off Germany in a penalty shoot-out. Future Liverpool star Alexis Mac Allister shared the glory with him.

The Reds returned to action in the League Cup on 22 December, but thanks to a Kevin De Bruyne masterclass Manchester City ran out 3-2 winners, sending Liverpool – the holders – out of the competition. Klopp's men had twice come from behind, but a Nathan Aké goal just shy of the hour mark put paid to their resistance.

We returned to winning ways after Christmas with victories away to Aston Villa on Boxing Day, and a 2-1 win over Leicester at Anfield on 30 December. Stefan Bajcetic scored his debut goal in the win at Villa Park. The win over the Foxes was accompanied by increasing speculation that Liverpool were about to sign Manchester United target Cody Gakpo. The capture of the Dutch striker would prove to be a rare highlight in January as Liverpool soldiered on through a miserable series of results that stretched into February. Defeats to Brentford, Brighton – who also dumped the Reds out of the FA Cup – and Wolves were compounded by injuries to Van Dijk and Konaté.

Liverpool therefore welcomed Everton to Anfield on 13 February, with confidence in short supply. Still, there's nothing like a victory over the old enemy to give you a morale boost. Hollywood star Will Ferrell was watching on from the corporate suites, as was former Liverpool chairman Martin Broughton. The Reds were without defenders Van Dijk and Konaté, while midfield maestro Thiago was out for weeks with a hip injury. However, the game saw Cody Gakpo score his debut goal for the club.

Talk of Liverpool's search for investment, after reportedly abandoning plans to sell the club, were rife, along with a mooted summer transfer budget of £300m. A report in *The Athletic* ranked Liverpool as the Premier League's number one sustainable club.

However, the credibility of the index was undermined by the fact that Everton came in second.

Evertonians, who had just got used to life without former manager Frank Lampard, were only slowly coming to terms with their club's growing fiscal crisis. The appointment of Sean Dyche was perhaps a symbol of their revised ambitions. Despite all that, with the former Burnley man winning his first game in charge and with Liverpool struggling, the Blues arrived at Anfield with hope in their hearts.

In what was possibly the most Everton moment ever, Liverpool's Mohamed Salah scored after the Reds turned a James Tarkowski near miss into attack. Darwin's pace was frightening as he took the ball and raced forwards, delivering a ball of sublime quality for the Egyptian to finish. After the break, another incredible breakaway involving passes between Robertson, Salah, Alexander-Arnold and Gakpo gifted the Dutchman a tap-in for his debut goal.

This was a game that also featured a standout performance from Stefan Bajcetic, who, despite his tender years, ran the midfield for Liverpool. Salah heaped praise on him at the end of the game, declaring him 'our best player'. The match was also another example of the link-up play between Salah and Darwin, which was already bearing fruit. The pair were now creating a goalscoring opportunity for each other every 52 minutes, on average.

In the stands, Liverpool fans were in triumphant mood, and as the clocked ticked down the Anfield faithful indulged in a chorus of 'this is your last trip to Anfield'. It may have been wishful thinking, but it would have stung the Blues, who were locked in another relegation dogfight.

This was Klopp's 250th win for Liverpool and, as we filed out of the stadium, there was a sense of recovered optimism. Given our previous form it made little sense but, just maybe, another push for the top four was possible.

This was another flag day, and the boss and the players lauded the atmosphere. Jürgen told the waiting media, 'I am in love with the atmosphere they created.' At full time he ran towards the Kop, fists pumping and face etched with passion. 'I'd have done anything for these supporters, except remove my clothing,' he said, after he was asked what motivated him to do it. 'Our people deserved it,' he added.

UEFA Report into Near Disaster at Paris Final Exonerates Fans

In mid-February 2023, there was a leaked copy of UEFA's report into their horrific handling of the Champions League Final in Paris. As expected, it completely exonerated Liverpool fans, going even further in stating that the behaviour of Liverpool supporters, far from being responsible for the chaos before and after the game, actually saved lives.

While it was disappointing that the report had been leaked to the press before supporters who had been traumatised by the events could digest it, the sense of vindication was enormous. Reacting to the report, Jürgen Klopp said:

> I think it's super-important that, finally, it's official, let me say it like this. I'm not sure, at least in my life, there was never a case with more evidence, where I knew more about [it] when I was not directly involved, because I was on the other side of the wall in the stadium, pretty much.
>
> But families, friends, they were all there and everybody knew how our supporters behaved, but it really feels good, it feels just right that it's now official and everybody knows it now because there were so many things said after the game, which we knew they were wrong.
>
> It was just lies. So, I'm really happy that it's finally said officially.

The authorities' attempt to shift the blame on to the victims of the chaos they alone created was eerily similar to our experiences after the Hillsborough disaster. The key difference here was that so many people had mobile phones, and the world's media was there to see and record the whole debacle. We didn't have that in Sheffield in 1989.

Klopp singled out the role played by journalists in ensuring that the same attempt at a cover-up couldn't succeed this time:

> The only good thing in all the bad things that happened there is that many journalists were there in that crowd. So independent, no Liverpool shirt, just being there and wanting to do their job, and they knew exactly that it was wrong as well, and I think

that helped because otherwise they probably all would have to go through that as well. I think we were really lucky that not more happened.

It was a day of, I'm not sure how you say it, but the day of 'goodwill lies' – when you have to lie to protect the other person. Because we all had messages from our people outside before the game and then the game got delayed, so we started looking at the smartphone again, 'What's happening?' We knew because people couldn't get in and everybody said, 'No, I'm fine, I'm fine …' and nobody was fine. Nobody was fine.

Then the game started, and I heard from people that everybody who was in the stadium was just there and thought, 'I made it somehow, wow.' It was not the mood you are in when you want to watch a Champions League final.

He ended by thanking the Liverpool fans who were caught up in the chaos for 'staying calm' on a night when the football felt irrelevant:

Thank you. Staying calm in a situation where nobody really can stay calm, tear gas in your eyes, pressure from up front, from the side, from behind, being locked in between thousands of people and not pushing like crazy, staying calm, is a massive thing to do and an extremely difficult thing to do.

And then getting out of it, and getting blamed for that, it's horrible. It's really horrible. So, there are some jobs to do, and I hope they do it properly because these kinds of events should be a pure joy to watch.

You pay a lot of money, it's a lot of work to qualify, then you go there, everything is a positive mood and in the end you're just happy to arrive somehow in the stadium when you made it.

That Klopp completely understood and spoke so eloquently, addressing our sensitivities around the incident and its aftermath, was significant. It meant so much.

Speaking to the club's official website, Liverpool FC CEO Billy Hogan took part in a Q&A, outlining what the report meant and what to expect next. In it, he expressed his sadness that the events had happened at all and acknowledged the terrible impact it had wrought on supporters, and the club's relief that the right conclusions had been drawn. He spoke of a sense of pride in the club's supporters:

> So, just a sense of pride in terms of our supporters and the behaviour of our supporters. I think if you read the report, it's mentioned a number of times in terms of being called a near miss. And frankly, I think if it wasn't Liverpool supporters, people might have reacted differently.
>
> I think the history that we have as a club going back to Hillsborough really made people behave and, you know, I think the sense of our supporters policing themselves in the face of what was incredibly heavy-handed policing. I was in those crowds, and I saw the behaviour of our supporters, and that is the reason why it was a near miss and why it wasn't an actual disaster.

Nine thousand supporters had given evidence of their experiences to Liverpool Football Club, many forced to relive the trauma of the day. The club had submitted those to the UEFA panel and delegations of supporters' representatives, including Joe Blott of Spirit of Shankly, Ted Morris of Liverpool Disabled Supporters Association, themselves caught up in the chaos that night, and Ian Byrne MP, who gave evidence at the French Senate. Those submissions and representations had been hugely influential.

The Spirit of Shankly, Liverpool Supporters' Union, issued the following statement, and it was unequivocal in terms of what it felt the key lessons from the report were:

> Spirit of Shankly today welcome the findings of the Independent Panel Inquiry into events surrounding the UEFA Champions League Final in Paris on 28 May 2022 in which Liverpool fans have been cleared of blame and responsibility for the horrendous situations that occurred in and around Stade de France that night.
>
> What should have been the highlight of the season for travelling supporters of Liverpool and Real Madrid – in UEFA's

words a 'festival of football' – turned out to be a maelstrom of chaos and alarm that led to some fans fearing for their life.

The blame game began even before a ball was kicked, and in the immediate aftermath those supposedly in charge – UEFA and the authorities – had no hesitation in pointing the finger at supporters.

But now with the publication of the report, it is clear, the fans bear no culpability with the panel concluding 'overarching organisational failures' were the root of what went so badly wrong. A remarkable absence of joint working between the major stakeholders – UEFA, the French authorities, and French Football Federation – from when the final was moved to Paris, in February, up to and including the day of the match itself resulted in pandemonium.

UEFA and the authorities sought to deflect any responsibility with the panel stating: 'The public response of UEFA in the aftermath of the problems on the night and in its subsequent evidence to the Senate was striking in its orientation to protect itself. It was a serious error for UEFA to assume it could avoid accountability for a foreseeable near disaster at its flagship event.'

Joe Blott, as chair of the supporters' union, issued the following statement on Tuesday, 14 February 2023:

I welcome the findings of the Independent Panel Inquiry into events surrounding the UEFA Champions League Final in Paris on 28 May 2022 whose report is published today.

I particularly note and welcome that Liverpool fans have been cleared of blame and responsibility for the horrendous situations that occurred in and around the Stade de France that night.

For his part, Ian Byrne MP said:

I have written to Secretary of State urging her to call for a full apology and retraction from UEFA and President Macron, and to call on the UEFA President to consider his position. I have also urged her to seek a commitment from UEFA that all panel recommendations will be implemented.

Club captain Jordan Henderson gave his reaction also:

> The Paris report needs to be a turning point for the treatment of football fans. No one should have their safety jeopardised by inadequate organisation. The sooner action is taken, the better.

Thanks to the tireless campaigning efforts of supporters, and the willingness of journalists to report what they saw honestly and faithfully, the truth was secured in the weeks and months that followed the near disaster in Paris.

Those same campaigners, and supporters' groups such as Spirit of Shankly and Liverpool Disabled Supporters Association, also ensured that fans received refunds and those who made personal injury claims received compensation as a result of their experiences that night.

Whether UEFA and the Paris authorities have truly learned the lessons of that night remains to be seen. The acid test will be whether they can ensure that such events never happen again.

Liverpool 7-0 Manchester United

Historic Humiliation for Red Devils as Liverpool Run Riot

This was an oasis in a season that at times felt arduous. It was raw abandon and joyous, hysterical laughter. And it was historic.

Yet, as 5 March got underway, the mood couldn't have been in sharper contrast. In the pub before the game, the conversation was all about the adages of laws and averages, and how United were surely due one after we'd hammered them so often in recent seasons. Would this be their turn to return the favour?

The warning signs were there. United had beaten us 2-1 at Old Trafford earlier in the season, and our form had been decidedly inconsistent throughout the campaign, leaving us in a deserved fifth place.

There's a sort of ritual in the pub before a game. I and my mate John Stulberg always fix each other with a knowing stare and one of us says, 'I'm nervous about today.' The other (could be me or him) replies, 'Me too.' Then another mate, Keith Williams, invariably says, 'I'm not. I don't know why, but I feel confident. I think we'll win. I've just got a feeling.' It doesn't matter if he's right, the moment he utters those words, I relax. Because he usually is, mostly. Yes, I probably only remember the times that he's spot on, while consigning the times he's not to the dustbin, where all bad memories go. Of course, it's just magical thinking, but it somehow calms me down. Such is the rhythm of football for me.

On this day, Keith was confident. He was the octopus picking a winning team in a World Cup and I waited for his proclamation to arrive, like a plume of white smoke above the Vatican signifies the confirmation of a new Pope. It did, and we could all enjoy our pints and look forward to meeting up after the game, when we'd shake hands and marvel at how Keith had called it all along. Rituals and habits.

Even with his miraculous sixth sense, though, even Keith couldn't have forecast this result. It was literally without precedent. And for what we were about to receive, we would be eternally grateful.

Throughout February, the UK had been gripped by industrial action, with a reported half-million workers on strike. The nation was gripped by the tragic disappearance of Nicola Bulley, with many becoming amateur internet detectives and spreading wild conspiracy theories. Meanwhile, an elderly couple in London were dreaming of the day when they got to don glittery crowns and enjoy the biggest party of their lives, while people who couldn't afford to heat their homes made plans to stand outside, hoping for a glimpse of them.

As we wandered up to the ground, bellies full of beer and bladders lighter for that last trip to the loo – rituals and habits – we moaned about all of that. Well, it kept our minds off the game and the butterflies in check.

The Reds' form had been uninspiring, but there had been moments. Defeats to Brighton and Crystal Palace were followed by 2-0 victories at home to Everton and away to Newcastle. I'd experienced intense hope and optimism when Liverpool had raced into a 2-0 lead against Real Madrid at a packed and expectant Anfield, only to see the Madrid players shrug off the setbacks and set about a 5-2 demolition job that was as demoralising as it was brilliant.

Klopp's message to supporters after that defeat felt like a life lesson: 'The better we behave in times like this, the better things will be after that and the more useful the bad times will be.' They were wise words, but it was still hard to accept how far behind Madrid we'd looked in that game.

I'd bemoaned our lack of squad depth as we struggled to a goalless draw at Palace, only to reclaim belief after a 2-0 win against Wolves. The season was roller-coaster, and we were about to hit the highest point of the ride.

When I look back on this game, I find it impossible to believe that at half-time United were still in it. It was just 1-0 to the home side, who had gone ahead on the stroke of half-time through Cody Gakpo, who finished off an Andy Robertson cross. It was a goal greeted with wild relief and celebration. It was a perfect time to score, we thought. But it was no guarantee of the utter rout that was to follow.

In the second half, Liverpool gave a performance for the ages, and Mohamed Salah became the club's record Premier League goalscorer as the Reds simply overwhelmed United. It was thrill-ride for us, and for the United fans the realisation of their most terrifying nightmares, with many of them choosing to see out the game on the concourse in the Anfield Road end.

The goals came like an avalanche, burying United and leaving a drowning Ten Hag without a straw to clutch upon. First up after the interval was Darwin Núñez, whose header diverted a Harvey Elliott centre into the net, then it was Salah's turn to torment the United defence, setting up Gakpo for his second, before joining in on the act himself to make it 4-0 with 24 minutes still on the clock.

United's following must have feared the worst and, sensing what was to come, fled for the exit signs, wishing they'd stayed in bed that day. They escaped the agony of seeing Darwin Núñez grab his second, and Mohamed Salah notching Liverpool's sixth. It was all so unbelievable, impossible, and yet happening before our eyes.

Anfield was in ferment, as songs rolled down from the Kop. The Main Stand and the Anfield Road end joined in, starting their own, and the noise, out of sync and delirious, filled my head. I knew my pride and joy was matched only by the enemy's embarrassment and pain.

I watched replays of the game for days after, and laughed aloud when I heard Gary Neville's in-commentary attempts to downplay the significance of the rout. At 5-0 he said that this was not an era-defining, existential defeat. The players could recover from this. It would have to be six or seven for it to be truly damaging, he opined. Cue Salah, and then a glorious finish from Bobby Firmino two minutes from time. The goal by Bobby had special poignancy, given he'd announced on the previous Friday that he'd be leaving the club at the end of the season. Si señor.

Our celebrations combined with laughter. So comprehensive was United's defeat, so era-defining and historic was it, that you just had to laugh. This was Liverpool's biggest win over United in the history of the fixture, surpassing their 7-1 victory in the 1895/96 Second Division season, when United were still called Newton Heath.

Perhaps showing a sliver of compassion for his vanquished opponents, Klopp resisted the Kop's demands for fist bumps. Such triumphalism might have been kicking a man while he's down, but this was our most fierce rivalry after all. Liverpool supporters would show their counterparts no such mercy for weeks to come.

It was a high point for sure. And Keith called it, you know.

Reds Run-In Fade-Away Sees Them Out of Champions League Football

After the highpoint of the United rout, Liverpool's inconsistency took control and we wouldn't taste victory for another five games. Then, in typical fashion, it would see them follow mediocrity with brilliance. The drubbing of Manchester United at Anfield made what followed even harder to rationalise. The defeats to Bournemouth, Real Madrid and Manchester City, followed by draws against Chelsea and Arsenal meant that we went into the away game against Leeds United with hope at an all-time low.

However, the Reds had shown some bite and pride in the 2-2 draw with Arsenal on 9 April. Arsenal had roared into the game, looking every inch title challengers. They ran Liverpool ragged, racing into a two-goal lead after just 28 minutes, and it felt like Liverpool had no interest in the game. The crowd's mood was turning from frustration to anger, and all of it was directed at the players in red. It was a recipe for disaster. However, there's a feature of Scouse culture, a philosophy that allows us to lambast our own when we think they deserve it, but woe betide any outsider that tries it. We can close ranks in lightning-quick fashion.

That moment arrived when Arsenal's Granit Xhaka attempted to strongarm Trent Alexander-Arnold. As angry as we were with the Scouser and his team-mates for the dreadful performances they were putting in, none of us were having anyone trying to bully the Scouser in our team. Our reaction was instant, deafening and sustained. Arsenal boss Mikel Arteta, pacing the touchline and doing his best Pep Guardiola impression, must have known what was coming, and his heart must have shrunk as Anfield awoke in spitting fury.

The BBC captured the moment in their post-match report:

> Liverpool had produced an insipid performance and were being outplayed until Xhaka unwisely chose to tangle with Alexander-Arnold, the incident injecting Jürgen Klopp's side with the energy and inspiration they had been lacking – and crucially bringing the Anfield crowd into play.

Within 15 minutes, a rejuvenated Liverpool were back in it through Mohamed Salah. Half-time came too soon and much to Arsenal's relief. They were rocking and the Reds had found new belief. Driven on by a ferocious and partisan Kop, they launched wave upon wave of attacks at the Anfield Road end. We sensed this could be the moment when Klopp launched his assault on top four, just as he had two seasons earlier. Every game, every season sometimes needs a spark. Maybe this was it.

In the second half the Reds laid siege to the Arsenal goal, which seemed to creak in front of a loud and vociferous Kop. Salah won and missed a penalty, and with it the chance of an equaliser. Undaunted, we cranked up the decibels, and the players lifted their heads once more and kept going. In the end it was our boy from Brazil, Roberto Firmino, who rescued the point, with just three minutes to go.

The joy that greeted the goal was matched only by our despair as Arsenal's keeper Ramsdale saved brilliantly as Darwin raced clear, then produced a stunning fingertip save from Mohamed Salah, before pulling off what seemed like an impossible stop, preventing Konaté from bundling the ball over the line with only seconds left. We felt robbed of another storied comeback.

This was a game that had everything but the three points. And amid the chaos of that fightback there was even time for a linesman to elbow Andy Robertson in the face. TV replays appeared conclusive and damning that Constantine Hatzidakis had responded to Robertson's protests at a decision by elbowing the player on the chin. There was an investigation, which, of course, amounted to nothing, leaving us and the player incredulous. Our faith in match officials and their governing body couldn't have been lower, or so we thought.

Throughout Liverpool's struggles this season, the fanbase had convulsed, divisions opened up between those perceived to be on the side of the owners and those who wanted rid of them. Then there was the tiny minority of amnesic supporters for whom nothing is ever good enough, and who were questioning Jürgen's position. You rarely if ever met these people at a game, but they seemed much louder than their numbers should allow on social media. An ever-watchful media, having seen such debates online, began to ask difficult questions of the boss. Amazingly, given everything he'd achieved, he was asked about the possibility that his time may be up. 'I cannot leave. I will not leave,' came his reply. 'If you believe in me, we will have great times again.'

Elsewhere, Manchester City faced Premier League charges of 115 counts of financial irregularities, and Pep Guardiola launched a strange rant about Steven Gerrard's slip in the title-defining game against Chelsea back in the Rodgers era. He would later apologise but it was clear that Liverpool had taken up permanent residency in the Spaniard's head.

In April, Liverpool, after diving to the bottom of the fairground ride, were once again ascending the roller-coaster. The visit to Elland Road brought another flurry of goals, with Liverpool running out 6-1 winners. The goals flowed from Cody Gakpo, Mohamed Salah (2), Diogo Jota (2) and Darwin Núñez. However, the win did little to improve our league position, with the Reds languishing in eighth place.

Klopp's men had eight games to capture fourth. They'd come close, but six wins and two draws left them short. A 4-4 draw on the final day away to Southampton left Mohamed Salah devastated. His social media was an apology to the Reds faithful and a pledge to put things right in the season to follow.

Jürgen found the positives and, as he'd done before, turned our disappointment into a rallying cry. He embraced our Europa League qualification and vowed to build a new Liverpool, his second great team.

Liverpool 2.0: Reinventing Klopp's Reds

Liverpool FC August 2023–January 2024

One Klopp Interview Is All It Takes
Klopp Restores Faith with Call to Arms

Such was the meltdown on social media throughout the summer of 2023 that some of us were thinking of throwing the towel in. Depending on where you turned, Liverpool were either too frugal with their cash or spending money like it was going out of fashion. The controversy over Jordan Henderson's move to Saudi Arabia had Reds bickering and it was all starting to feel a bit too much.

The world of social media can infect your psyche and have you doubting the evidence of your own senses. What we all needed was a reminder of who we are, what's important and, well, a metaphorical slap in the face from the boss. It took Jürgen Klopp, talking to the club's official *We Are Liverpool* podcast, to snap me out of my pre-season funk.

After a couple of years in which we soared to new heights before plunging the depths of a quadruple near miss, to the misery of Paris, followed by a campaign riddled with what ifs, buts, maybes and abject displays, crowned only by an all-too-late flourish that only partially lifted the gloom, I'd found it hard to summon the sort of pre-season optimism that occasionally approaches the delusional. Instead, I'd been sleepwalking into the 2023/24 campaign.

With a mastery of understatement that borders on genius, the boss described the previous season as a 'real knock'. He wasn't wrong, but paraphrasing the author Douglas Adams's description of Sundays as the 'long dark teatime of the soul' would have been a better fit. Liverpool's last campaign, coming hot on the heels of an exhausting and forlorn quest to become the greatest team that ever kicked a ball, was indeed enough to blot out my soul.

Thankfully Jürgen is made from different stuff than me. 'I'm on fire,' said the boss, with that trademark grin you can't help but love, as he summed up his resolve to right wrongs and make the next season one to remember, 'in the best way possible.'

Football is now a sport in which you can only truly guarantee success with the wealth of a nation state, and expensive lawyers. So, as delusional as I can occasionally be, I certainly wouldn't be holding Jürgen to his promise. Yet I did feel inexplicably lifted by it. Hopelessly romantic. Maybe. But I didn't think I was entirely guilty of blind faith

– the boss did have form when it came to rising from the ashes of a disappointing campaign.

The boss, a massive fan of the *Rocky* movies, has always had an uncanny ability to experience lows and consistently climb from the canvas and fight on to victory. Few managers could recover from the ignominy of the Kyiv final in 2018 to boldly proclaim, the very next day, we'll win it next year, before going on to do just that. He'd perform the same feat after missing the Premier League to City by a single agonising point in 2019. 'Trust us,' he said, explaining how he understood that some supporters might have once again become doubters, as they watched their team fall from a metaphorical cliff last season.

There are those much wiser than me who have pointed out the errors of Jürgen's ways. His alleged stubborn streak and apparent loyalty to players who are supposedly past their best aside, I'd still argue that his ability to learn from mistakes and setbacks made him more than worthy of our trust. The failure to evolve the midfield over successive seasons may have led to a need for something of a hasty revolution, but the signings of Alexis Mac Allister and Dominik Szoboszlai for less than the cost of a Man City substitute looked smart. Also, the rehabilitation of Curtis Jones at the end of the last campaign was one of that season's few bright spots. Even with the loss of Fabinho, and Jordan Henderson's apparent conversion on the road to Saudi Arabia, there was renewed hope that the club and Klopp were on the case and working to solve those issues ahead of the big kick-off. Jürgen's statement that 'transfers will happen' before the new season meant, to me, that he at least had confidence in the direction the club was taking on recruitment. And that would do for me.

I was steeled for a fall, of course I was. You always must be. But once more I could feel that old energy returning. The lethargy of the last year was fading, replaced with that familiar nervous energy as the first game approached. I didn't realise how much I'd missed that feeling. If Jürgen's words could have this effect at a distance, I could only guess at the impact he was having on the players as they got ready to go again.

Among the many reasons to be cheerful at the start of the season was the completion of the new Anfield Road stand. The impressive development meant that as Liverpool welcomed Bournemouth on 19 August, they'd do so in front of more than 60,000 supporters. This was something no Liverpool side had experienced since 1952, when 61,905 saw the Reds beat Wolverhampton Wanderers 2-1 in the fourth round of the FA Cup. Imagine the noise back then. 'It would be good if they could fill them [the new seats] with the right ones,' said the boss, clearly hoping the decibel count inside the ground would benefit from the stadium expansion.

Anfield has always been about more than bums on seats. You're not there to be an observer; you're there to support as loudly as you possibly can. Jürgen had given you your orders. The manager's words in that podcast were as timely as they were effective and, for me at least, they banished the gloom of that long dark season of the soul.

We *would* go again, filled with renewed energy and focus, exciting youngsters making their way, others finding new maturity, thrilling signings, and the promise of more. That interview reminded me why I was still glad that Jürgen is a Red.

The first game was just around the corner. I could not bloody wait.

Leaving on a Jet Plane
No Escape from Transfer Window Madness

A month is a long time in football, two months is an eternity – 24-hour news cycles and the unending insanity on social media can play havoc with your mental health. The incessant demand for Liverpool, or more specifically the owners, to spend the GDP of a small nation in a futile attempt to compete with the petrochemical clubs means that many can never be truly satisfied.

Yesterday's success in the market counts for nothing. Go back eight months, or a year, and you might as well be discussing ancient history. I like ancient history, to be fair, but I'm part of a dwindling band of dreamers, it seems. I long for those days when the signing of Darwin Núñez for £85m was heralded as a masterstroke, when the 'net spend boys' retreated into their basements for a few hours at least, and when the capture of Cody Gakpo for £44m represented evidence of Liverpool's prowess in the market and proof of Manchester United's dithering.

They were fun times.

As August 2023 arrived, I set off with the family for a holiday in Greece safe in the knowledge that, during June and July, Liverpool had been 'kicking arse and taking names in the transfer window', getting their business done early and without fuss. At least that had been the collective view of the online ones.

Liverpool had acquired Alexis Mac Allister in a deal that frankly beggared belief – £35m for a World Cup winner, in today's market! All were agreed, it was genius. Next through the door, just a month or so later, and to huge fanfare, came Dominik Szoboszlai. Liverpool weren't messing around; they'd just stumped up £60m and got the deal done.

For two glorious months, the internet – or the parts of it that I frequent – had been a wholesome place. The 'Top Reds' – I've never been sure if they're the goodies or the baddies in this melodrama – were in the ascendency, and the 'FSG Out family' appeared to be on mute. The uproar over Liverpool's abandoned pursuit of Jude Bellingham seemed to abate and, for what must have been minutes, there were no planes over Anfield. No toys were thrown out of prams, and I could barely wait to refresh my feed. Frankly, the thought of a four-hour plane flight with my phone in aeroplane mode and without access to the minute-by-minute rumour mill left me feeling a little strung out. By the end of the holiday, I'd be longing for a stint stranded on a desert island, Wi-Fi free and blissfully ignorant.

I should have known better than to let myself get sucked in. How had I been so naive? Those of us who know the football internet land like the back of our hands should understand that its a nuance-free zone, where such tranquillity can disappear faster than a footballer's principles.

Liverpool's pursuit of Romeo Lavia, the Southampton midfielder, best known to me as the guy who set up a goal for us at the back end of the 2022/23 season, could best be described as protracted and unsuccessful. Less charitable people would call it shambolic and doomed to failure. However, it should be pointed out that most of the people with hands clenched in fists of rage actually knew very little of the player until news of the Reds' interest emerged, and even then questions had been raised about his suitability to fill the gaping holes in Liverpool's midfield. Now it seemed some of them couldn't live, and the club couldn't survive, without him. That's the way it is in internet land, where nuance goes to die.

The deal had taken slightly less than the time it takes to buy a house to reach its disappointing end, which was deemed to be catastrophic, embarrassing, worrying and a sign that Liverpool was now a small club or, worse still in the eyes of the net spend brigade, cheap. In what strikes me as bizarre form of logic, many of our supporters seem to switch allegiance to the selling club during transfer negotiations. 'Just pay the asking price' is the usual cry. If you do, that's good; haggle a bit, and that's bad. It has always made me wonder why we need a director of football at all. Just employ a bot that fires off a bid at exactly the figure the selling club wants – job done.

The problem is, of course, that we now live in a world where football clubs exist that can do just that, and Liverpool are not one of them. So, the apparent binary choice facing us is a life under the yoke of the Moneyball-obsessed and deeply risk-averse FSG, or a transfer of ownership to a nation state with more stains on its conscience than Boris Johnson – assuming he has one, of course – and all we have to do is exchange our soul and become just like everybody else.

The only thing truly shocking about claims that FSG are risk-averse in the transfer market is that anyone is genuinely surprised about that. They came with a reputation for employing a statistical approach to recruitment that aims to – wait for it – reduce risk and maximise return. At the Red Sox, they knew they couldn't compete financially with the New York Yankees, so they decided to try to be smarter. It worked for a while. Whether they've succeeded or not long term depends on which side of the fence you're on, and there are obviously only two sides.

Objectively, it's been a mixed bag. Not truly terrible and not truly great, overall. At the Red Sox, there has been discontent for some time, and more recently FSG have been criticised for turning their baseball team into 'underdogs'. At Anfield, similar criticisms have been levelled. To be fair, some of it's justified. When it comes to spending, FSG are too risk-averse, in my view. Allowing the midfield to age and disintegrate without reinforcements was negligent.

Can I say that without being crammed into the 'FSG Out' box? Can I add that this is the same ownership model that delivered Jürgen

Klopp, Virgil van Dijk, Alisson, Mo Salah, Diogo Jota, Luis Díaz, Darwin Núñez and Mac Allister, as well as a slew of trophies, including the holy grail of the Premier League, without being called a 'Top Red'? Probably not, yet both statements are true.

I was beginning to tire of it all. The roller-coaster of the transfer window – filled with adrenaline-fuelled highs and hungover headaches – might be fun for some, but for me it was not football, it was a game of monopoly and one you can never win at that. Then came a bombshell tweet – or is it an X now? – from one of the doyens of 'in-the-know journalists', and I was strapped in for the ride again, screaming that I wanted to go faster.

I'd been lying next to the pool pretending to read a book while fighting off the urge to fall asleep, the sun burning my legs as the sound of splashing and children's gleeful laughter wafted in and out of my fading consciousness. *Should I get another beer?* I half-thought, half-dreamed. Then a snore snapped me into wakefulness. My son, who had been scouring social media, shook my arm and thrust his phone in my face, his eyes wide and wearing a grin on his face that suggested 'you really want to see this'.

Liverpool had matched Chelsea's bid for Moisés Caicedo, which meant that the 'penny-pinching' Reds had offered in the region of £95m to Brighton & Hove Albion for a player, a potential deal that would smash the club's transfer record to pieces. Visions of a midfield that consisted of Dominik Szoboszlai, Alexis Mac Allister and Moisés Caicedo danced before our eyes. This was a midfield rebuild we could get behind, an expensive one, yes. But for not much more than the cost of one Jude Bellingham, Liverpool looked set to create a midfield that would be the envy of the Premier League. There was a time when the thought of going toe to toe with Chelsea in the transfer window would fill Liverpool fans with a sense of impending doom, but surely the Reds represented a much more attractive option to Moisés than Chelsea.

At least that's what I thought as I lay back on that sun lounger and dreamed of what might be.

What followed was what amounted to a cross between fantasy football and Russian roulette. Chelsea, apparently encouraged by Caicedo's agent, who in turn had also egged on Liverpool to bid, threw everything they had at the deal, believing, correctly it turned out, that the player preferred Stamford Bridge to Anfield.

Billy Hogan, who had been led to believe a deal was on, personally took over negotiations with Brighton and submitted counter-bids that would have taken Liverpool's spending into the stratosphere. However, the early optimism soon turned to dread as the inevitability of Chelsea getting their man began to sink in.

Worse still, the Londoners, fuelled by a cash injection from Todd Boehly who was quickly establishing himself as a master of creative accounting, announced that they'd also pursue Liverpool's apparent second-choice target, Romeo Lavia. The Reds attempted to match Chelsea in their pursuit of Lavia, but the player, seemingly miffed at being dangled on a string by Anfield's moneymen while not minding that Chelsea's bean counters had done the same, chose the bright lights of London over the floodlights at Anfield.

It was a disaster well, not a disaster, as you, I and other sane people would define one. It wasn't as if Liverpool had gone bankrupt or, say, got relegated, or anything truly disastrous. However, in the world of football social media, the fact that Liverpool had missed out on two players none of us had even dreamed they'd pursue just a matter of weeks earlier was nothing short of a complete catastrophe.

Soon accusations that the bid had all been part of an elaborate publicity stunt abounded. Apparently, FSG were so terrified of accusations of penny-pinching from anonymous accounts on X that they manufactured fake bids north of £100m. To be honest, though, I was more annoyed at myself for getting sucked in again.

I'd somehow navigated the cognitive dissonance involved with finding such sums of money being lavished on a single player, while the country was in the grip of a cost-of-living crisis, obscene, while simultaneously becoming excited by the fact that Liverpool seemed to be showing some genuine ambition. Yes, when it comes to the Reds, I can do hypocrisy like the rest of them. However, there are limits.

Did I want my club offering ten-year contracts to potential targets to circumvent profit and sustainability rules? Absolutely not. Did I accept that this meant we'd always fall short in any transfer tussle with the oil-rich clubs or when competing with those who seemingly have more money than sense? Yes, reluctantly, but I was at least comforted by the Reds' apparent preparedness to spend big when the opportunity to acquire significant talent presented itself. Others will never be satisfied.

But why did it take so long? Why did we allow it to happen in public? Why even bid when the player clearly wanted Chelsea? Well, to be fair, Liverpool had previously developed a reputation for 'stealth signings' but not every deal can or will happen like that. That's especially true when the selling club or the players' agents have another agenda or want to apply pressure to the buying club by leaking details of bids to the media.

Those claiming the prolonged and failed attempts to recruit Caicedo and Lavia marks some fresh stage in the terminal decline for Liverpool would do well to recall the botched purchase of Virgil van Dijk. Liverpool had been forced to pull out of that deal and were forced to pay a premium to get him months later. If any player transfer was evidence that life is rarely black and white but shades of grey, then this is the one. Virgil was simultaneously evidence of our competence and incompetence in the transfer market, and on the much-vaunted (by me also) Michael Edwards's watch.

Even by recent standards, it seemed unfair to me at least to single out Liverpool's multiple bids for Caicedo and Lavia as reason to proclaim the end of a dynasty. Are they the only ones to find themselves on the wrong end of a selling club's stubborn resolve? Were we witnessing the demise of Bayern Munich because their opening bids for Harry Kane went straight into Daniel Levy's shredder? Were Chelsea no longer a serious club because they found themselves still a few bob short of signing Moisés Caicedo and were dragged into bidding way more than the player was worth by Liverpool? The answer was obviously no, wasn't it? Or maybe it was complicated.

None of this should be new to people of a certain age, people like me. Anyone who lived through the 1990s or indeed the better part of the last 20 years will attest to numerous transfer sagas, failed pursuits and prophecies of doom. Life on the old forums at the start of the new millennium was usually feverish this time of year, and threads that spanned weeks were common. The era of the 'in the know', the often anonymous and cryptic stranger who fanned the flames of internet angst with claims of 'smoke screens', and deals that were so imminent they happened yesterday, only to collapse in a mysterious haze of bullshit and bluff.

It led to outpourings of rage against the club, which back then meant attacks on then CEO Rick Parry's character, hairstyle and dress sense. In the end, none of it made a bit of difference once the first ball was kicked, when phoney football ended and the real game kicked off. It's a shame that this has successfully evaded the collective consciousness of so many for all these years.

By the time I returned home from that family holiday in the sun, I longed for the closure of the transfer window, when all the wailing and gnashing of teeth would finally subside for five minutes, and we'd all have to make do with the squad we had and trust the manager to work his magic. A time when Liverpool fans everywhere set aside their differences and throw their full weight behind the lads and the boss. A likely story. *I'll give it until 1 September*, I thought.

I do love football.

Stage-of-Life Blues
But Reds Are Flying

September 2023 would be a month of contrasts for me. It saw the Reds notch up 16 goals across the month, with six conceded. It ended with a gut-wrenching defeat to Spurs, and with me facing down my own mortality.

Sat in front of my GP on a warm autumn afternoon, his face a picture of grim concern as he told me I was facing weeks of uncertainty and a series of embarrassing and uncomfortable medical investigations, it felt like my world was collapsing around me. Like many in the country, the Covid lockdowns had a dramatic impact on all aspects of my life, including lifestyle and diet. My levels of daily exercise plummeted and I'd piled on the pounds, or as my diplomatic father-in-law had once put it, 'Christ, Jeff. You're twice the man you used to be. The belly on you!' As we emerged from government restrictions, I'd found myself locked into a pattern and, although I tried to ignore it, I was becoming increasingly physically and psychologically unwell.

Now, here I was being told that, although my doctor 'didn't think it was cancer', it was better to be safe than sorry. That word – *cancer* – hit me like a hammer blow and, despite his reassuring tones, it kept echoing round my head. Suddenly, it became hard to think of a future, to imagine anything beyond a crisis that, out of the blue, was now swallowing me whole.

Just days earlier it had all been so different. I was still full of the joys of a new season, with remnants of holiday memories lingering pleasantly in my mind. The Reds had blasted through August with two wins and a draw. I'd watched the 1-1 draw against Chelsea in a bar in Greece. I realised that, not for the first time, I was watching a game between the two sides on foreign shores and surrounded by their supporters. The atmosphere was fine, though, and I could even manage a laugh when my son told me that a lad younger than him had given way to him in the queue for the toilets, saying in a thick cockney accent, 'Go on, my son.' That phrase, accompanied by drunken laughter, would become the soundtrack to the rest of our holiday. 'Fancy a beer,' Joe would say, as I sat on the sun lounger. 'Go on, my son,' I'd reply. 'More feta, son?' I'd ask. 'Go on, my son,' he'd reply. And so on. You have to imagine a faux cockney accent perpetrated by two Scousers, one that lies somewhere between Dick Van Dyke in *Mary Poppins* and David Jason's Del Boy character, to get the full effect. You had to be there.

The draw had been disappointing, especially after we'd battled the Londoners in the transfer market. However, as we walked back to the hotel bar to join the rest of the family, taking in the warm night air as we strolled, it felt so good that all the faff of the summer was over and football was back.

I was back in time for the first home game of the season, against Bournemouth and revelled in the 3-1 victory, while raging at Alexis Mac Allister's dismissal. It would eventually be overturned, but the growing sense that match officials couldn't be relied on was growing irresistible.

Seven days later, the Reds travelled to St James' Park to take on the Premier League's other, less successful, petroclub. It would be a day that would live long in the memory. Newcastle had broken into the top four, claiming a place in this season's Champions League. Many feared they'd soon join Manchester City in a Premier League duopoly backed by Middle Eastern fossil-fuel dollars. I honestly felt they'd overachieved, helped in no short measure by Liverpool's collapse and Chelsea's absence from the so-called 'big four'. I had no faith in Eddie

Howe to follow up the previous season with a title challenge, and felt we had the beating of them.

We did, of course, but the result may have been more emphatic but for the intervention, once again, of the match officials. In the 28th minute, Virgil van Dijk saw red for a foul on Alexander Isak. The referee suggested that Isak was denied a goalscoring opportunity, despite the fact the player was running away from goal and Liverpool had cover. Television cameras clearly showed a furious Virgil branding the decision 'a fucking joke'. We all agreed.

Liverpool had gone a goal down when Anthony Gordon produced a brilliant solo effort to send the home crowd into raptures. Just three minutes later the Reds found themselves down to ten men and facing a raucous home crowd who had sensed their moment to rub salt in the wounds.

This was the second game in succession in which the Reds had seen a player dismissed. Van Dijk's reaction towards the match officials would later be studied in detail by the FA, and his resultant ban extended. It was hard for me not to sympathise with our No.4, and the sense of injustice was infuriating. As Virgil would say, the red card was a 'fucking joke'.

In days gone by, such a setback would have caused Liverpool to lose their heads and their shape. Not Klopp's Reds, though. Instead, they stayed in the game, and where Eddie Howe got every tactical decision wrong – taking off Gordon, his most potent threat – Jürgen's substitutions turned the game. If the second-half introductions of Harvey Elliott, Diogo Jota and a debut for Jarell Quansah built a bonfire under Geordie vanity, the introduction of Darwin Núñez lit the flame.

It was a virtuoso performance from the bench from the Uruguayan, whose two goals in the final ten minutes of the game drove a stake through Newcastle hearts. Each looked a carbon copy of the other, with Darwin capping fine runs with two powerful finishes past Nick Pope, from similar angles. As he celebrated wildly in front of the home crowd – who it's fair to say were *not* impressed – the away end, located somewhere in the clouds, were jubilant. Núñez has enjoyed a mixed reception from Liverpool supporters, but it's moments like this that have earned him a cult following, and I'm a fully signed-up member.

Liverpool were developing an annoying and unsustainable habit of conceding the first goal in games. However, at least for now, they possessed enough firepower to blast back. How long could that last.

On 30 September, Liverpool travelled to the Tottenham Hotspur Stadium to face Spurs. Once again, the Reds fell behind first when Son Heung-min put the home side in front on 36 minutes. Klopp's men levelled in first-half stoppage time before succumbing to a sickening Jöel Matip own goal in the sixth minute of added time. However, that was but a fraction of the story.

Matip had laboured magnificently in defence as the Reds mounted a brilliant rearguard action with only nine men. That a Liverpool side, so depleted, had managed to hold off Spurs for so long should have shamed the home players and supporters. Instead, they celebrated the win like any cup final victory. It was gut-wrenching.

The Reds had seen two players dismissed in highly controversial circumstances. Curtis Jones went in the 26th minute after the referee was shown a still image of the youngster's boot contacting his Yves Bissouma's leg, rather than the whole context. Diogo Jota later received two soft yellow cards, with one later rescinded. These decisions were bad enough and would lead to apologies from the PGMOL. However, they couldn't come close to the shocking injustice meted out to Liverpool and Luis Díaz in particular.

Liverpool were denied an opening goal, when a clearly onside Díaz had his effort disallowed by the on-pitch referee, despite evidence, which emerged later, that VAR at Stockley Park were aware the goal should have stood. Recordings would later reveal a state of utter chaos as one official, upon realising that the game was continuing with Díaz's goal ruled out, attempted to correct the mistake, only to be overruled. To compound matters, the goal had been disallowed without the VAR team showing the customary offside line graphics. The sound of the referee, Hooper, congratulating his video assistants for a 'good process' would have been laughable if it wasn't such a rancid injustice.

Instead of the Reds going into half-time 2-1 up and with 11 men on the pitch, Cody Gakpo's goal on half-time would have put them in front, instead of on level terms. Who would have bet against them winning the game from that point on. Instead, they faced the second half level, and with only ten men.

It's undeniable that a 'serious human error had occurred', as the PGMOL called it in its subsequent apology to Liverpool. We can all accept that such things happen, but rarely are they so egregious and consequential. In such circumstances, it seemed obvious to me that the game should be replayed. Of course, when Klopp later suggested as much, he was met with a barrage of abuse and criticism from ex-players and rival supporters alike. His peers would also desert him, despite knowing they'd have said the same if they found themselves in the same position.

Nobody was suggesting that every contentious call should lead to a replay, just that when one so rare and unprecedented takes place, the integrity of the result must be called into question. On such decisions, league titles are decided. Liverpool came out swinging, threatening to explore any and all options in response to the debacle. In truth, it felt more like sabre-rattling, and their protestations eventually faded away with the promise of improvements in the system employed and assurances it was a one-off.

The result left Liverpool in fourth spot and, as they faced October with fire raging in their bellies, a siege mentality was brewing.

The chaos of that game and the seething sense of injustice surrounding the result had acted as a glorious distraction for me. It took my mind off what was happening in my life, which – somewhat self-indulgently – felt even more chaotic and unfair. I guess all of us, as we age, have the symptom we dread. For some it may be a pain in the chest that signals an imminent heart attack, or a lump or bump that could be cancer. You bury those thoughts in the darkest recesses of your mind – most of the time – you reason it's probably nothing and you move on. Life is too busy to get it checked out, and who wants to spend hours in a waiting room only to leave feeling like a hypochondriac, right? That was me before Tuesday, 26 September 2023. I couldn't ignore my symptoms, though, and in truth, looking back, I'm so glad I didn't.

Although what followed was months of uncertainty and, if I'm honest, fear, it was still the biggest turning point in my life and I'm better off now for it. For a while, though, I was terrified. In a classic 'good news/bad news' scenario, I was eventually told that I didn't have cancer. I'd felt certain that I did. However, while they were looking for the 'big C', they stumbled upon a swelling in an artery – an aneurysm – and, to cap it all, that had been the last thing anyone had expected to find. I was going to have to live with it, and my lifestyle would have to change.

Psychologically that was hard, but I'm learning to see all this as possibly the best thing that could have happened to me. I'd never have known about the aneurysm if I hadn't become ill, if I hadn't swallowed my fears and gone to see the doctor. I'm told men are terrible at seeking medical help, and they put things off in the hope 'it will all go away if you ignore it'. I can be like that too, most of the time. Take whatever you want from this episode, but I'll always be glad I chose not to ignore it this time.

I'm not the first to experience one of these stage-of-life moments, and I won't be the last. Others face far worse challenges than I have. At times like these it's the constants in your life – family, friends and colleagues – that sustain you. Football, or more specifically sharing it with friends, was part of my recovery. And, of course, writing also helped. Most of all, though, I think the lessons I'll take away from that time are about what you do when life gives you an opportunity to change direction and do things differently.

Within just a matter of months, I'd look into the eyes of a tired-looking Jürgen Klopp, as he stared down the barrel of a camera and effectively told us all that he'd hit his own time-of-life moment. He could not and would not ignore it. It was time for him to do things differently.

I felt that I could completely understand where he was coming from.

Liverpool 5-1 West Ham United

Hammers Crushed at Anfield

On 20 December, Liverpool dished out a hiding to David Moyes's West Ham at Anfield, the Reds running out 5-1 winners. As I left Anfield and made my way home in the cold night air, all in the garden seemed rosy. I'd returned to work after an extended period away and was feeling better than I had in a long time.

I'd made several lifestyle changes that meant dramatically reducing my alcohol intake, which didn't turn out to be as difficult as I'd imagined. However, the look of horror on the face of Joanne – one of the wonderful bar staff in the Cabbage Hall – when I ordered a diet coke instead of the usual pint of lager did make me question my choice for a moment. I decided dying from embarrassment was better than, well, dying.

Liverpool had been making progress on all fronts. A win against Everton at the end of October, in the middle of the chaos wrought by Storm Babet, had heralded a run of eight wins, three draws and just two defeats from 13 games in all competitions. However, the goalless draw with Manchester United on 17 December should have served as a warning sign that the Reds' season was about to hit the buffers. The campaign was starting to take its toll on a Reds side that had been carrying too many injuries and was too reliant on youth. And, although we didn't realise it in December 2023, Liverpool 2.0 was ahead of schedule and punching above its weight.

In the news, Luis Díaz's father, having been held to ransom by Colombian captors, had been released, much to the relief of everyone. The Anfield Road expansion was coming along after the collapse of the company responsible for construction, leading to delays, and its opening date had been pushed back to the New Year. Everton had received a ten-point deduction for breaches of the Premier League's Profitability and Sustainability Rules and were now second from bottom on goal difference. Blues fans launched a campaign, accusing the Premier League of corruption, despite Everton admitting they'd breached the rules. I wasn't sure if the punishment was corrupt. But I did feel it was excessive. If ten points is the benchmark for being found guilty of a single charge, heaven help Manchester City if they're convicted of the 115 charges they face. They must surely be looking at a future in the local Sunday League. Of course, I won't hold my breath.

The attendance for the visit of West Ham was a record for a Football League Cup tie at Anfield, beating the 53,051 at the fourth-round tie against Tottenham Hotspur on 25 October 2016. And the Reds put in a dominant display, thrashing the visitors 5-1.

Dominik Szoboszlai opened the scoring with a superb 25-yard effort, which rocketed into the bottom of the goal as the game approached the half-hour mark. It was a breathtaking strike of sheer quality and the Hammers simply crumbled from that moment on.

Ten minutes into the second half, Curtis Jones's clever footwork on the edge of the six-yard box saw him bamboozle Alphonse Areola and lash a shot through the keeper's legs. I took pleasure in that goal after enduring endless criticism of the youngster from a nearby Kopite for whom Jones can do no right.

Cody Gakpo made it three on 71 minutes, bagging his eighth goal of the season. Although Jarrod Bowen claimed what would ultimately be a consolation goal on 77 minutes, Liverpool were moving through the gears now. Mohamed Salah made it four when he raced clear of the visitors' defence and finished, before Jones finished off an excellent run by adding his second. The Reds were launching waves of attacks now, and Elliott, Gakpo, Alexander-Arnold and Salah all came close to adding to the tally.

Only Fulham now stood in the way of another appearance in the League Cup Final, and a potential record-breaking tenth win. Liverpool would see off their challenge in the semi-final with an aggregate 3-2 win, which was far closer than it should have been. We didn't care, though. Now there was a scramble to win tickets, and a trip to Wembley to organise.

Reds Buckle Up for Klopp's Last Stand

Liverpool FC January–June 2024

Klopp Stuns Liverpool with Bombshell Announcement

'And the tears come streaming down your face
When you lose something you can't replace.' – Coldplay, 2005

It was our 'Shankly moment', our 'Dalglish moment'. These were the words so often used to describe the news that Jürgen Klopp would be leaving the club at the end of the 2023/24 season. Just as it had in 1974, and again in 1991, the announcement came without warning and to the sheer disbelief of Liverpudlians everywhere.

I was in work when a colleague silently thrust his mobile phone in my face. It took a second or two for the screen to come into focus and for my brain to make sense of the headline on the BBC's breaking news page: 'Jürgen Klopp to Leave Liverpool at End of the Season' it declared carelessly, seemingly oblivious to its impact. There was no warning shot, we weren't gently walking down the stairs, we were being hoofed off the top step.

It was difficult, impossible to comprehend. I wondered whether it was a fake site, my 'yer joking aren't yer' moment. But it was true. The news we'd all known would come one day but hoped it would be a long way off had arrived.

'It's not that I want to,' said a forlorn-looking Klopp, 'it's that I have to.' Then, 'I'm running out of energy.' I knew how he felt. As much as I was heartbroken, I recognised burnout when I saw it and understood the desire to switch off from it all, walk away and enter self-preservation mode.

Maybe, Jürgen wasn't quite at that point yet, but he didn't have long before he'd get there. In the months since the announcement, I've come to feel grateful that he made the decision while he still had juice in the tank to finish the season, and that he gave us time to get used to the idea.

I spoke to numerous supporters in the days following the announcement and found that I wasn't alone. Lifelong Red, Alicia Lorena McDermott:

> I was in Chile when my father told me the news of him [Klopp]
> leaving. I had mixed feelings; on the one side I was sad as I
> always thought he may stay just that little bit longer, but also

I was happy for him. For me, Jürgen Klopp reinstated the roar of the Liver Bird, reignited its firepower, rekindled its never-say-die spirit, reinstalled its pride and position, and reminded it of its identity.

Paul Amann, founder member of Kop Outs:

Jürgen was perhaps the most intense human I've ever met. His authenticity of passion and purpose are aligned in a way that you'll find in few people and even fewer politicians. He understood the psyche of our city and its people, tapping into that in how he chose to speak.

He chose to speak out against hatred, not to try and target hate-mongers directly, but to empower us as fans to take them on, to use our vast strength in numbers, to tap into our spirit of mutuality and solidarity, and to do the right thing.

He brought the best out of players by somehow infusing them with his energy, which they then translated to improved performance. His technical area theatrics were those of any enthused passionate fan. His affable hugs and easy smile also belied a granite resolve and adamantine certainty of purpose; he was nobody's fool.

Hearing of Jürgen's departure was intense. A chasm of doubt opens up where there was the certainty. A sense of loss akin to grieving is felt. His integrity in departure leaves no doubt that this is his choice. That energy he infuses in our team and us as fans couldn't be infinite; it's his honesty in recognising this that commands yet more respect.

Chet Muraji is a student of the history of our club and a full-time carer for his mother. He told me how he received the news he'd been dreading:

I was at home with Mum and awaiting a visit from her carers, they were due at midday.

A notification from Liverpool Football Club pings up on my phone, and I immediately open it. It's a video interview with Klopp at the Kirkby Training Complex.

There was the usual preamble, then Jürgen's face: 'Ah yeah, I have to. Um …' he paused, and I knew at this moment this was not going to be good. '[…] I will leave the club at the end of the season.'

I was right. It wasn't good. Not good at all.

Gerard Kenny, another lifelong Red, told me he found it hard to think of the club without Jürgen Klopp at the helm:

He has put his heart and soul into managing Liverpool FC. He has delivered what he promised and will always be in the hearts of Liverpool fans around the globe.

Ian Golder, a Kop season ticket holder, and an old school friend, told me how he was trying to maintain a philosophical outlook:

I'm sort of looking at the positives now. I was shocked when I got the news as I think I always thought he would see out his contract.

Ian had initially wondered whether the announcement was a result of a fall-out with the owners but had quickly realised that the boss had simply had enough.

I think in the short term the announcement is galvanising the whole club rather than working the opposite way. I'm feeling it will be a great end to the season. I think he's leaving an incredible squad for the next manager, and I see it as a Paisley moment rather than a Souness one.

Dermot Nolan, a Liverpool supporter from Ireland, told me how he was taken aback by the news:

It was a 'where were you' moment. I felt a bit gutted and sad, and it took me back to the summer of 1974 as a ten-year-old, and my mother told me it's been on the news that Bill Shankly is retiring from Liverpool as manager. I couldn't believe it until I heard the sports news on the radio myself.

How would we replace him? We'd just won the FA Cup. But although it's sad to see Klopp go, there's a sense of pride and reflection of all he has done for the club and indeed the city. Like Shankly, you can't replace the special aura, but I'm confident we'll get in another manager to build his own ideas to our great club.

Susan Taylor is a Liverpool supporter whose father, Johnny Wheeler, captained the club in the pre-Shankly era:

In my father's 90th year, Dad was invited back to the club as the oldest living captain. He was presented with a signed portrait of himself. It said, 'Dear Johnny, if it wasn't for players like you, LFC wouldn't be the club it is today YNWA, Jürgen Klopp.'

Her message to the boss would be: 'Jürgen Klopp, LFC would not be the club it is today, without you! YNWA.'

Peter Simpson, another lifelong Red, told me how a tweet about Klopp's decision was shared with him by a friend:

My mate gets a lot of things wrong, so my first reaction was that he'd got his wires crossed but it was real this time.

Peter told me how he shared the news with his wife, and how they both spent the rest of the morning shocked and absorbed by the news as it unfolded:

It took me back to when Kenny Dalglish resigned in 1991. I was only a schoolboy then but the feeling this time was exactly the same. My dad couldn't break the news to me back then and how would we break it to our kids now?

As it turned out, both of our children already knew, probably through the power of social media. Our eldest, Katy, took it well enough, but our nine-year-old, Adam, said that his 'heart hurt'.

It's been a privilege for us all to see Klopp and his coaches oversee one of the most successful and joyous eras in LFC history. In fact, the teams of 2018/19 and 2019/20 are up there alongside some of the best club sides ever. Jürgen, you'll be missed and, as our Adam said, 'Our hearts hurt.' Probably forever.

Lee O'Connor is a Kopite who travels home and away with Liverpool:

The day Jürgen announced he was leaving at the end of the 2023/24 season, I was in work when I heard the news. I even had to stop for a second to think what date it was, hoping it was April 1st, and it was all some kind of wild hoax.

I suddenly became that kid on the streets of Liverpool, in the summer of 1974, who famously refused to believe Granada's Tony Wilson when he gleefully told him that Shankly had announced his resignation.

From the day Jürgen Klopp walked through the door at Liverpool, you just knew something special was about to happen. His impact was immediate, that culture of togetherness he fostered throughout the club can never be overstated.

From that first press conference he had us all, players and supporters alike, eating out of his hand. He completely transformed the club from top to bottom with his influence, humility and personality. The ethos he created both on and off the pitch is immeasurable when I think about it. Over the next nine years we felt invincible, and nothing was impossible.

I've often said that Jürgen Klopp to me and my generation is what Bill Shankly was to my dad and his generation. His impact was that profound. Not only a fantastic manager but, more importantly, a fantastic human being. Build him a statue and get it outside the Kop. Jürgen Lives Forever.

David Moen, a Liverpool supporter from Monaghan in Ireland, told me how the comparisons between Jürgen and Bill Shankly rang true for him:

From the very moment he uttered the words: 'I'm a very normal guy from the Black Forest. I'm the normal one, if you like,' you knew we were to embark on a special journey. How special. It has been beyond our wildest dreams.

I can go on and on about the many special days and nights Jürgen and his Redmen have given us, all are well documented. We all have a particular highlight; imagine that, having the luxury of choosing a favourite moment among the many we've experienced under Jürgen during his Anfield journey.

It's likely to never be repeated at that level again. How blessed we were as Reds to have lived to see his era, the new Shankly. He has more than earned the right to be mentioned in the same breath as the great man. He was the normal one, we are the lucky ones.

Kevin Woods, another friend from my schooldays, and a lifelong Liverpool supporter, shared his sense of utter shock with me:

It was like one of those 'where were you' moments. I was sat at my dining table delivering a PAYE class to a group of trainees. My phone pinged; it was a message from my WhatsApp group telling me the news. I nearly broke my neck in my haste to find the remote control. There it was, BREAKING NEWS.

Did I cry? Yes, I did. In fact, I burst into tears a few times over the next couple of days. This may seem strange for a 50-odd-year-old man who went to Heysel, Hillsborough, and who has lost his mum and dad over the last couple of years, and nursed his wife through cancer, but there it is.

The esteem this man is held in is unrivalled. I've seen managers come and go over the years, but this is different. It's now a cliché, but it was like somebody had passed away.

Steven Scragg is a writer for *These Football Times*, podcaster, author of several football books and a Main Stand season ticket holder:

I was painting a door when the news filtered through, a kind of bottle-green colour. It's a good solid wooden door and it will eventually adorn the front of our house, but every time I open and close it, I'll probably end up thinking of Jürgen Klopp.

I had a similar relationship with the pages of Ceefax, when it came to the blow of the blunt weapon that was Kenny Dalglish's

February 1991 resignation. On that occasion, it was initially news that seeped through via an urgent bulletin on the radio at work, but the main image that stayed with me was being stood near the bus stop on the way home, peering through the window of a local television retailer, reading more information from the pages of Ceefax.

These things stay with you, and the gut reaction to the news of Klopp's impending departure took me right back to that shop window and Ceefax, in February 1991. Page 303. While the summer of 2024 was his original exit plan, that two-year contract extension to 2026 had allowed us the luxury and comfort of a buffer zone, kind of an agreed overdraft facility. January was a shit month to rescind it, Jürgen.

John McMenemy, a Liverpool supporter from Scotland:

Having been a big Bundesliga fan for years, I was already well aware of Jürgen, his qualities and infectious character. I was beyond thrilled when he came to Anfield.

Despite the size of Liverpool FC, I still view our club as a family, and with Jürgen's announcement it feels like a loved one is leaving home. But I know this man is leaving us stronger than we've ever been, and his mindset, philosophy and winning mentality will remain with the new boss.

It takes a lot for hardcore football fans to come to tears. There will be tears when this man leaves. It's a measure of the respect, affection and gratitude for the boss.

George Scott, a reserve player for Liverpool during the early 60s, one of Bill Shankly's first signings and my co-author on the *Lost Shankly Boy*:

Shankly was the right man, in the right place, at the right time, and with his socialist ideals of everyone working for the greater good and sharing in the rewards, he was the perfect fit. The devastation of the people on the red side of Liverpool on hearing the shock of Shankly's resignation in 1974 was off the scale.

Fast-forward in time to 2015, and another messiah came to Liverpool. He, like Shankly, was the perfect fit for the club. Jürgen Klopp, without doubt in my mind, was the modern version of Bill Shankly; everything about Jürgen, in my view, was the mirror image of Bill. His passion, his humour, his belief in his players, his love of the city and the supporters, his political ideals and, above all, his winning mentality.

Over half a century later, in 2024, we all felt that same shock and sadness at hearing the news that Jürgen would be leaving the club.

How lucky the modern generation of Liverpool fans have been to have witnessed through Jürgen these past nine years the memories and glories that their fathers and grandfathers enjoyed in years gone by. Thanks for the memories, Jürgen.

Adrian Killen is a lifelong Red who lived through the Shankly years and who, as an avid archivist and collector of Liverpool FC memorabilia, has seen it all. He told me how he was trying to stay philosophical about the news:

The Klopp resignation was one of these moments when you'll always remember where you were or what you were doing. The Munich disaster, the Kennedy assassination, man on the moon, the Shankly-Dalglish resignations, Heysel, Hillsborough, the memories will always linger.

I was working in the garden on the day and came in the kitchen for a cuppa and heard what sounded like a caller on Radio Merseyside saying he couldn't believe the timing of this and just when he was building a new team of players. I obviously was all ears at that point and then to my astonishment I learned the fact that Jürgen was calling it a day at the end of the season.

To say I was in shock would be an over-exaggeration. I've seen it all before and the club has always carried on, irrespective of any individuals, be they players, managers, directors or even fans like us. At my age, I've become very philosophical and can put things into greater perspective.

There are greater things to be worried or concerned about than who will be our manager next season. Whoever it is and whatever the results, I'll still be there every game (all being well) cheering our team until my time comes.

David Goulding, a Liverpool supporter who travels home and away to watch the Reds, had this to say:

For me and our Stu [David's brother], this represents the end of an era. We've seen a few of those down the years. He's a bit older than me, so he remembers the end of the Shankly era. My first era ended with Sir Bob.

Since then, we've been blessed more than any other supporters. Jürgen for me and our kid represents another changing of the guard in an uplifting way. For our boys, though, this is more than the end of an era, it feels for them like the end of life as they know it. My lad's first game was the 4-3 victory over Dortmund. His last was against Wolves. In between those, he has seen us win the league, been to Paris, Kyiv and Madrid. He has had boss weekends under the Wembley arch too. Now, there's nothing. Unchartered territory. We walk on, with hope in our hearts.

Lee Tracy is the grandson of Tom Bromilow, the legendary Liverpool captain of the 1920s. Lee told me:

A hundred years ago my grandad, Tom Bromilow, was playing in the 'Untouchables' team of the 1920s; my roots and connection with LFC go back a long way.

Like many things in life, you get used to something good being there for a long time, you almost forget it can and will end at some time. Jürgen Klopp felt like a member of the family, out there day after day trying to guide the team to the next success.

That passion he possessed and demonstrated without fail for those years. Then the shock hit as he announced this would be his last season. A void, like a bereavement, set in and it was hard to imagine life beyond. It can and will go on, but it can never be the same. Thank you will never be enough.

Linda Ellston, another veteran Liverpool supporter of the Shankly era:

> Jürgen stepping down is a shock, but the man is a genius; it has taken its toll on him, he made us the envy of all, the man is a legend. He deserves a statue next to Shanks. He's the reincarnation of the man I adored. Who can replace those fist bumps?

Jeremy Latimer is the son of legendary Liverpool player Peter Thompson:

> The manager won trophies, but the man won hearts and souls and healed wounds we've carried for decades. Klopp resurrected the Holy Trinity with a smile as broad as the Rhine. His legacy will be our continued constant belief in 'our team', 'our club' and 'our community'. To simply hold our heads up high is everything. Jürgen, you are Liverpool and Liverpool is you.

Peter Kenny Jones is a football historian and the author of *Liddell at One Hundred* and *Sweeper Keeper: The Story of Tommy Lawrence, Scotland and Liverpool's Legendary Flying Pig*. Peter is in no doubt about Jürgen's place in the history of the club:

> Jürgen Klopp is, without a doubt, the most significant figure in Liverpool history in my lifetime. When Steven Gerrard left the club, I was sure that no other player or manager could ever touch his legacy, but I was wrong.
>
> The good memories with friends, family and fans can never be taken away, but it was the way in which I reacted to the news of his departure that made me realise how much I loved him.
>
> It was comfortably one of the worst pieces of news I've ever received and, after days of locking myself away in my garage, I felt like it was the end of the best period of my life as a Liverpool supporter.

What Jürgen managed to do on his final game at Anfield, though, as I failed to fight back the tears on the Kop, was make me look forward to a future without him. It's true that life will go on and the Reds will challenge for trophies again and we will all be fine. However, as much as Liverpool will be okay, we'll never replace Jürgen because he truly is one of a kind.

Arnie Baldursson is a founder member of the LFC History website and author of *The Liverpool Encyclopaedia*. He told me how he'd once met Klopp:

Jürgen was as charming as expected. He laughed aloud a couple of times, signed a note to my taxi driver so I could get a free ride to my hotel and stunned me by shouting: 'Go on Vikingur!' which is a team from Iceland, my home country. His charisma is immense, and I was so impressed by Kloppo, the name by which he signed my copy [of the matchday programme].

I was in a state of shock when I read on Twitter that Klopp was going to leave the Reds. It had been only minutes since the news was released and my first reaction was that this was a cruel hoax, but a link to his interview on the official site killed any hope I had. I was stunned when Kenny Dalglish resigned in 1991. I was too young to remember when Bill Shankly left in 1974.

Klopp is the modern Shankly for Liverpool fans and arguably one of the biggest legends in our history. I shed a few tears as I watched him say goodbye to the Anfield crowd as his departure moved closer. I've admired players and managers of Liverpool but never been so emotional about one person at the club as Kloppo. He'll be forever in my heart.

David Wilkinson is a painter and decorator from Bradford who has supported the Reds since 1975:

I just loved watching the old teams and the entertainment on the pitch. Passing on the history to my children means the world. The culture of the city and its people mean the world to me. No better place in the world.

When the boss said it was time to go it was that Shanks moment again. The old TV clip where nobody believed it was happening; same with Kenny too, I suppose. Inside I'm broken and upset, bit like when talking to my 19-year-old son as he said, 'It's all I've ever known really, Dad.'

Why would he want to leave all this, especially with the rebuild on its way? But at times, my god, he has looked so tired. So, we must respect that. To me he wasn't a boss but a father figure, and no wonder players would run through a brick wall for him. He gave us a rebirth and for that I will be forever grateful. He now needs his rest with his family, and we move on.

Raul H. Cohen Llaguno is the host of *YNWA World* podcast, and a Liverpool supporter from Mexico:

I started watching football when I was nine years old. By the time I was 15, I thought I'd seen it all. How wrong was I? The Jürgen Klopp era is the era I've enjoyed the most.

In 2010 I got the chance to go to Germany and to a Dortmund game, when Jürgen was coaching that team. It was an amazing experience because I got there early, I was the first fan in the stadium. Some of the players said hello, but others did not. Jürgen came right over to me and asked where I was from, and when I told him I was from Mexico, he smiled and told me to enjoy the game. I immediately fell in love with Jürgen and his style of play.

I enjoyed everything about the period with Klopp. Of course, we were finally winning silverware again, but I enjoyed the style, the way the team was playing. Many games the team played like that. But what I enjoyed the most was all the atmosphere that Jürgen created, not just in Liverpool but worldwide.

Thanks to social media I got to meet lots of fans around the world, and we were living the games together through WhatsApp, through Facebook and watching them. And during the lockdown, Jürgen Klopp made it easier because my family, we were watching all the Liverpool content together and it made it easier. It brought us joy during that difficult time.

So, in all my years following Liverpool, the Jürgen Klopp era is the best.

Neil Mulvaney is a Liverpool supporter who travels home and away to watch the Reds:

When Jürgen first came to Liverpool, I was optimistic about him, but I didn't expect him to do the things he has done here. His trophy haul, working against the financial and on-field juggernaut that is Man City, is quite astonishing really. Our title win was a brilliant memory. The team was relentless that season and they were rewarded for their non-stop intensity – all of which is thanks to Jürgen and his man-management. It's no exaggeration that the best football I've ever seen Liverpool play on a consistent basis was under Jürgen.

When we beat Barcelona in 2019 it was because Klopp had made us their equals. He'd taken a team that wasn't good enough to qualify for the Champions League and pulled off one of the greatest comebacks of all time. The turnaround in mentality at the club in that time was amazing. That's all down to Jürgen Klopp and his motivational skills. Who else could convince a team that we had a chance against Barcelona in those circumstances?

For me, Jürgen is the modern-day Bill Shankly. Without question, the man is the best Liverpool manager in my match-going lifetime and, in my view, in the top three of all time. I'm eternally in his debt for the memories he has given me.

David King is another Irish Red, and an early years service manager:

Shankly famously said 'it's far more important than that' when asked if football was a matter of life and death. We all know that this can seem like an extreme view; however, when the news broke of Klopp's departure at the end of the season, I have to say it was this quote that was at the forefront of my mind. For years

I've watched the archive footage of the reaction to Shankly's retirement. Now I know, first hand, how those interviewed felt.

David told me how dealing with the news was similar to grieving the loss of a loved one:

> Just before the news broke officially, a picture of Klopp arrived on my phone via WhatsApp, simply informing me 'Klopp's stepping down'. I immediately denied this as farcical.
>
> Anger followed later that day. How could he? I couldn't focus on anything. The anger didn't last long, though. After all, Jürgen owes us nothing. It was then I started the bargaining stage.
>
> If we win the league, he'll stay. If we win a few cups, he'll stay. More money, better conditions, bigger transfer budget, maybe Ulla will make him see sense – surely a combination of the above will see him change his mind.
>
> Soon depression started to sink in, a few days later. Constant news around the announcement, messages from people I haven't heard from for years, checking in on me to see if I was okay, made me realise that this was like a death. It was this realisation that opened the door for acceptance. It took me at least a week, if not longer to accept Klopp's decision and to turn my focus on to the positives.
>
> I always tell my children, 'Don't be sad that it's over, be happy that it happened,' and it was time for me to listen to my own words. It was time for me to realise that I'm so glad that Jürgen is a Red, and always will be, regardless of who is paying his wages.

Tony Zeverona is an engineering lecturer, and chair of Prescot Cables Football Club. Tony is a veteran of away days all over the world and has seen it all:

> The news broke while I was in work, and I couldn't believe it. My mind went back to when Shanks announced his retirement. I'd been looking forward to seeing Liverpool 2.0 under Klopp, with his new signings making an impact again.

Jürgen is a people's manager and gets the mindset of Liverpool and its supporters. His style of play and his emotional connection with the fans place him on the same level as Shanks. So, inevitably, our WhatsApp group went into meltdown. I instantly recalled all the highs and the pride of following Klopp all over Europe.

Garry Williams is a lifelong Red:

The August 2014 pre-season game at Anfield against Borussia Dortmund was the first time any of us would have seen Klopp in the flesh. He stood at the halfway line, legs apart, tracksuit, yellow cap, staring at the Kop, I thought. He wasn't, he was watching our players during the warm-up.

He had an aura about him; 14 months later, he was our manager. The hype that followed had never been seen before. It was love at first sight and we were all aboard. He even called out fans for leaving early, which I loved. He changed our mentality and appreciated how we could influence a game.

I got over the setbacks quickly because Klopp said we'll be back, and you knew this was just the start. Allez, Allez, Allez, and one year later we're European and are world champions. We've lost the best manager in my lifetime.

Mook San Lim is a Liverpool supporter from Penang, Malaysia:

Klopp coming to Liverpool was akin to the time when Shankly first appeared. Liverpool Football Club was in need of a leader with the character and charisma and Klopp was it. What a journey it has been in the last nine years.

He's won the lot and led Liverpool back to its perch. We're all believers now. We all knew that this day [Klopp stepping down] would come eventually but, nonetheless, it still comes as a great shock; more so when there were some rumours earlier that he may stay beyond 2025.

Liverpool owes him an immeasurable amount of gratitude. He said that it doesn't matter what people think of you when you come in but rather what people think of you when you leave. Klopp's revered stature in our history is guaranteed. We will definitely miss him.

The news hit all Reds hard. Some struggled to deal with it, while others attempted, with varying degrees of success, to adopt a philosophical stance. The stage was set for an emotional game against Norwich City at Anfield on Sunday, 28 January 2024.

Liverpool 5-2 Norwich City
Canaries Overwhelmed on Day of High Emotion
Only one topic dominated conversations on Merseyside in the days following Jürgen's shock announcement that he was to leave at the end of the season. I continued to struggle with the idea of a Liverpool without him. And even though they were likely celebrating the departure of a man who had become their nemesis, even those on the blue half of the city found themselves uncomfortably consumed by the news.

His impact across the community has been immense, and he'd become part of the fabric. It was impossible at this point to imagine the post-Klopp era. What would that look like? Who could possibly fill his shoes? People mentioned the name of Xabi Alonso early on, and his record in Germany had been impressive. But even thinking of life without Jürgen felt like a betrayal.

We knew the game against Norwich City in the fourth round of the FA Cup was going to be difficult to get through. There was an overwhelming desire to send the boss a message that we'd miss him but we understood. That we were grateful for all the success but wanted the best for him, as he always wanted for us. It was, to all intents and purposes, like saying a very long goodbye to a family member.

Klopp's reception before kick-off was packed with emotion, raw and powerful. And the players responded by sweeping aside the visitors. Darwin struck the woodwork before Curtis Jones headed the Reds in front after 16 minutes. James McConnell, another youngster making his full debut under Klopp, provided the assist.

The Canaries had the cheek to equalise, but Darwin made no mistake when finishing off an assist from Conor Bradley to put the

Reds back in front minutes later. It had been a frantic start, with three goals in under half an hour. In truth, given the emotion surrounding the game, it was exactly what we needed. The more incident and drama, the less time we had to dwell on Klopp's bombshell.

The second half continued to deliver, with Diogo Jota and Virgil van Dijk putting Liverpool 4-1 up and seemingly in complete control. But the drama continued with Norwich's Christian Fassnacht seeing a goal chalked off by VAR for offside, before a stunning Borja Sainz effort made it 4-2. The Reds were never in any real danger, though, and Ryan Gravenberch's headed goal deep into stoppage time gave the result the respectability it deserved.

We'd serenaded the boss throughout the game. He always insisted that we wait until full time but, given the circumstances, even he must have expected it. In the build-up, Andy Robertson had joked that Jürgen was 'going to lose that one', referring to Klopp's rule about singing his name.

The occasion clearly got to the boss, and he was visibly emotional at full time, telling the waiting media, 'I'm not made of wood,' and 'I had to hold myself together.' Those were feelings shared by all those of a red persuasion that day.

In the opposite dugout was Klopp's close friend, David Wagner. Half in jest, he'd asked the Liverpool manager for a 'massive rotation' before the game. Jürgen had replied, 'I'm not sure that will help,' such was his belief in his youngsters.

As we left Anfield, it felt like Jürgen was leaving more than a great 11. The performances of his young ones had shown us a strength in depth that we hadn't dreamed possible at the start of the season. Hindsight now tells us that this potential wouldn't be fully rewarded this season, but for a while anything seemed possible. The kids were dreaming big, and it was about to pay off in ways they could never imagine.

Reds Clinch Tenth League Cup
Klopp's Legacy on Show

> *'Virgil van Dijk at the bottom of a pile of red joy.'*
> Peter Drury, Sky Sports

It was another cup final day that started ridiculously early. February was almost over, but the air still carried a chill. Yet, as I wiped sleep from my eyes and rose from my pit, there was no denying the warm and fuzzy feeling in my belly that only a trip to Wembley, or maybe Christmas Day as a kid, can produce. I'd made this trip countless times, but it has never become old.

At 6am a small crowd of us gathered at the Twelfth Man pub that stands in the shadow of the Kop. It was cold and still dark. I paced the pavement in a failed effort to stay warm as cars and taxis arrived in a steady stream, unloading their cargo of people and crates full of ale at its doorstep. The crowd grew and laughter mixed with excited chatter filled the air, as people barely awake just a few moments earlier came alive. We were on our way to Anfield South and there was a trophy to be won.

There was the usual scramble for seats on the coach, the rattle of bottles and phone calls to missing mates who had missed the alarm and may yet miss the trip. Then reinforcements at the Rocket Pub, crowned by a glorious red sunrise – perhaps an omen – and then we were off.

I was making the trip solo this time, but you're never really on your own on an away trip. Familiar faces at service stations and the common experience and language of supporters of the same persuasion are what make the football away day a unique experience for me. You maybe get that at a festival, but for me there's nothing like travelling to watch your team on the road. And when there's silverware at stake, it's a different level.

We arrived early and Wembley Way was yet to feel the weight of tens of thousands of hopeful supporters. Despite that, the queue for BOXPARK, designated as the Liverpool fan zone, was impossibly long. Up on the walkway outside the green zone turnstiles, another area designated for supporters to while away the hours before kick-off was similarly packed.

If I'm honest, I wasn't feeling it this time. Even before the team news filtered out, I had a sense of foreboding. Regular readers will know that I'm not a believer in magical thinking, usually. However, when it comes to football, I confess to allowing superstition, dreams and premonitions to take up an unhealthy amount of space in my mind.

I don't know what it is. Maybe it's some form of pattern recognition, but I often get a sense of the outcome before a game has even kicked off. Of course, there's a heavy dose of bias involved because I probably only pay attention to the times when I'm right, so it's probably a good thing that I'm documenting here one of those occasions when my 'sixth sense' got it spectacularly wrong.

Nevertheless, as I wandered around Wembley, killing time in the dreary drizzle that welcomed us to the capital, I had an overwhelming sense of pessimism. Could we really beat Chelsea a third time under the Wembley arch in the space of two years? I didn't fancy our chances. Lightning, they say, doesn't strike twice. What odds on a third bolt powering the League Cup into Virgil van Dijk's hands? Then there were the injuries to contend with. I'd have felt more confident going into this game with a fully fit Trent Alexander-Arnold, Andy Robertson, Dominik Szoboszlai and Mohamed Salah. The kids had so far acquitted themselves well, but this was Wembley, it was a cup final and it was against Chelsea.

The chaos at the turnstiles only added to my increasing sense of gloom. Ours, located in the green zone, seemed to open too early, prompting frantic exchanges between stewards, while other supporters struggled with the vagaries of an electronic ticketing system. Where had we seen that before?

If I was struggling to locate my mojo, I wasn't alone. As I stood in the queue for an insanely priced can of Stella Artois on the concourse of the sky-high level 5, I struck up a conversation with a couple of supporters who had just seen the team news.

'If this was at Anfield, I'd be more comfortable,' said one woman. 'The pitch is smaller, we're closer and we can get behind the lads and influence the game. It's harder at Wembley. You're too far from the pitch.'

'There's not much on the bench,' said the other, a former Anfield steward and a veteran of many cup finals over the years. 'Difficult for Klopp to change the game with substitutions today,' he said, reflecting on the paucity of experience on the subs' bench.

I couldn't disagree. And it did nothing for the nerves. By now, though, the singing had started, and it lifted me a little as I made my way to a seat that seemed impossibly far away from the pitch. Despite that, I wouldn't have swapped it for a seat on the couch at home. Not for all the Stella Artois at Wembley.

The 2024 League Cup Final was full of subplots. From the distinctly unromantic Moisés Caicedo story to the infinitely more endearing prospect of Conor Bradley, deputising for arguably the best right-back in world football, at just 20 years of age, bidding to become the first Northern Irish player to win a trophy for Liverpool since the incomparable Elisha Scott did so in 1923.

In this, as in so many matters, Klopp knew best. In the days after the dust had settled on that final, I managed to find a quote the manager made to the BBC back in 2020: 'The dream is to have all the boys from the academy, a team full of Scousers, they would fight like crazy, we want to be the sport for everyone with a Scouse soul.' While Conor may not have been born in Liverpool, Northern Ireland may be as close as it gets. And, on that energy-sapping pitch in the London Borough of Brent, he and his young team-mates proved they all have a Scouse soul.

What followed defied logic and expectation. The match stats don't tell even a fraction of the story. Somehow, despite boasting a squad sprinkled liberally with youth and inexperience, Liverpool dominated possession and had more shots on goal than Chelsea. However, both sides could easily have won the tie in the regulation 90 minutes.

As the game progressed, it was Liverpool who saw the odds, already stacked against them, begin to lengthen. Van Dijk had what looked to me to be a perfectly good goal ruled out by VAR, after Wataru Endo was adjudged to have blocked Chelsea defender Levi Colwill from challenging the Reds' No.4, or simply doing his job to put it another way. And, earlier in the game, the Reds saw Ryan Gravenberch stretchered off after Moisés Caicedo's first-half tackle somehow escaped a booking. His replacement would give a performance full of energy, grit and determination, showing the world of football why, at least as far as the Kop is concerned, there ain't nobody like Joe Gomez'.

Just as he did in the two previous finals against Chelsea in 2022, Caoimhín Kelleher came to Liverpool's rescue on several occasions. The greatest compliment I can pay him is that with him deputising in goal, we've barely missed arguably the best goalkeeper in world football, Alisson Becker.

The first half was a simmering pot of tension and anxiety, with both teams threatening to take the lead. Kelleher saved brilliantly as Cole Palmer went close, before Cody Gakpo saw a goal-bound effort cannon back off the post, and Raheem Sterling had the ball in the net, only to see it ruled out by VAR. It looked clear from my vantage point in the sky but, after watching it back countless times since, I've struggled to locate the part of Nicolas Jackson's anatomy that was offside.

In the final act of normal time there were more acts of heroics from Kelleher and the Reds' defence, and the match ended goalless. So, once again, we faced the agony of extra time and, heaven forbid, penalties. I wasn't sure my heart could take it.

'This is where experience tells,' said the guy next to me. 'Have we got the legs? Can he change it from the bench?' With that he shook his head. 'I can't see it,' he said.

I nodded, my stomach a tangled knot of nerves. In that moment, I only thought of enduring the journey back on a coach and, worse still, work the following day after the misery of a cup final defeat and nursing thoughts of what might have been. It seemed in that moment, before extra time commenced, that our whole season, whether Klopp went out with a bang or a whimper, hinged on the outcome of the next 30 minutes. Maybe it did.

However, in big moments like this the truly great managers rise to the occasion. They make the right choice, say the right things and turn disadvantages into advantages. In that additional half-hour, Jürgen Klopp proved to be the poster boy for that characteristic. Mauricio Pochettino, not for the first time, showed himself to be the polar opposite of his rival. While Klopp elevated his Reds' team to new heights of resilience and power, plumbing previously unknown resources, Pochettino shrank, and his players' will to win evaporated.

The Chelsea manager would later reveal that, with Liverpool relying on an increasingly inexperienced 11, he'd seen an opportunity to win the game on penalties. His decision to hang on for that eventuality would prove disastrous. During the first 90 minutes, Klopp had already taken off Bradley, replacing him with another youngster, Bobby Clark. He also removed such experienced heads as Robertson, Mac Allister and Gakpo, replacing them with James McConnell,

Kostas Tsimikas and Jayden Danns. During extra time, he then took off French international Konaté, bringing on young Jarell Quansah.

For all the post-match debate about the average age of the respective squads, Chelsea's was younger, but few rival supporters considered the fact that Liverpool's squad contained a litter of players who had little or no experience of first-team football. The same couldn't be said of Chelsea, whose squad had been assembled by an ownership whose strategy resembled that of a drunken sailor on shore leave with a pocket full of bounty.

One of those Liverpool kids, Jayden Danns, almost won the game, forcing Chelsea keeper Djordje Petrovic to tip over his header. Harvey Elliott also saw his headed effort miraculously saved.

As the game marched inexorably towards penalties, the focus switched to the vast banks of terraces around the stadium. My heart was racing, and, in my gut churned expectation and dread. I could feel my blood pressure rising in my cheeks and I stood anxiously awaiting our fate, my hands clasped behind my head. As my gaze lifted temporarily from the action, something in the stands opposite me caught my attention. I'm not sure if this is exactly how it happened, but in my mind's eye this is how the most remarkable show of belief and support since Istanbul in 2005 played out.

Away to my right, in the Chelsea end, I could see a smattering of mass-produced blue flags wafting passively. However, our supporters had begun to wave scarves in the air. It started as a low buzz from a handful of fans and then grew into a crescendo of the haunting and uplifting anthem 'Allez, Allez, Allez' that swept through the massed ranks of Reds in our half of the stadium.

Emotion threatened to sweep me away. 'Bob Paisley and Bill Shankly!' I bellowed, with a tear in my eye. 'The Fields of Anfield Road!' Now a lump in my throat. 'We are loyal supporters, and we come from Liverpool!' I felt like crying now, but couldn't let that happen. Our whole end was singing, a sea of red-and-white scarves swirled, whipping up the energy levels in the stands and, we hoped, transmitting belief to the players on the pitch.

It was a truly awe-inspiring display and Chelsea had nothing to match it, not in the stands and not on the pitch. To paraphrase an old Anfield adage from the days of Shankly, hard work, passion and belief will always beat talent, when talent lacks hard work, passion and belief. I'll never forget that moment, ever. It felt to me, in that moment, that we'd win the game. When our supporters, the manager and the players are moving in perfect synchrony like that, there's no force on earth that can stop them. After the game, Joe Gomez would describe the impact of that moment on the players:

> Honestly, I'm not one for cliches, but I generally think we have the best in the world [supporters]. It's credit to them. I hope they realise that and how much it means to us. We just get a boost and it helps us so much. That is one thing we are all grateful for.
>
> When you have a comparison like that, it's a 50-50 stadium and you can see how evident it is, how superior our fans are in comparison. It's credit to them.

In commentary, the ever-poetic Peter Drury waxed lyrical as a wave of support swept around the Liverpool end of the stadium:

> The sense of understanding from Liverpool supporters is unsurprising. They get it, they know what they're watching here.
>
> They [the players] require encouragement and love and they're getting it – and Liverpool are responding to it.

Ian Doyle, representing the *Liverpool Echo* team at Wembley, took to social media to express his admiration for the efforts expended by all those of a Liverpool persuasion:

> No matter what happens in these closing 15 minutes, this has been one of the most remarkable final performances I've ever seen from #LFC. The courage and belief they have in each other is astonishing – and then there's the talent. They have been tremendous.

Alexis Mac Allister would later say that there is 'nothing like it' when it came to Liverpool's incredible support. He would add, 'Liverpool fans are different to the rest of England.'

Jürgen Klopp would later sum up the impact of the fans in those final moments in extra time. 'There were moments when it was really tough,' he said, 'but the fans sensed it and dragged us up by the bootlaces. It was truly sensational.'

The young Reds on the pitch were now enjoying themselves. Perhaps unencumbered by the weight of expectation felt by their Chelsea counterparts and buoyed by the belief placed in them by their manager, they took the game to their opponents, fashioning a host of chances.

Then, two minutes from time, a Bobby Clark shot-come-cross was deflected behind for a Liverpool corner. Up stepped substitute Kostas Tsimikas to take it. What followed appeared to me to take place in slow motion. It was as if I barely had time to set myself for the set piece, to mutter my superstitious mantras, to hope or expect. The ball floated towards the centre of the penalty area, and I see Van Dijk rise, then in an instant the ball is in the net. I catch a glimpse of the outstretched hand of the keeper, I imagine the despair in his eyes.

I couldn't possibly have seen it from that distance – and I lose control. We all lose control. Fans watching at home saw injured players running down steps and charging towards the pitch, making a mockery of the wounds that had kept them from featuring. One of them, Darwin Núñez, almost knocks over a hobbling Curtis Jones before vaulting over the advertising hoardings.

I feel pain in my shins as I almost fall over the seats in front of me. Somehow, I manage to steady myself, and then I'm hugging and dancing with strangers to my right, left, behind and in front of me. It's bedlam, pandemonium ... whatever word you can conjure to describe unadulterated abandon and joy, that will do.

There was just two minutes for us to hang on. Virgil hadn't been denied his moment as match-winning captain. The kids had fought for and won their right to compete at the highest level, and Jürgen was staring down the barrel of another incredible, improbable moment of destiny.

Away from the stadium, Reds would hear ex-United left-back Gary Neville describe extra time as 'Klopp's kids versus the Billionaire Blue Bottle jobs'. A great soundbite, yes. In truth, either side could have won, and only one could. But when the time came, I believe that only one manager, one team and one set of supporters believed that a win was possible. That for me, in a tight game with the odds stacked against Jürgen's Reds, made all the difference.

Little wonder that Klopp would describe it as 'the most special trophy I've ever won'. Our concourse wisdom had suggested Liverpool wouldn't be able to change from the bench, but Klopp did. We feared the fans couldn't influence from terraces so far from the pitch, yet we had.

Henry Winter, writing for *Times Sport*, summed up the sense of togetherness at the club:

> Before Jürgen Klopp went up for the trophy lift, he left instructions that all the team's matchday staff should gather for the celebrations on the pitch. He wanted them in all the pictures, sharing the moment, all in it together.

Nothing could epitomise that more than the emotional rendition of 'You'll Never Walk Alone', during which the players and fans united in glorious communion. Klopp had become the third Liverpool manager to win the League Cup two or more times. He now ranked alongside Bob Paisley and Gérard Houllier in that respect.

Merseyside football reporter for *The Telegraph*, Chris Bascombe, wrote on X – formerly known as Twitter:

> Had the privilege to report on every LFC final since 2001. For sheer courage, perseverance, and refusal to give in, that was up there with a certain game in 2005.

I couldn't agree more. This was one of many games for the ages in my career as a Liverpool supporter. I can't find the words here to adequately express my gratitude that I was there to see it.

Tragedy and Poverty Chants
Whataboutery and the Self-Defeating Nature of Tribalism
On Saturday, 2 March, Liverpool travelled to the City Ground to face Nottingham Forest. The Reds were top of the league, and in one of those do-or-die sequence of games that could be both thrilling and

utterly exhausting. That meant, with the game heading into the ninth minute of stoppage time and still goalless, fingernails had been chewed to their beds, and nerves were frayed almost to breaking point. When Darwin Núñez, a 60th-minute substitute, scored the winner, emotions took over and Liverpool's away end went berserk. So too did the Forest fans, with some taking it too far. At one point, Liverpool full-back Andy Robertson had to rescue a small child from behind the dugout as grown men tried to get at the match officials.

The last few weeks had been remarkable. We'd watched in awe as the Reds rose from the ashes of a difficult defeat at the hands of their title rivals Arsenal to claim top spot. After clinching the League Cup, and with Liverpool still in the FA Cup and Europa League, talk of another tilt at a quadruple had resurfaced.

As I looked back at the foothills of February, it was hard to imagine that a chastening defeat to Arsenal at the Emirates could herald an ascent. And all this with the first team decimated by injury and little more than a posse of kids riding to the rescue. It was a great story. One the football world should at least grudgingly admire, if not wholeheartedly celebrate.

Oh, to live in a world where football is a glorious escape from the madness of 'real life' and where our rivalries are sharp enough to make us wince yet still be able to go home with a smile on our faces. Where defeats leave wounds that do not feel fatal. For the record, I don't believe that world has ever existed, certainly not in my lifetime.

The rage from Forest fans was understandable. Losing any game with the last kick of the ball is sickening. Who hasn't raged against a perceived refereeing injustice, only to wake up the next day and wonder whether maybe it was really a case of six of one and half a dozen of the other? Certainly, Paul Tierney got many things wrong in that game, and those decisions went both for and against Forest. However, the sight of a young kid having to be rescued from the stands by a Liverpool player as an angry group of supporters vented their spleens at the officials, Liverpool Football Club, its fans and anyone else who got in the way was as depressing as the moronic poverty chanting they'd engaged in throughout the game.

There's a historical symmetry in the fact that we should be discussing Forest fans in this respect. This year marks the 40th anniversary of the miners' strike in the UK, an often bloody battle between the country's coal mining communities, the police and the state. Its dark legacy hangs over those mining towns to this day. In those places, wounds span generations and refuse to heal.

I remember the Kop chanting 'scab, scab, scab' at Forest fans in the 80s. Nottingham, of course, was the home of the Union of Democratic Mineworkers, to this day blamed by many in the trade union movement for helping to break the strike. A 'scab' is someone who crosses a picket line and betrays their comrades.

Liverpool back then was embroiled in its own fight for survival against the Thatcher government. For most of us, the miners' strike represented another front in that fight, and we knew whose side we were on.

Sadly, though, I'm also old enough to remember Liverpool supporters chanting about the Munich air disaster, loudly and in our thousands. And, while thankfully those disgusting songs are absent from today's Kop, you may still hear the odd moron regurgitating this bile on an away coach or in a pub before or after a game. This illustrates the Jekyll and Hyde that exists within all people and all groups. Football supporters are no different, why would they be?

The chants of 'scab' aimed at Forest fans at Anfield in the 80s felt like a symbol of our class consciousness and of working-class solidarity. Yet the Munich chants were the antithesis of that spirit, and although I honestly didn't make that connection back then, we were guilty of the same divisive behaviour we condemned in others.

Fast-forward four decades and Liverpool fans have for the most part dropped the tragedy chants. It's jarring to recall how few who stood on the Kop in the 80s would have batted an eyelid as thousands of their peers belted out a song revelling in the Munich air disaster, save perhaps those old enough to recall how horrific it was. But that's how it was back then. We were flailing around at anyone we felt we had a beef with; sometimes we punched up and, when we felt the mood called for it, we punched down. In the years that have passed since those adolescent days, I believe that the crowd at Anfield has grown up.

Two football tragedies and their aftermath have taught us and the generations who have followed that tragedy chanting should be left behind, but it has also sharpened the political consciousness of those who travel home and away. Chants of 'fuck the Tories' by Liverpool supporters are commonplace at Anfield and at away grounds around the country these days, and, of course, the national anthem is roundly booed at cup finals. In addition, Reds have been heard chanting 'Maggie's in the mud' at games. This, of course, is a reference to the fact that former Tory Prime Minister Margaret Thatcher, the architect of the all-out assault on working-class communities like Liverpool 40 years ago, is now dead. Her role in the 'managed decline' of the city and the cover-up of the Hillsborough disaster has never been forgotten on Merseyside. Her legacy in the city means she's despised by many, and her party has never recovered electorally in the area as a result. It will perhaps surprise many that prior to her term in office, the Tories frequently had councillors elected to Liverpool City Council, while today they have none, and that's unlikely to change for the foreseeable future.

Many in polite society would argue that taking pleasure in the death of another – even Thatcher – is beyond the pale. Perhaps so. I admit that, as a grown-up who has now lived long enough to experience the pain of grief and loss, I'd rather we didn't scrape that particular barrel even if I understand why some do.

Oh, to live in a world where football is a glorious escape from the madness of real life.

It's naive in the extreme to expect any group of people who have suffered at the hands of a political leader and their party, as the city of Liverpool has at the hands of Thatcher and subsequent Tory governments, to follow the rules of polite society. The damage done to Liverpool and other communities – like those embroiled in the miners' strike – by the policies of Thatcher and successive Tory governments is generational. The lessons of those years have been passed down in families and will never be forgotten.

Others have cited what I believe to be a false equivalency of Liverpool supporters booing the national anthem and singing about Thatcher's death, and the poverty and Hillsborough chants sung by rival fans on terraces around the country. One supporter, posting on X, had this to say after some Reds had criticised Forest fans for poverty chanting two minutes into the game:

This will probably get me pelters but I'm going to post it anyway. I've seen numerous messages from Liverpool fans suggesting that Forest fans were singing the 'Sign On' song to them at yesterday's match.

I'm not going to dispute that as I wasn't there and I've heard it sung myself, certainly not saying it's right but they are up in arms about it.

One week earlier these same fans decided to boo our National Anthem at Wembley as well as break into a chorus of 'Lizzie's in a box'.

My answer, your hypocrisy is off scale, don't start moaning about other fans who goad you when your own standards are in the gutter.

Another supporter lashed out at Scousers complaining about mass unemployment becoming the subject of terrace banter by claiming he'd been made redundant five times, and he never 'whinged or moaned'. You should have, mate. You should have fought and campaigned against those responsible. You'd have had every right to.

Are Liverpool supporters guilty of hypocrisy, though? My observation is that while Liverpool fans rail against the establishment, its heroes and its symbols, such as Thatcher and the national anthem, others choose to mock ordinary people who suffer because of the policies of that same establishment. While Liverpool supporters are punching up, they're punching down.

This whole discussion is symptomatic of wider issues in society, of course it is. Football has never existed in a vacuum and societal problems will always play out on terraces inhabited by tens of thousands of ordinary people every week. They don't leave their experiences, biases or beliefs at the turnstiles.

Oh, to live in a world where football is a glorious escape from the madness of real life.

The reason I object to poverty and tragedy chanting is less about it being 'offensive' to me – that seems such a passive and weak word in my view – and more to do with a feeling that these chants are self-defeating. The same people who complain that Liverpool supporters bring politics into the game and disrespect their country, its leaders, flag and anthem are bringing politics into the game by resorting to bigoted stereotypes and mocking the same social inequality many of them experience for themselves daily.

Those chants don't 'offend' me as much as they depress me. They speak to a section of society that has either never been prepared to call out the mess we're surrounded by daily, or who have given up on the idea that things can be any different. For these people, the highlight of their weeks is a desperate race to the bottom in which poverty and tragedy are fair game for terrace banter, and nothing ever changes.

For the sake of balance, I could aim this criticism at some of our own supporters. I'd also agree that there are many supporters of other clubs around the country who feel the same way I do about politics, football and life. They disown those in their own ranks who sing about poverty or tragedy at football matches.

Most football supporters of all clubs can identify with their rivals. Why wouldn't they? We all lead similar lives, have the same problems and love our teams. We understand the importance of our clubs to our respective communities too.

Forty years ago, Thatcher and the Tories sought to undermine our communities and our game by sowing division wherever they could. The miners, minorities, football fans and cities like Liverpool were seen as the 'enemy within'. Many fell for it then, and it seems there's no shortage of people willing to take the bait today. So, while I'm not asking for us all to sit in a circle with our tambourines, singing 'Kumbaya', it would be good if some could at least recognise that if their lives are in ruins, they should be angry with the politicians whose decisions ruined them, not supporters of another football club.

And if your club is in ruins, then it's probably the people currently running the game that should bear the brunt of your ire, not Scousers and not people struggling to survive a cost-of-living crisis.

Like a New Signing
Michael Edwards Returns to the Anfield Fold ... Well, Sort Of
There was a time when we all believed, or at least said we believed, that the only people who mattered at Liverpool Football Club were the players, the supporters and the manager. Not necessarily in that order. On 13 March 2024, after weeks of speculation, the return of Michael

Edwards to the Liverpool fold was greeted like a new signing by Reds everywhere. So Shankly was wrong, the directors do matter really.

In truth, the great man knew that, of course he did. But he never missed an opportunity to galvanise and unite the three elements of the club's 'holy trinity' to gain maximum advantage over 90 minutes in a football match. And when the referee blows the whistle to signal the start of hostilities, there is little the directors of the club can do to influence the outcome.

Of course, we've all been painfully aware of the impact, for good and bad, that the people who run the club have. Some would say that since the calamitous ownership of Hicks and Gillett we've been a little obsessed with the people who run the club. For what it's worth, I remember being mildly disgruntled that former chairman Noel White (1990–91) had a little too much to say for himself. I, like many Reds at the time, preferred the strong silent type.

To be fair to Edwards, he'd always done his talking in the transfer market, quietly collaborating with the manager and the owners to assemble the club's first title-winning team in 30 years. It was only in the latter stages of that rebuild that many Reds even knew who he was. When he left, it was like we couldn't live without him.

We could, obviously, but with Jürgen Klopp announcing his departure at the end of the season, this was the most pivotal period in the club's history. Just like Shankly's resignation, Klopp's departure represents a crossroads. An inspirational leader who had rebuilt the club physically and psychologically was leaving and which path the owners and directors chose from that moment on would be pivotal.

In 1974, Liverpool chose a familiar face and a safe pair of hands to lead the club on to the next level. They picked Bob Paisley. Now, 50 years on, a new set of owners have pulled off a similar trick, or at least we hope so.

Of course, Michael Edwards isn't the manager. But he *is* someone well known to the ownership and the club's fanbase. He has a proven record of success, and he's trusted. With the club shaping up to make its biggest managerial appointment since 1974, Edwards's appointment felt like a shrewd move. The 44-year-old returned to the club in a role much broader than the one he previously held, having turned down the opportunity to reprise his previous job. As CEO of football operations for FSG, he'll oversee the ownership's expansion into global football. His remit includes but is not limited to Liverpool Football Club. He appointed a new sporting director but would also set FSG on the path to multi-club ownership.

Edwards, who had spurned overtures from both Chelsea and Manchester United, wasted little time in identifying the man who would lead Liverpool's rebuild in the post-Klopp era. Identified early on in negotiations, Richard Hughes was swiftly installed as the club's new sporting director on 20 March. The appointment had been trailed in the media for weeks and came as little surprise to supporters and journalists. Hughes was a former technical director at Bournemouth and well known to Edwards. The pair have a very busy in-tray, and top of the pile of jobs as far as Liverpool fans were concerned was replacing Klopp, possibly the hardest act to follow in football right now.

In a statement issued after his return, Edwards revealed just how much FSG had wanted him, and detailed the task ahead:

I am very grateful to Mike, John, Tom, and the ownership group for offering me the opportunity to take on this new leadership role within FSG. I was humbled by the desire and persistence they showed in wanting to work with me again. This is definitely not something that I take for granted given their track record across sport and business.

It was vital for me that, if I did return, it had to be with renewed vigour and energy. In practice, this means having fresh challenges and opportunities. As such, one of the biggest factors in my decision is the commitment to acquire and oversee an additional club, growing this area of their organisation. I believe that to remain competitive, investment and expansion of the current football portfolio is necessary.

With Liverpool, I will oversee the required reinforcement of football operations, with a number of essential leadership positions needing urgent attention. I know from personal experience what a wonderful job Mike Gordon has done with day-to-day oversight on behalf of his fellow owners. Going forward I'm looking forward to working with FSG's Board of Managers. Also, in assuming this role, I fully understand that it comes with great expectations, and I therefore intend to identify, hire, and subsequently empower leaders who meet and embody the club's values and ambitions.

Having served the club previously I need no reminder of how much emotional investment is made by supporters in the city itself, as well as across the UK and the world. I am looking forward to getting started.

Jürgen Klopp was asked about the appointment of Edwards during his pre-Sparta Prague press conference and spoke of his relationship with and respect for Edwards. He acknowledged that the pair had already spoken but dismissed any notion that the CEO of football might attempt to persuade him to stay at the club, in response to Sky Sports' Vinny O'Connor:

We had that conversation, yes. Michael and I, we always had a really good relationship. It was always very good on a professional basis anyway, really good, and a lot of good things happened obviously in the time that we were here together. Michael decided to do something else and now he's back I am happy.

I said it a few times, I want to see the club in the best possible place after I leave, so everything we can do as long as I am here, I will do. After that, other people have to do it and I think it's a top solution, honestly. A top solution.

Our conversation was great, we spoke about a lot of things, about what I think about different things, players and stuff like this, the situation in the club because I was in all the time while he was not in, so what had changed and what might have to change. These kind of things. A really good talk and, as I said, I think it's top news for the club.

When asked directly whether Edwards had attempted to convince him to reverse his decision to leave, the boss was dismissive:

No, because – and it is very important in the job – he is not dumb. It's not a subject to talk about, to be honest. Can you imagine I changed my mind now? Can you? Of course not. I cannot say what I said … It would be like, 'Never, ever for another club in England,' and then signed for next year for a neighbour or whatever, or whoever needs a coach. That would be completely crazy.

I don't say these things without thinking before. It would mean I started only now realising how great this club is. I know it all the time. It is, for me, the best club in the world and I leave it anyway – that's why I tried to explain. I just want the club to do as good as somehow possible. I am really sure we created a basis with the right people in charge, and Michael is a top choice.

That was that, then. In truth, by this stage, I – and I suspect most Reds – had begun to make peace with Jürgen's decision to leave. We could all see that the job was starting to wear on him, and to expect him to stay when his energy levels had been exhausted was unfair. He'd at least given us a heads-up of sorts, left a fantastic legacy, with possibly an even greater finale to come. So, at least mentally, I was beginning to prepare for life without him.

The idea that he'd somehow miraculously – or ludicrously to be more accurate – change his mind and announce that he was staying felt wrong and absurd. That didn't stop certain social media accounts and click-bait aggregators from promoting the idea relentlessly, though.

Richard Hughes, a Scot and reported Liverpool supporter, wouldn't officially join the club until 1 June; however, it was widely reported that, alongside Edwards, Hughes was already working with FSG on future plans for the club. He'd have undoubtedly spoken to Jürgen too. Confirming his appointment, the club had this to say:

Liverpool FC can confirm the appointment of Richard Hughes as the club's new sporting director, a post he will take up at the end of the 2023/24 season.

The 44-year-old will join the Reds after leaving his role as technical director at AFC Bournemouth, where he enjoyed a decade of successful stewardship of the south-coast club's football operation.

Hughes will officially take over responsibilities at the AXA Training Centre on 1 June in advance of the 2024/25 campaign having been appointed by Michael Edwards, who was recently named Fenway Sports Group's CEO of Football. The pair had previously worked together during Hughes' playing career at Portsmouth.

Hughes said:

> I am incredibly proud to be offered this opportunity. Liverpool FC is a unique club and I'm grateful to be given a chance to serve it in this capacity.
>
> People rightly talk about the rich history this organisation can boast, but it is the present and future which really excites me. Jürgen Klopp is leading an outstanding team and squad and alongside that the commitment to young players and their pathway to the first team is also outstanding.

His comments about the development of youth players were particularly reassuring. In recent years we'd grown accustomed to the conveyor belt of talent passing from Kirkby to Anfield. The idea that all of that may be torn up by a new manager who wanted to do things his way had been a concern. However, Hughes talked about working with the existing team at the AXA Training Centre 'to make good decisions'.

Edwards spoke of his delight at Hughes's appointment, a man he'd clearly earmarked in his negotiations with the owners:

> I've known him for half of my life in a professional and personal capacity and he is absolutely someone who embodies the best values of Liverpool FC. I trust him completely.
>
> He has outstanding judgement and a track record of making smart decisions which benefit the organisations he represents.
>
> Both Richard and I are aware of the weight of responsibility that comes with working in this capacity for a club such as this. The fact he is excited and energised by the challenge ahead is important.

It seemed Liverpool and FSG were preparing well for a future without their iconic German manager. Of course, time will have the ultimate say on whether these were 'good decisions' or not. But, as we moved relentlessly towards the season's run-in, I was bizarrely beginning to be thankful for that traumatic day in January when the boss tipped us the nod that his time as boss was coming to an end.

That probably sounds crazy. But imagine if he'd left it until the summer. At least now, I reasoned, the club could quietly rebuild in the background and be ready to hit the ground sprinting in June. And hopefully fit in a bus tour of the city, with some shiny trinkets to show off. Now that would be the perfect send-off for the boss.

Dreams Dashed

Liverpool 2.0's Brave Quadruple Charge Falls Short

To their eternal credit, Klopp's new Liverpool went into the final few months of the season chasing glory on all fronts. They'd barrelled on despite the engine hissing and a couple of the tyres looking flat. A group of plucky youngsters had practically carried the malfunctioning truck this far, but as the road grew longer, signs of an imminent breakdown were hard to miss.

The Reds looked in good shape as they completed January with impressive wins over Norwich City in the fourth round of the FA Cup and Chelsea in the Premier League. After the defeat to Arsenal, February brought a 3-1 victory over Burnley, played in front of a record attendance of 59,896. The Anfield Road expansion project was now nearing completion. The Reds followed that up with a 4-1 drubbing of Brentford, then the same scoreline against Luton Town, in which Jayden Danns made his Premier League debut. Liverpool were flying and optimism was growing.

On 28 February, Liverpool's youngsters featured in a 3-0 victory over Southampton at Anfield, in the FA Cup fifth round. *The Athletic* described the Reds' academy set-up as a goldmine, claiming that clubs around the world were already studying it as a template. As if proving his point, Liverpool's scorers that night were a pair of 18-year-olds, Lewis Koumas and Jayden Danns. Also appearing from the bench that night was Kaide Gordon aged 19, and Trey Nyoni, who was just 16. The win set up a quarter-final clash with Manchester United.

In the Europa League round of 16, Liverpool pummelled Sparta Prague into submission, racking up an 11-2 aggregate scoreline, with youngster Bobby Clark having the time of his life in the home leg. He scored one and assisted in another.

Lying between those two ties was the visit of Manchester City to Anfield on 10 March. Billed as a do-or-die match, the tension in the run-up to kick-off was intense. The attendance for this match was a record for a league match at Anfield, beating the 59,896 against Burnley a month earlier, and equalling the gate for the visit of Luton Town on 21 February.

There was little to separate the teams, a second-half Alexis Mac Allister penalty cancelling out a first-half opener from John Stones. Liverpool, who had already been leapfrogged by City, now sat in second place. However, yet again it was the finer details that would cost the Reds, and by that I mean the officiating. Mac Allister was denied a second clear-cut penalty late in the game when City's Jeremy Doku booted the Argentine in the chest. It occurred inside the penalty area but a VAR review concluded no penalty, to our utter disbelief. If that had happened anywhere else on the pitch, it would have been a foul and a red card.

A draw with Manchester City can never be seen as a bad result these days. They're a juggernaut, and regardless of how they arrived at their position atop of football's pyramid, you have to fight like crazy to earn every tiny advantage over them. It's this fact that makes the title win of 2020 all the more remarkable. However, not for the first time, we left a game of football with the unavoidable sense that we'd been robbed, and thoughts that it was going to leave us painfully short in the hunt for Klopp's second championship, and the kind of send-off he deserved, began to gnaw away at me.

Liverpool were paired with Atalanta in the Europa League quarter-final, with the first leg at Anfield. Victory in the tie would set up a semi-final with either Benfica or Marseille. That left open the possibility of facing Xabi Alonso's (the man tipped to replace Jürgen at the time) Bayer Leverkusen in the final in Dublin.

I'll be honest, it was all starting to sound preordained to me, and I didn't see Atalanta as a serious barrier to a glorious trip to Ireland at the end of the season. That would have felt like a home game, but I should have heeded the old warnings about counting chickens before they'd hatched.

Before that, on 17 March, was the sixth-round FA Cup clash with Manchester United, at Old Trafford. In what was a crazy and ultimately desperately frustrating game, Liverpool succumbed to an 87th-minute equaliser after leading 2-1 at half-time. Harvey Elliott restored the lead after 105 minutes, but two late, late strikes, from Marcus Rashford and Amad Diallo in the 112th and 120th minutes, sent United to the semi-finals. It was heartbreaking for a Liverpool side who had given so much, despite the absence of so many first-choice players for so long.

The dream of a clean sweep was officially over. In truth, it had been an impossible fantasy for a while now. With the unerring benefit of hindsight, Liverpool 2.0 had been overachieving, way ahead of schedule, and it was to their credit that they'd carried the possibility of a fantasy ending to Klopp's reign this far.

The Reds struggled on, winning their next two games in the league against Brighton and Sheffield United, and as they set up for their second game against United in little over two weeks, it felt like they might have rallied for the final push. However, a 2-2 draw at Anfield was mourned by an army of crestfallen but appreciative Reds at the final whistle.

Liverpool were now second in the table, behind Arsenal on goal difference, with City lurking ominously in third. The Gunners faced Manchester United in their next game, while Liverpool were at home to Crystal Palace. We needed a favour from the old enemy but, despite their recent success against us, they didn't look capable of upsetting the Gunners' apple cart.

A dream ending to the season was still possible, but the wheels were now coming off, and the Reds were trundling along – tired, broken and seemingly running out of ideas. The season had caught up with us. It was painful.

However, as news swirled of potential candidates to replace Jürgen Klopp, I couldn't imagine anyone I'd rather see in the Reds' dugout for the run-in than the self-titled 'normal one'. Nevertheless, stories of Xabi Alonso and Ruben Amorim as potential successors came and went, as if oblivious to my attempts to deny the inevitable.

Also in the news, bloodshed in Gaza filled our TV screens and drew protests around the world. The Horizon scandal, in which innocent Post Office workers had been wrongfully imprisoned for theft, spoke of another fiasco in which the failures of the powerful had been hidden and the blame shifted to the victims. Meanwhile, a horse called I Am Maximus won the 2024 Grand National.

For the Reds, our hopes of adding even more glitter to Liverpool's resurgence now rested on the Europa League. It felt well within our grasp and the visit of Atalanta held no fear for me. Back then I'd clearly underestimated how low on fuel Klopp's Reds had become. The 3-0 home defeat to Gian Piero Gasperini's men was surely the greatest night in the Italian side's history and one of our worst. It was well deserved on both counts. Liverpool were poor, but Atalanta's coach got everything right and earned his moment in the limelight.

April then brought further misery as the Reds crashed to a shock 1-0 defeat at home to Crystal Palace, which saw hopes of a title win all but disappear. I remember one moment during that game, with the Reds a goal down and chasing an equaliser, when the lad next to me turned and said, 'We won't lose this. We'll come away with a point.' I doubted he was correct this time but reminded him that a point 'wouldn't do'. We just looked at each other and shook our heads.

On the managerial front, Feyenoord's Arne Slot had become the favourite to succeed the boss, with Liverpool's hierarchy in negotiations with his club. They'd reach a successful conclusion by the end of the month, allowing Liverpool to enter the home stretch with Klopp's replacement sorted. It was a testament to the man that Jürgen's long goodbye had allowed Liverpool to plan the future in relatively calm circumstances. He had, from the moment he joined us, acted always with the best interests of the club and the city at the forefront of his mind.

It was still difficult to think about a Reds side lining up without the German in charge, but the seeds of acceptance were beginning to germinate. We understood that Jürgen had given his all, and nobody begrudged him a rest and a new adventure or two. He'd earned his last stand in front of the Kop and, despite the team's struggles, we all knew we had to give him the greatest send-off possible.

For now, though, all our hopes were pinned on another legendary European comeback, this time in Italy on 18 April. A Mohamed Salah penalty in the fifth minute sparked optimism, and a revival seemed possible, at least for a moment. But the Reds failed to build on it, and Atalanta soon regained their grip on the game and the tie. It was a masterclass from the Italians and Liverpool just couldn't shake themselves loose.

We'd have to make do with the League Cup, which was, of course, still one more trophy than most teams had to celebrate. However, Klopp's earlier suggestion – in the heat of that Wembley win back in February – that if we had just one trophy to parade, we would, seemed well intentioned but misguided now. The truth was that the club, Jürgen nor any of us had the appetite for that now. We'd have our celebrations, but they'd be to honour almost nine years of glory, not just a single season's. We'd do that in our home, together, at Anfield.

Everton managed a rare and unlikely win over Liverpool, on their own patch on 24 April. And although hopes of a league title were now slim at best, the defeat at Goodison meant that nothing short of a miracle would see the Premier League trophy returning to Anfield. The Blues were now safe from relegation and felt they could sing 'you lost the league at Goodison Park'. So low have their expectations fallen that becoming a fly in Liverpool's ointment and avoiding relegation has become a virtue. The DVD and T-shirts would be available in the club shop within 24 hours. Maybe.

The truth is they deserved their win, and I was prepared to take my lumps even if I wasn't happy about it. Living with an Evertonian – my wife is a Blue in case you didn't know – means that these oh-so-occasional setbacks feel more painful than they should. But I guess I had it coming.

The Reds fought out a 2-2 draw away to West Ham before a chance came to wreak revenge on Spurs for their shameless celebrations at the end of their VAR-inspired victory in the capital. The game began in celebratory mood, a dress rehearsal for the final goodbye, perhaps. And in the Anfield sun the Reds set about demolishing Tottenham Hotspur in an hour-long blitz that saw Klopp's men roar into a 4-0 lead.

Spurs had been given a glimmer of hope that they could reach the Champions League places after Aston Villa fell to defeat at the hands of Brighton. Some kind of fight seemed inevitable before the kick-off. That Postecoglou's men had waited until they were four down before mounting one was a surprise. Their two-goal salvo in the space of five second-half minutes came either side of the replacement of Alexis Mac Allister with Ryan Gravenberch. The Argentine had been running the show up to his departure, and the fact that Liverpool didn't possess a replacement of similar quality for the tiring midfielder was telling.

When Son Heung-min added to Richarlison's 72nd-minute strike just two minutes after Mac Allister left the pitch, the signs were ominous as the crowd threatened to fracture. However, Liverpool held on and the Kop regained its composure as the final whistle approached. As the minutes ticked by, the atmosphere began to ratchet up a notch. It was almost as if we were in some sort of rehearsal for the final game against Wolves in just a fortnight's time.

The season had been long and tiring, filled with magical moments and no shortage of challenges. At times, for me at least, it had felt exhausting, and overshadowed to a degree by personal angst. But in those moments, after Son had made the score look far more respectable than it should have, I felt some of the old emotion return.

I hadn't realised it had gone. I'd been so swallowed up by my own 'last stand' that I'd somehow not noticed that some of that spark had faded. Here I was, having been so comprehensively transformed from a doubter to a believer nine years earlier, having to rebuild that faith once again, in football and in life.

Now I was engulfed in song. It rang out from all four corners of the ground, as supporters ran through Jürgen's song book with a kind of rumbling passion that lifted me as much as I hoped it had lifted the boss. Life sometimes feels too hard to bear, our struggles can consume us if we let them. When – as I often am – we're alone in our own heads, it threatens to do just that.

We're helpless without others, without community and camaraderie. That's what the Kop has always given me. Football has throughout my life been about those moments when I'm part of something much bigger and more powerful than I could ever be on my own. So often it has filled up my batteries and given me strength to face the randomness and cruelty of life, to see joy, passion and feel like I belong somewhere. If only for 90 minutes.

Liverpool fans gather in a Paris park ahead of the Champions League Final against Real Madrid.

Reds fans in front of the Eiffel Tower. Photo by Gareth Dixon and courtesy of The Red Archive.

Liverpool supporters in Paris. Photo by Iain Robertson and courtesy of The Red Archive.

Peter Kenny Jones and friends at Paris. Photo by Jake Atkin and courtesy of The Red Archive.

Fan park scenes. Paris 2022. Photo by Matt Preston and courtesy of The Red Archive.

More Reds enjoying the Paris sights. Photo by Michael Shellien and courtesy of The Red Archive.

Celebrating the boss in front of the Eiffel Tower. Photo by Shairley Young and courtesy of The Red Archive.

Conwy Reds in the Stade de France. Photo by Shairley Young and courtesy of The Red Archive.

Jamie Webster entertains the Reds in Paris. Photo by Shairley Young and courtesy of The Red Archive.

Paris is a sea of Red. Photo by Shairley Young and courtesy of The Red Archive.

Peaceful Liverpool supporters held under an underpass in crammed conditions for prolonged period. Actions like these by the Paris police would later be condemned by independent reports. Photo by Simon Helsby and courtesy of The Red Archive.

The Champions Wall at Anfield is updated to reflect Liverpool's 10th League Cup win in 2024.

A distraught fan displays a cut out of Jürgen Klopp in their Liverpool Garden after the boss announcing he is leaving at the end of the season. Photo courtesy of Yvon Wardale.

Ian Rush Mural on Anfield Road in the shadow of the Main Stand as Anfield awaits Klopp's last game in charge.

My FA Cup semi-final ticket.

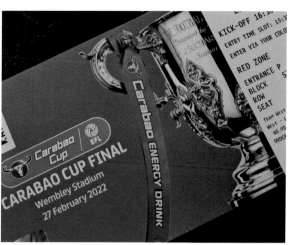

My League Cup Final ticket

Me at Wembley League Cup Final in 2024.

Reds on their way to Wembley 2024.

Wembley awaits Liverpool and Chelsea.

A mural on Anfield Road near to the Flat Iron pub places Klopp amongst the managerial greats.

A slimmed-down-version of me after my health scare, with friends John Stulberg and John Whitehead in the Cabbage Hall pub before Klopp's last game.

An advertisement outside the Kop on Walton Breck Road before Klopp's final game in charge.

Kop artist Peter Carney working on his Klopp farewell banner. Photo courtesy of Peter Carney.

Peter Carney's banner on the Kop ahead of Klopp's final game. Photo courtesy of Peter Carney.

Another Peter Carney creation, which would be displayed at Klopp's final game. Photo courtesy of Peter Carney.

Fans outside Anfield with a Klopp banner prior to his last game in charge. Photo courtesy of Peter Carney.

Doubters, Believers, Conquerors banner as viewed from my seat on the Kop before Klopp's last game.

'THANKS JURGEN, LAD!' – a stall on Walton Breck Road prior to Klopp's last stand.

David Goulding and his family and friends enjoying the sunshine before Klopp's last game.

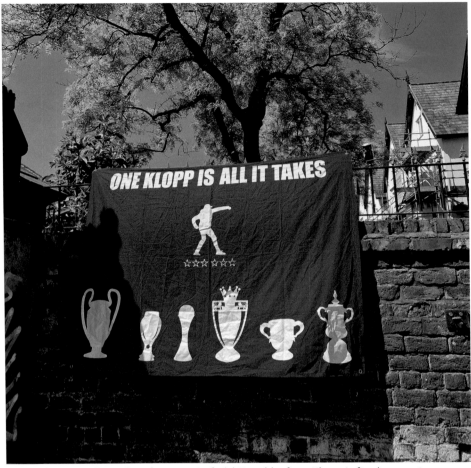

'One Klopp Is All It Takes' banner Anfield Road before Klopp's final game in charge.

A packed Anfield Road before Klopp's last game.

'That Was Grea,t Liverpool!' a temporary Klopp mural for Klopp's last game.

Peter Collis, Danny Leather, Joe Zeverona, Tony Zeverona and Neal Sanders on Anfield Road before Klopp's final game. Photo courtesy of Tony Zeverona.

The Kop prepares for Klopp's last stand.

View of the Kop from my seat in Block 109 of the Kop.

The view from the bottom of the Kop as Kopites get ready for Klopp's last stand.

Banners at the ready for Klopp's last stand.

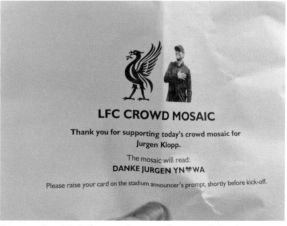

My card, which formed a small part of Andy Knott's wonderful Danke Jurgen crowd mosaic.

Me and the legendary Alan Kennedy in the Arkles pub, Anfield.

Lucky supporters form a queue to see 'An Evening with Jürgen Klopp' and say a final emotional farewell to the boss at the Liverpool Arena.

'An Evening with Jürgen Klopp' at a packed-out Liverpool Arena.

I'd lost that almost a decade earlier, and I'd come close to losing it again. I realised how priceless it was now more than ever. I knew also that men like Jürgen, and Shankly, Paisley and Dalglish before him, had been responsible for so much of that. If the footballing gods hadn't seen fit to reward Klopp's last stand with the trophies and medals he so richly deserved, then he'd get his just rewards from us on the Kop and from an army of believers all over the world.

Anfield Bids Farewell to Jürgen

An Emotional Final Game

And just like that, we'd reached the end. On 19 May, Anfield was ready to say farewell to the 'normal one'. I was anything but ready as I set off for the game. The sun was shining, the skies were clear and it was everything an end-of-season game should be. Except this was no ordinary campaign finale.

The streets around the stadium had filled up early. Kick-off was hours away and streets that would normally have been empty save for the vendors setting up stalls were now crammed with people who just wanted to soak up the atmosphere, pose for pictures in front of the murals, now too numerous to count – many of them dedicated to the boss – and welcome a team bus carrying Jürgen Klopp for the final time.

News of tickets changing hands for thousands of pounds had been rife for months; this was the biggest show in town. No amount of money would have persuaded me to part with my ticket.

Crowds gathered in front of a giant screen on Paisley Square, packed out pubs and filled chippies and cafes to bursting point. Banners hung everywhere and in the car park of the historic Sandon pub a party had started. Its music and sounds carried on a light breeze down Walton Breck Road as I walked along.

I wandered around the ground, taking it all in and reflecting on the last nine years. And on the traumas of lockdown and its impact on me and my family's mental health, my own health problems and how for the first time in my life I'd come face to face with my own mortality. I thought of the people I'd lost and the challenges we'd all faced together.

I also remembered the glory of that first Premier League-era title win, the magic of Madrid and how Origi's goal had ended the tie against Spurs, sending Reds all over the world into ecstasy. Bobby Firmino winning us the World Club Cup and the domestic cup double. We'd conquered all of Europe, and under Jürgen we'd won the fucking lot.

The Klopp era will be remembered long into the future. The incredible games, the trophies, the wonderful moments and the sense of pride and belief he restored are the touchstones, but there was a backdrop to all of that, for all of us. Klopp has been there through it all, a source of constancy and humour. He has so often been a voice of sense in an insane world.

For that reason, Jürgen is woven into all our life stories. A football manager, yes. But one who felt like a family member to all of us. He arrived in troubled times and led us out of that. He was a voice of compassion and reason during the pandemic when life felt so cruel and unreasonable.

Saying goodbye was going to be tough, but we'd done it before. Most football clubs consider themselves fortunate to have had one figure like Klopp in their entire history. A generational manager, someone who transcends football and inspires a community to come together and dream big, work for each other and share in the rewards. To find the jewels in the ruins of defeat and use them to go again.

In Shankly, Paisley, Dalglish and now Klopp, Liverpool Football Club has been truly blessed. In my lifetime I've witnessed greatness and have had to say farewell to some incredible heroes. And each time the club has moved forward, finding a way to be great again. We will once more, I know. But as I gazed up at a Klopp mural on the side of a terraced house on Skerries Road, it was difficult to see how.

In the run-up to the game, Klopp had been in fine form. He'd turned up late to a press conference, apologising to the assembled journalist. He smiled and said, 'Let's face it, who gives a shit.' It was greeted with great hilarity. A viral video showed him receiving a painting from artist and Liverpool fan Abigail Rudkin. As ever he went the extra mile and insisted on making the video with her, creating memories she'll never forget. Another would show Jürgen reading fan letters. It was all so emotional, and the sense of history being made before our eyes was everywhere.

Eventually, it was time to go through those turnstiles. There was, after all, a game of football to watch.

This was the day that Manchester City would be crowned champions, Arsenal would finish runners-up and the Reds would end the day in third place. It wasn't the ending we all wanted for the boss, but it was every bit as emotional and celebratory.

The backdrop to this game would see Prime Minister Rishi Sunak, who had insisted he had a plan, forget to take an umbrella with him as he stood drenched in Downing Street to announce a general election on 4 July, much to the horror of the rest of his own party. In football, the Premier League announced that there would be a vote on whether VAR should be scrapped, at their annual meeting in June. We could all dream.

None of that was important, though, not on 19 May 2024. I was at Anfield and couldn't imagine being anywhere else.

A flag day had inevitably been declared, and a pre-match mosaic designed by the incredible Andy Knott spanned the Lower Anfield Road, the Sir Kenny Dalglish Stand and the Kop. The words 'Danke Jürgen YNWA' were spelled out on cards lifted by supporters in all three ends of the stadium, as our anthem rang out. It was perhaps louder and sung with more passion than usual. Klopp reacted emotionally, touching his hand to his heart.

Regulars at Anfield will have passed Andy selling the fanzine *Red All Over the Land* on the corner of the Kop and the Sir Kenny Dalglish Stand. He's now as much a fixture on matchdays as the flagpole that shares the space with him. Speaking to *This is Anfield*, Andy discussed the plans for Klopp's mosaic:

> We couldn't put 'Jürgen said to me' because it would be too small, it wouldn't have the effect. Try and keep it simple with bigger symbols is the best way to do it.
>
> The design doesn't take that long because I have a grid sheet now, so as long as I know what I want to put into it, I will fit it in.
>
> I'm normally nervous on the Hillsborough ones because it means so much; however, I was hoping this day would never, ever happen, but we're here doing it for Jürgen.

I always wake up early on the days we're doing it, nerves, anticipation or whatever it may be. I don't think we've had one where it's not turned out how it should. For me, it is a labour of love.

Andy is one of many artists and creatives whose work will go down in the history of Liverpool Football Club. So too will Peter Carney, the Kop's artist in residence. He and his helpers had made a trilogy of banners to mark the occasion. He told me:

We made three banners for Jürgen's leaving. They read, TA JÜRGEN LA, I FEEL FINE, and THANX10. TA JÜRGEN LA was the title of our main banner. The main message running through the banners is that we can't thank him enough.

Remarkably, Peter had procured the cloth for Jürgen's banners from a fabric shop in Paris. He'd stumbled upon the store while attending the Champions League Final against Real Madrid:

Walking the back streets of Paris on the afternoon of 28 May 2022, I came across a fabric shop with stacks of West African wax print bundles in the window. To me, that was like walking past Woolworths window in the weeks before Christmas. I had to have a nose, even though I had no intention of buying. An hour later, I walked out with a bundle of cloth with a design that immediately said to me 'Jürgen's leaving banner'.

Peter's banners and Andy's mosaic would form a stunning backdrop to Jürgen's 491st and final game in charge. The match was almost a sideshow to the main event, which was all about a final farewell to a living legend.

Fittingly, Liverpool ended the Klopp era with a performance that symbolised everything he'd strived to create over the past nine years. For those interested in such things, his team created a massive 5.20 worth of expected goals, as they bombarded the Wolves goalmouth.

The visitors suffered their first setback midway through the first half, with Nélson Semedo receiving a red card for a foul on

Mac Allister. The referee initially waved a yellow, only for VAR to upgrade it to red, giving Gary O'Neill his post-match talking point. The Argentine midfielder opened the scoring for the Reds just seven minutes later.

With Klopp's song echoing around the ground for the entirety of the match, Liverpool continued to do their jobs professionally. A win in his final game was the least he deserved, and Jarell Quansah made sure of it with a goal just before the interval. Liverpool then saw out the remainder of the game with the minimum of fuss.

As we entered the final five minutes, the whole ground erupted into chants of:

I'm so glad that Jürgen is a Red
I'm so glad he delivered what he said
Jürgen said to me
You know we'll win the Premier League
You know he said so
I'm in love with him and I feel fine.

Sung to the tune of The Beatles' hit 'I Feel Fine', it grew ever louder as the final whistle approached, until it reached a deafening crescendo, which was surely heard across Stanley Park. Seated in the dugout, an emotional Klopp struggled to hold back the tears.

The man had led us to our fifth top-three finish in the last six seasons, and he'd ended his Anfield reign with the highest win percentage – 62 per cent – of any Liverpool manager in the Reds' history.

Writing in the matchday programme, Jürgen would say this of his last campaign:

We aimed for the moon and ended up in the stars. This is a club that is ready to take the journey in a new and exciting direction, not one that is ready for the journey to come to an end.

We now knew that his replacement would be the Feyenoord coach, Arne Slot, and he had big shoes to fill, the biggest. However, as is typical of the boss, Jürgen led a chant of his successor's name during the post-match farewell ceremony.

I made my way down to the front of the Kop to make sure I got close to the boss and the players as they made their way over at the end of the celebrations. A stage had been erected in the centre of the pitch and the sense of anticipation built almost from the moment the referee signalled the end of the game. Emotions felt raw, and I don't think anyone felt ready for what was to come.

In what has become a mark of the man, the ceremony would be about more than him. Refusing to hog the limelight, he shared his final moments as Liverpool manager with his departing backroom staff. It seemed like a microcosm of the Klopp era, indeed every era in which the Reds have been successful. It was about the collective, not the individual, and it was also about the future, not the past.

Then it was finally Klopp's turn. The roar of approval and applause was predictable but no less impactful on the boss:

> I'm completely surprised. I thought I was already in pieces, but I am so happy. I can't believe it, about you all, the atmosphere, the game, about being part of this family, about us.
>
> How we celebrated this day, it's just incredible – thank you so much. It doesn't feel like an end. It feels like a start. Today, I saw a football team playing full of desire. That's one part of development. That's what you need.
>
> This attention is uncomfortable but, in this time, I realise some things. People told me that I turned them from doubters into believers – but that isn't true. We have this stadium, training centre and you – the superpower of world football!

We'd laughed, sung and cried together over the past nine years. The emotion of it all was overwhelming. But from my vantage point in the Kop it was difficult to hear Jürgen clearly through Anfield's ancient PA system, but the moment had lost none of its power.

I'd watch it back later on television, shedding more than a few tears as I watched Jürgen's final fist pumps in front of an adoring Kop and realised it was over. Finally, over.

Jamie Carragher told Sky Sports:

This has probably never been seen at a club before. You have such great success that the memories last a lifetime. They will never forget you.

To be manager over 20 years and to never be sacked, or lose your job, it shows the relationships he's built.

He created the best team in world football over a two-year period. The only team to break Man City in a season. The title was won in November – that's how special it was. He created it.

Trent Alexander-Arnold broke down in tears as he attempted to answer questions from the media. Klopp had been all he'd known, and Klopp had given him his start in football, lifting him to dizzying heights.

Despite a third-placed finish, Anfield remained the biggest show in town. Manchester City were being presented with the Premier League trophy live on TV, yet viewing figures showed that many more people tuned into Klopp's emotional and historic farewell.

All that remained for Jürgen, and a lucky 11,000 fans, was an intimate gathering at the city's M&S Bank Arena on Liverpool's waterfront. The event, billed as 'An Evening with Jürgen Klopp', took place on 28 May. Tickets were as rare as hens' teeth, but I was surprised in the days leading up to it when my son called to say he'd secured two tickets.

It was an incredible night and left memories that will last a lifetime. 'I really don't think there is another city in the world who would do something like this, it is not possible,' Klopp said at the end of the night, after cheekily promising to return for a parade, should Manchester City – charged with 115 breaches of Premier League rules – be stripped of the titles they won while Klopp was manager.

No amount of trophies won as a result of City's billions could ever mean more than the joy that Jürgen Klopp has brought to Liverpool. I wouldn't swap any of them for the time we've spent together with the boss over the last nine years. I wouldn't have wanted to swap Jürgen for any manager in world football either.

An unbreakable bond has now been forged, and I feel it will last forever. Just as an older generation of Reds talk with great reverence of Shankly, today's Liverpool supporters will tell their children and grandchildren of the brilliance of Jürgen Klopp. His name now stands alongside the greats in the club's history and his legacy is assured.

Afterword

Jürgen's Legacy: He Made the People Happy

'*It doesn't matter so much what people think of you when you arrive. It matters more what they think of you when you leave.*'

Jürgen Klopp

In the days and weeks following Jürgen's departure, countless column inches, radio and television broadcasts, social media posts and podcasts have borne witness to the impact the German has had, not only on Liverpool Football Club and the wider city, but also on the Premier League.

Summing up his legacy is therefore a challenge. How can I find anything unique to say, when so much has been said by so many already. I don't think my words alone are sufficient to do justice to the man's legacy.

So, I've opted to turn this chapter over to supporters, journalists, authors and content creators, sharing with you their thoughts and emotions on what the man meant to them and the club. They come from everywhere – England, the Netherlands, Poland, Japan, Mexico, the United States and beyond. However, regardless of where they follow the Reds, you'll notice common themes in their assessment of Jürgen Klopp.

Les Jackson is the author of *A Life Well Red: A Memoir Edged in Black*. Les is a veteran of the Shankly era, who thought he'd never see the likes of the great man again, until Jürgen arrived:

> My first game following the Reds was in 1968, when Bill Shankly had already been in charge for nearly a decade. He was already my hero by then and the days he retired and then died are two of the saddest I can recall. A true socialist and man of the people whose legacy was laying the foundations of the club we know and love today.
>
> I thought his ilk had gone forever. Just over 40 years later Jürgen Klopp arrived, and, to a great extent, Shanks was reborn.

His impact on me, as a man about to embark on his sixth decade, was no less than Shanks's impact had been on a young boy still in his first.

Another 'man of the people' perfectly in tune with the Scouse psyche, his legacy is surely building on those foundations laid by Shanks, bringing another era of sustained success and uniting a fractured fanbase, which quickly warmed to his enthusiastic and larger-than-life persona. To coin a phrase: 'He was made for Liverpool, and we were made for him.' I will miss him.

Mike Holt, a Liverpool supporter, is host of the successful *Going the Match* podcast:

Jürgen Klopp for me will always be remembered for his attributes as a human being first and foremost, and that speaks volumes. How one man can reassemble the 'holy trinity' of the players, staff and supporters in one common goal to strive towards the greatness of the football club, not many managers have the skillset in this day and age to be able to do that.

Jürgen for me embodied all the values and feelings we as supporters hold close to us and that is why he will always have a special place with us.

All a supporter ever wants is for the players and staff to show every level of passion, determination, endeavour, fight and love that you would give. Jürgen understood that and, more importantly, he delivered it. For the first time in my life, I always felt our club was in safe hands. I felt comfort in knowing the right man was at the helm. It didn't matter what happened on the pitch and how many trophies we won.

Professor Stephen F. Kelly is a novelist, the author of Shankly and Dalglish biographies. His latest book studies The Beatles' impact on the global music scene – *How the Beatles Rocked the World*:

I remember early on in Klopp's reign Liverpool drew 2-2 with West Bromwich Albion at Anfield. It was a dour performance by the Reds but at the end of the game Klopp made the players come down to the Kop end, where they all held hands and saluted the fans.

Some of the players looked a bit bemused as to why they were celebrating but Klopp was insistent. The Kop, of course, responded with a loud chant of 'Liverpool'. The next day the back pages mocked him, wondering how he could make the players celebrate in front of the Kop when they hadn't won.

The press and fans elsewhere didn't understand. But the point was that Klopp understood the Kop, the city of Liverpool and what the soul of Liverpool Football Club was all about. It was Klopp's way of acknowledging the Kop and showing that we were all in this together. He wanted to form a bond with the Kop.

It was the kind of thing that Shankly might have done. And that's what summed Klopp up for me. It's hard to think of any other manager who could have won the hearts of Liverpool fans in the way that Klopp did, and that occasion summed it all up. Suddenly Klopp wasn't just another manager but was someone special.

Not only has he been an outstanding manager for Liverpool, but he came to understand the city, its culture, its politics and its people in much the same way as Shankly had.

Tracey Murray is a lifelong Liverpool supporter and the daughter of legendary Reds goalkeeper Tommy Lawrence:

I've supported Liverpool all my life. I now know that legacy comes from foundations. My dad's team in the 60s built the foundations for the Liverpool team of the 70s that would dominate the competition for the next two decades.

I think history will repeat itself with Klopp's departure and we'll have him to thank for that even more as the years go by.

In the past, on the rare occasions we didn't live up to our high standards, I would be devastated. I remember losing against Manchester United while I was a young teen and faking time off school because of the embarrassment I felt. Although

I look back at it and know it was slightly dramatic, it showed how much it meant, and I wasn't the only one like this.

This feeling faded away and our expectations dropped, and it's fair to say that the city and the club didn't have that belief until Klopp arrived. Don't get me wrong, we had some great seasons in the 2000s and we won trophies – Istanbul 2005 remains one of the greatest comebacks I've ever seen – but it always felt like we were underdogs.

Klopp changed this. From the very moment he stepped through the door, no longer were we here to take part, we were there to win. Even with the squad he inherited and the years required to get it into the shape it is now, the players started giving their all and the fans knew it.

I see many similarities between Klopp and Shankly. I hope Arne Slot will be Jürgen's Bob Paisley. Legacy needs a foundation.

Frank Carlyle is a lifelong Red, a local Liverpool historian, author of several books and host of *The Frank Carlyle Show*. He has seen it all down the years:

When Jürgen Klopp was appointed manager of Liverpool Football Club, I knew from the beginning we had a vastly experienced man and, most importantly, a winner. He proved me right, ending our 30-year wait for the league title.

Klopp promised the Anfield faithful he would win a trophy within four years. What still resonates with me is the Madrid and Spurs Champions League Final in my birthday month of May. I was in total bits when Jordan Henderson lifted 'Old Big Ears'.

However, the game that still brings goosebumps every time I think about it or see highlights was against Barcelona at Anfield. Three goals down from the first leg and having to score four goals to defeat a very good Lionel Messi side. And we did it! And I was in bits yet again.

There were other finals too, both domestic and European, and it wasn't all plain sailing, especially in Europe. Nevertheless, in Jürgen's nine-year tenure he brought the glory years back to the club. One of Jürgen's quotes that will never leave me is simply about himself and the fans: 'On and off the pitch we have created memories that will last forever.'

Thank you, Jürgen Klopp, for our trophies, thank you for your passion, thank you for the unforgettable moments and memories of your illustrious nine-year tenure. Thanks most of all for bringing back our pride. The city's door is always open for you, Ulla and the rest of your wonderful family.

Chris McLoughlin is a football writer for Reach Sport. His work has been published extensively in print and online. If you subscribe to the *Official Liverpool FC Magazine* or read the club's matchday programme, you'll have read Chris's work:

Jürgen Klopp is our modern-day equivalent of Bill Shankly. That's how it feels to me. I was only three years old when Shankly died, but I grew up in the 1980s hearing the stories of him and watching *The Official History of Liverpool FC* VHS over and over again. I was awestruck by him.

His aura. His accent. His words. His confidence. The way in which he was idolised to the point where Kopites would bow at his feet. How he sat tapping the Football League trophy while drumming it into us that it was 'our bread and butter'.

He was an inspiration, but that footage made me wish I'd lived through his Anfield era. Now I feel like I have lived through the modern-day version.

Klopp was not Shankly. He was a first-rate version of himself in a completely different world. But, like Shankly, he had the power to harness the Anfield crowd, to think in the same way as so many of us, to build teams that combined hard work with quality, emotion, with belief.

He oozed charisma and confidence. He had family values and a sense of humour, but also a steely edge and a fierce winning mentality. He built a collective spirit where every man gave his all on the pitch and the Anfield crowd gave their all off it. He also delivered success.

Between 1962 and 1966, Shankly led Liverpool to the Second Division title, two First Division titles and a maiden FA Cup. Between 2019 and 2024, Klopp led Liverpool to a sixth European Cup, a first Premier League title, a maiden FIFA Club World Cup, an FA Cup, two League Cups and a UEFA Super Cup.

Both were given time to build. Both had setbacks along the way. Both retained the faith of Liverpool supporters. And both delivered multiple successes by combining key signings, such as Ron Yeats and Virgil van Dijk, Ian St John and Mo Salah, with talented homegrown youngsters, like Ian Callaghan and Trent Alexander-Arnold.

Like Shankly, Klopp has left Liverpool FC in a much better place than he found it. That's his legacy, as are some of the incredibly talented young players he has left behind, but there's a significant difference. Whereas Shankly built a second great side that was fully established and became champions before he stepped down, Klopp's Liverpool 2.0 was still under construction. And whereas the Reds had continuity in the 1970s and Bob Paisley stepped into the massive void Shankly left behind, Klopp's modern-day boot room departed with him and thus a completely new era under Arne Slot and his backroom staff has begun. Which makes it feel to me like Klopp is an impossible act to follow, but then I imagine Kopites were saying the same in 1974 …

Paul Moran, another lifelong Red, is also the son of legendary Liverpool stalwart Ronnie Moran. Paul's experience watching Liverpool and his insights behind the scenes of the Shankly era make him ideally placed to judge Klopp's legacy:

Having watched Liverpool FC for over 50 years, including during the brilliant years that my dad was associated with the first team, the main thing that Jürgen Klopp brought back to me was the excitement of simply going to the games. It was rare during his time at the club that we played a game that didn't mean anything or had little consequence to the season's outcome.

Trophies are always nice but, although we won every major title during his time, my main Jürgen Klopp memory is the way we played, the way we defended and attacked and the sheer entertainment the team brought everyone lucky enough to watch the games, whether in person or on TV. Thanks, Jürgen and good luck, Arne.

Rado Chmiel is a freelance translator and interpreter, and a writer for the *Polish Reds Magazine*. Rado also translated Raphael Höningstein's *Bring the Noise* into Polish. Rado spoke emotionally about the impact Jürgen had on him as he went through a difficult spell in his life:

Dear Jürgen, Ich danke Ihnen für alles große momente! This is how I could start my love letter to Kloppo – the phrase means: Dear Jürgen, thank you for all the great moments [...] I think he would appreciate me trying to speak German to him.

Jürgen Klopp was well known to me before he joined Liverpool in October 2015. I am originally from Poland, and he was the creator of the mighty Borussia team, which included three of our then-best players from abroad: Kuba Błaszczykowski, Łukasz Piszczek and, of course, Robert Lewandowski.

When Klopp took over Liverpool, I was over the moon. I knew what style of play he preferred and what a character he was, but I wasn't ready for this ride at all. We all know the football part and we should be grateful for everything that happened on the pitch.

But I also must thank him for what he has done off the pitch. He showed us the human face of football. He was honest, he was open and when he made mistakes, he admitted them and learned the lessons to make himself and his teams better. And this is Jürgen during all of his life.

I was lucky enough to speak a few times with the Boss and I am not shy to say that Klopp, even if he wouldn't know it, helped me to overcome my demons. I was afraid of attending the therapy to improve my mental health, but Jürgen's attitude of being grateful for every little thing happening in life, his life philosophy, and his perception of admitting to mistakes and learning from them gave me enough strength to find necessary help I needed and overcome my depression, panic attacks and anxiety.

Jürgen's attitude helped me to overcome my low confidence in myself and to become somehow proud of what I have already achieved in my life as I was at the point where all those translations and chasing my dreams meant nothing for me at the darkest time of my illness. I will be forever grateful to him for everything.

Jacqueline Wadsworth is a historian and author. She's also the granddaughter of Liverpool legend of the 1920s Walter Wadsworth:

Jürgen Klopp made me feel that I was always on the winning side – whether we were winning or not – and that's because he was a natural-born leader. His charisma spilled way beyond the bounds of the club and the city of Liverpool, into the homes of fans like me in the provinces, and the joy and pride he inspired on so many occasions is something I'll never forget.

It was his personality that was key to his and the team's success. His loyalty to and faith in his players was often repaid by performances that were truly off the scale … who will ever forget our miracle comeback against Barcelona in 2019!

Jürgen will be sorely missed, but he left at the right time – with the fans still wanting more.

Keith Salmon is the author of *We Had Dreams and Songs to Sing*. He explained what the Klopp era had meant to him:

You might find it strange, but my memories of Jürgen Klopp are bookended by two nondescript performances in the Europa League. It was a bone-chilling night in Augsburg, Germany in February 2016, a goalless draw. And it was off the pitch that I saw the Jürgen effect. There was a real belief in the one thousand hardy souls who followed the Reds that night.

It was only the start of the journey, we had already seen enough to know this was going to be fun. Roll it forward just under eight years and before Jürgen shocked us all, I was in Toulouse, France, alongside my lad Charlie and another thousand believers; while it was poor on the pitch, off it the experience was amazing.

In between, Jürgen had us dining at the top table with Europe's elite, three Champions League finals in five years, with unbelievable trips to Kyiv, Madrid and Paris, and we had the time of our lives. Charlie was on the journey and has eaten his way around Europe. Croissants, bratwurst and tapas – this was his future and that was thanks to Jürgen and his boys. I can never thank him enough.

We believed in him and, most importantly, he believed in us. What a partnership, and we had the time of our lives, the best time to be a Red.

Yumiko Tamaru is a photographer, writer and secretary of the Official Liverpool Supporters Club of Japan:

The best thing about Jürgen is that he created the bond between the team and the supporters. It was something I had never seen before him. I am an international fan living in Tokyo, but even a fan like me, who can only watch Liverpool matches through a TV screen, could feel the unity he created.

The first time I felt it was when he took the players up to the Kop end and gave a bow after we secured a 2-2 draw with West Brom in his first season. Watching that through TV at 3am in my room in Tokyo, I felt like I was there on the Kop, celebrating the draw with Jürgen and the players. I never imagined that I would feel such a strong connection with a Liverpool manager.

I know that some people say he should have won more trophies, but even if we won nothing, I would still feel thankful to him for entertaining us with such an exciting attacking football and connecting all the fans around the world together.

Dr David Webber is a senior research fellow and occasional writer on the political economy of football:

In October 2015, Liverpool Football Club was an institution bound by the weight of its own glittering but increasingly distant history. Cut adrift upon a landscape now ruled by oligarchs, petrostates and venture capitalists, England's most successful football club felt rudderless, lacking purpose and identity. Enter Jürgen Klopp.

Conscious of but not cowed by the mythology of this most unique of football clubs, Klopp promised 'a new way' of operating. Success was to be a collective effort, and everyone had a part to play. Echoing the practical socialism of the great Bill Shankly, the intensity and gegenpressing that would be a feature of Klopp's teams must, he insisted, be matched by that of a noisy and partisan Kop.

Klopp, however, was far more than a manager, and the German assumed a statesman-like presence in a league, the imprint of which by now was stretching across the globe.

Demonstrative and animated on the sidelines, Klopp was pure box-office for the Premier League. But beneath his own exuberance and the exacting demands he placed upon his players and supporters, Klopp was also so often a voice of reason and integrity.

No more clearly was this evident than during the Covid pandemic. As politicians in Westminster flailed and failed in their own response to this global crisis, Klopp provided reassurance, common sense and perspective. His was a calming influence amid chaos and uncertainty. Even with a 30-year wait to lift a 19th league title at one stage in jeopardy, Klopp urged the people to look after and out for one another.

The 'new way' that Klopp promised in his opening press conference proved to be the blueprint for the collective endeavour and success that followed. Shankly would be proud.

Matt Ladson, co-founder and editor of *This is Anfield*, also felt that Jürgen's legacy was about more than football:

Jürgen's legacy and impact at Liverpool extends far beyond simply the football or a list of trophies won. Football is about community, about people, a social experience and a representation of wider society. Within that, Klopp fully enveloped everything that was Liverpool FC, the supporters, the local community and the city itself. To be a Liverpool manager is more than simply being a football manager, you're an ambassador for the city, and nobody has understood that assignment more than Klopp in recent history.

Not just Klopp, but also his wider backroom team had an extensive understanding of the history and fabric of Liverpool FC. It was truly impressive how Jürgen, Pepijn and more could recite stories about Bob Paisley or Bill Shankly like a lifelong supporter could.

I had the absolute honour to witness Jürgen in press conferences and in other settings within the media landscape; so often there were little stories that showed the depth of his understanding of the club and people. One such instance was when 104-year-old Bernard Sheridan attended a post-match press conference and Jürgen went out of his way to approach him afterwards, insisting on a photo together. It wasn't coordinated; nobody told Jürgen, he just did it.

A true people person, a true leader, a true human and a great example and role model for all. Everybody can learn a little something from Jürgen.

Paul Salt is a broadcaster and presenter for BBC Radio Merseyside and has covered Klopp's reign. Paul reflected on Klopp's time at Anfield and the impact he's had on club and city:

I grew up in the 1980s as a Liverpool fan. There's no doubt about it, we were spoiled. One of my first memories was winning the European Cup in Rome in 1984. For so long I treasured that memory because I never thought I'd see anything like it ever again.

Then there was Istanbul. But that felt temporary. I also remember idolising Kenny Dalglish as Liverpool manager. I was devastated when he resigned. I never thought I would ever feel quite the same about a Liverpool manager.

Then along came Jürgen Klopp. For me he's the modern-day Bill Shankly. He just got Liverpool. A club whose fans put their manager on a pedestal more than any other. He was the figurehead, the leader and he wanted to take people with him on the journey. He was willing to fight the corner of the fans, the players, the club, and the city.

He got what it means to be a Scouser. I've not even mentioned what he did on the pitch! He leaves Arne Slot with a fantastic squad, but more than that he leaves Anfield with so many memories. He most definitely made it fun to go to the match again.

Jacob Hansen is a writer and podcaster at *Tribal Football*. He knew what Klopp would bring before the German joined us, and he hasn't been disappointed:

Having followed German football for years I was already a big fan of Jürgen Klopp when he signed for Liverpool, and I thought, *This is completely right.* It turned out even more right than I ever dreamed of.

Anfield became a fortress again. What a brilliant brand of football he created and what thrills he gave us. Critics say the trophy haul should have been bigger. What arrogance. Some supporters never get to win anything. We did, and with a manager we loved. The charisma, the humanity, the fighting spirit he brought with him.

I've loved every second of Kloppo's years with Liverpool, and future managers might win even more trophies, but in terms of personality his equal won't come by in my lifetime.

George Sephton has been the Anfield match announcer since the days of Bill Shankly. His voice has become the soundtrack of many a Kopite's match-going life. He's also the author of *The Voice of Anfield*. Having seen it all, George has been blown away by Jürgen's contribution:

The first thing he has left us, of course, is a lot of happy memories. Especially for me personally.

If I was making a list of the top 20 magic moments in my life, then Jürgen would be responsible for at least five or six of them.

That line-up for YNWA in front of the Kop after the Barcelona game. Although I suppose that applies to everyone. I had the privilege of sitting in my window right over that temporary podium when we collected the Premier League trophy.

From the surreal moment after his first home game as manager, when I said hello and he responded, 'Oh yes! You are the famous voice of Anfield,' to the moment after he'd come offstage at the Liverpool Arena, having finished his 'Evening with Jürgen Klopp', and he came over to me and gave me the proverbial Jürgen hug, it has been the stuff of dreams.

In the broader scheme of things, he has left Arne Slot a wonderful squad to work with. He has made sure that every eager and wet-behind-the-ears academy player realises that they have every chance of going on to great things with the Reds. It started with Trent Alexander-Arnold and has worked its way through to Conor Bradley.

He has brought the excitement and pure joy back to Anfield and cranked up the atmosphere in the stadium. At this moment in time, I miss him, and I'm not looking forward to matchdays without him around.

John Kennedy is a retired trainer and a Liverpool FC author. He has been following Liverpool since the days of Bill Shankly:

I was a teenager on the Kop when Bill Shankly was Liverpool's manager and remember well how special he made us all feel. The great man established a unique bond between the dressing room and the supporters, and Jürgen Klopp has resurrected that. History will record the trophies we won under his leadership, but future managers will do well to recognise how important the supporters are to the success of this club, and how Klopp was able to harness Anfield's potential energy into an unstoppable force – just as Shankly did.

We have some extraordinary memories from Klopp's reign, and I hope the new manager acknowledges the part the supporters played in that. Klopp certainly did, and I believe that, above all else, will be his legacy.

Jack Lusby is an editor at *This is Anfield*, and a writer for *FourFourTwo* magazine:

Klopp's legacy speaks for itself; the trophies, the way Liverpool are now known for playing and the belief among the fans shows the scale of the job he undertook over his almost nine years in charge. But his lasting legacy is how he emboldened the academy and made Liverpool a destination for young talent again.

You can look at the likes of Sheyi Ojo and Harry Wilson – who were among the first to debut under Klopp and have gone on to enjoy successful careers elsewhere – or first-team standouts like Trent Alexander-Arnold, Curtis Jones and, more recently, Jarell Quansah; his faith in youth has helped realise the work of those behind the scenes at the academy.

It's something the club should always be built around, and now his dedication to youth and the way so many others have bought into it gives Liverpool a foundation for success for potentially decades to come.

Kieran Smith is the founder of the Liverpool FC Historical Group, and co-author of *Untouchables: Anfield's Band of Brothers*:

The appointment of Jürgen Klopp brought a sense of something special to Anfield. When Jürgen first held court, he spoke, we listened. A prediction of winning a league title within four years came true. We never doubted his positivity, or his prophecies.

Never, in over 40 years of following Liverpool, have I witnessed a manager immediately become part of the fabric of the club, the city, its people. Football is often referred to as a religion. Shanks himself referred to Anfield as a church. If there's an example of a quasi-religious movement, then the Klopp era surely fits the bill.

His legacy goes beyond football. Of course, there are the trophies and memorable games. More than anything else, though, it's Jürgen's connection to the fans, the city and the hope he gave to so many.

Steve Hunter is Liverpool Football Club's official matchday commentator. As such, he's well placed to comment on Jürgen's contribution over the last nine years:

Jürgen Klopp is the modern-day Bill Shankly. He gave us some truly magical and unforgettable times we'll never forget. He won the Premier League title, he said so you know!

To commentate for the club on Klopp's Liverpool was incredible. The teams he built, the belief he gave and just seeing that wonderful beaming smile gave you that belief that anything was possible with this brilliant guy. If you look back to the incredibly tough times with the pandemic, just the reassuring words of Klopp made you feel that everything was going to be fine, and we would get through it together.

The parade the day after we lost the Champions League Final to Real Madrid told its own story. That was the parade that would have happened when we won the title. That was our way of saying thank you, Jürgen; he gave us back our pride and he's an honorary Scouser. Build a statue of this great man at Anfield.

Jordan Moore is a journalist working for ITV Ulster. Like so many, he has grown up with Jürgen Klopp:

Klopp first came to Liverpool when I was 17. At the time, I was just starting my A levels in physics, maths and history and was an aspiring astronaut. I'm now a 25-year-old man working as a journalist. Personally, and from a career perspective, I'm unrecognisable from who I was and who I wanted to be nine years ago. For Liverpool Football Club, it's a similar story.

Going back ten years, my feelings following the 2014 campaign that saw our title fight implode at Selhurst Park was one of an opportunity gone, and one that was unlikely to come again anytime soon. Throughout my early years, Liverpool won the odd trophy, but it was sporadic and usually more to do with luck or moments of individual brilliance more than anything else (Cardiff in 2006 always springs to mind). It meant hope of winning the league was just that, hope.

Now after every defeat in a final, or second-place league finish, the thought is 'we'll win it next year'. For me that's Jürgen Klopp's legacy. He took Liverpool from a team of sporadic success to expectant victors, or as I would have said in 2016, from the dirt to the stars.

Gold medals and silver cups are the measures of success in football. Subsequent Liverpool managers may collect more of these precious metals than Klopp, but it's always a lot easier to find them when someone else has shown you where to look.

Paul J Maychin is the co-creator, producer and presenter at Redmen TV:

There were those who watched the Bundesliga and had fallen in love with his Bayern-toppling Dortmund team. More still watched his side battle to the Champions League Final only to fall at the same, final Bavarian hurdle. The rest heard the phrase 'heavy metal football' and fell head over heels with the concept.

The only time I've ever watched German football was that brief insane period during lockdown when it was the only football. Despite my best intentions to watch it, my one-year-old son needed a bottle just after kick-off and I fell asleep while feeding him and missed the whole UCL Final. Heavy metal football sounded cool, but for me it was never about the style of his football, it was about his attitude towards football.

My first real experience of Jürgen Klopp was seeing him say 'fuck' in a post-match interview. It sounds stupid to say it, but I absolutely fell in love with him.

I've now spent a decade and a half covering Liverpool and football in general, longer still studying the media. Those interviews are normally a waste of oxygen; full of tried, tired, tested, boring, cookie-cutter platitudes. They're a microcosm of modern football. Safe, plastered with sponsorships and empty of personality. Here was a guy, though, that saw those yawn-worthy conventions and decided he would rather just be himself. And that's just what he brought to Liverpool, speaking personal truth with heart on sleeve.

Liverpool is a culturally rich city of passionate romantics and storytellers. It's also increasingly a city that's 'too cool to clap', and with the rise of the social media age, the Liverpool fanbase was also starting to fear the backlash of embarrassment. Too many near misses and too many stories about how good things used to be had left us with scarred psyches and fear in our hearts where once hope resided. After all, nobody wants to support the banter club.

Suddenly, though, here was a guy who took his players to the Kop to thank them for sticking it out to see a late equaliser against West Brom. West Brom!

The point being that some rivalries are bigger than others, and some games have more at stake, but he reminded us that all of it mattered! Every point, every goal, every kick, every touch. Suddenly the 'Kopite behaviour' shouts from our bitter blue brethren started feeling less like emotional hand grenades and more like the pea-shooter shots they actually were.

If the manager is going to run on the pitch and hug the goalie when we score a goal; if he's going to construct a team that will run through brick walls, and in style; well, the very least we can do is stand up, clap our hands, sing some songs and give every due ounce of appreciation possible.

Jürgen Klopp brought back the blind, passionate support and made it fun in the process. Now, none of us at Anfield are too cool to clap. Long may it continue.

James Nalton is a football and sports journalist who writes for several media outlets, including *Morning Star, Forbes, American Soccer Reverie,*

World Soccer, The Guardian, FotMob, and the MLS and BBC. James told me how Klopp had reawakened a dormant philosophy at Anfield:

> The transformation of Liverpool under Klopp was comprehensive, but in some ways, it was not a transformation at all – merely a return to something that existed previously. Something that had lain dormant in the foundations of the club, only occasionally reappearing since the 1990s but brought back permanently by Klopp for new generations to experience.
>
> It could be described as a 21st-century version of Shankly's Liverpool, but Klopp didn't labour to replicate former glories or mimic personalities of the past. It happened naturally and with its own character. The kind of connections forged at Mainz 05 and Borussia Dortmund made Liverpool a perfect next step for Klopp, just as Klopp was a perfect, much-needed appointment for Liverpool.
>
> A style of play instilled from the off still recalled an original blueprint set out by Klopp and his late friend Wolfgang Frank during their days at Mainz, updated for a new era at the top level. This was a welcoming, international version of Liverpool, with a manager who often spoke like a socialist at a time when right-wing UK governments were bumbling the country into isolation.
>
> An internationally successful Liverpool too, as regardless of the mood, such a story needs to be punctuated by trophies, finals and genuine title challenges. Though football as a business and science is unrecognisable from the Liverpool FC that came out swinging in the 60s, Klopp naturally tapped into important intangibles that are constant and enduring.

Joanna Durkan is an assistant editor at *This is Anfield* and has covered Liverpool throughout Klopp's time with the Reds:

> There are few greater ways to endear yourself to those involved at Liverpool FC than to embody everything it stands for from the very first day. It's no easy task to do it so seamlessly, but for Jürgen Klopp it felt effortless because he'd always been

that way – he didn't need to change, he simply just had to be himself.

Charismatic, self-aware, compassionate and competitive, it was always going to be a match made in heaven. That he had to 'fire' himself spoke volumes of his influence and the high regard in which he was held; he was the Shankly of a new generation. Those are words not written lightly, but it's the legacy he has left behind. He made dreams come true and allowed millions to create memories they'll cherish forever, with loved ones and the strangers embraced in the stands. There will be few like him again.

Kim Olthof is the author of *Our Liverpool Tattoos Around the World*. Based in the Netherlands, Kim has found a special place in her heart for the German:

When Jürgen Klopp first arrived at Liverpool, he immediately stole my heart. I mean, if you call yourself 'the normal one' in your first press conference you obviously have character, humour and an understanding of the needs of Liverpool fans. It gave me the feeling that I could trust this new manager as he knew exactly what he was doing.

This intelligent, but also incredibly honest man with a golden heart turned out to be exactly what everyone with a Liverpool heart needed. I see him as the Shankly of the new generation.

I am always proud to be a Liverpool fan, but these last years I have been glowing with pride. Like most Liverpool fans I went from doubter to believer again. And went from listening to stories from the Shankly era to an understander of the emotions that Liverpool fans had all these years ago. Jürgen not only brought me an enormous amount of happiness these last years, he also brought me closer to the older generation and made me complete as a Liverpool fan.

Gareth Roberts is known for his time on *The Anfield Wrap* and his appearances on LFCTV *Press Review* show. Gareth's latest project is *The Late Challenge* podcast. He told me:

My first match was September 1990. Kenny Dalglish was manager and Liverpool had lifted the title for the 18th time that May. The programme showed Peter Beardsley scoring against Manchester United in a 4-0 win at Anfield that month.

'Champions of the Football League' it declared. The Reds had won 10 of the last 15 titles. It was taken for granted. But the Liverpool league machine was about to break down. Three decades passed. Good times, bad times, but no league title.

Many wondered if it would ever happen again. It felt curse-like. Freakish. And it hung heavy. It did for managers. It got to players. It wormed into the Anfield mindset. We were desperate. And it was unhealthy. Over to you, Jürgen.

On day one he said it would happen. The mood shifted. Spirit grew. Belief came back. Passion returned. We saw smiles on faces again. Klopp made Liverpool feel like Liverpool again and he did it all by being himself. A normal man who likes a pint, who just happens to be a great football manager, an elite communicator and a genius at harnessing the power of the people.

An infectious ball of emotion who laughs, cries, gets angry and sad, who gets lost in the moment for the good and the bad – all because of football. Just like the rest of us. Just a man. But a man who won that title again. A man who made Liverpool great again. A man who made us believe, who made us laugh and made us cry.

Jürgen Klopp. He was made for Liverpool, and Liverpool was made for him.

Andy Marsden is the co-author of *Liverpool Football Programmes: The Definitive Collector's Guide*. Andy explained how Jürgen Klopp transformed a club in the doldrums:

He educated us on his brand of high-octane football – full of fun and excitement – to deliver trophies and conquer the world. This is only the beginning of how Jürgen Klopp transformed this football club. Take a moment to remember his talent for nurturing players, backroom staff and others at the football club. From Carol the tea lady, those working in administration, to the owners, he inspired them all.

We've shared in so many great moments, and long may we benefit from what he leaves us – a squad upgrade, an exciting youth development, a training complex to be proud of, and much, much more. Many of my elders said Shankly was the Messiah. Jürgen is the new messiah. He saved our club. He promised and he delivered. He re-energised us. His legacy will grace us for years to come. Anyone that has achieved all of this deserves a rest. Danke, Jürgen.

Carl Clemente is the author of *19: The Official History of Our League Champions*, and co-author of *Mr Liverpool: Ronnie Moran: The Official Life Story*:

I remember his first press conference, when he asked for patience. This fella is going to be here for the long term, I thought to myself, as he admitted he couldn't just click his fingers and bring the club immediate success. He was given time, and over the next few transfer windows he was able to put his historic team together, piece by piece.

On the pitch we started to see improvements in the style of football that was being played, which was very attractive to the eye, and which brought the team results by playing entertaining, attacking football.

Jürgen's team and managerial skills started to provide Liverpool supporters memories and stories to pass down to future generations, as our dads and grandads told us about the Shankly, Paisley, Fagan and Dalglish days. Final after final, trophy after trophy, Jürgen's team started to break records, left, right and centre.

I don't like comparing people in football; however, in my opinion, Jürgen is the modern-day Bill Shankly. Like Shanks, he made the people happy, not just by his style of football on the pitch, but by his personality, values and all-round goodness too. Like others from the Boot Room era, Jürgen 'just got it', which means, Jürgen understood the people, the history of the club and city.

For these reasons, I'll be eternally grateful to him for providing us with so many unforgettable memories and stories.

Darren O'Connor is the founder and host of the *Liverpool Connection* podcast. Based in Austin, Texas, Darren is a Formby expat. He holds Klopp in the highest regard:

> As a Liverpool supporter, I understand the deep reverence Klopp commands. His tactical acumen and success are undeniable, but it's his ability to connect with the fans on a personal level that truly sets him apart. He understands the culture and history of the club, respects the values and embraces the city's heart and soul.
>
> Klopp's reign has been a celebration of Liverpool's identity, where the intense bond between the club and its supporters has been magnified, epitomised by the anthem 'You'll Never Walk Alone'. The true depth of Klopp's influence at Liverpool is far-reaching, leaving a legacy that will be remembered for generations.
>
> As a fan, I see him as the embodiment of Liverpool's spirit – passionate, determined and relentless in the pursuit of excellence. His tenure is not just a chapter but a golden era in Liverpool's illustrious history, and for that I'm eternally grateful.

Steven L Wilson is the president of the Official Liverpool Supporters Club of Austin Texas. He explained how Jürgen had left his imprint on Liverpool, and sent a personal message to the departing boss:

> Jürgen, because of your energy and passion throughout your time at LFC, you've helped grow the worldwide network of Official Liverpool Supporters Clubs. The games were must-see TV and inspired many of us in the United States to make the jaunt across the pond to see you at the helm of our beloved club.
>
> I was blessed to be the president of the Austin, Texas chapter throughout your coaching tenure at LFC. What you have done for the city of Liverpool has been just as remarkable. Above the

wins and trophies, you brought back the passion and energy to the city from the very first day.

I was fortunate to be able to go to Anfield and see your first two home games – little could we realise what a journey we would all go on together. Thank you for being our gaffer, a great steward of the club, adding your name to the club's great managers, bringing us that long-awaited Premier League title, and helping a new generation to fall in love with the Reds.

John Pearman, founder and editor of the last surviving printed Liverpool FC fanzine, *Red All Over the Land*, spoke of Jürgen's impact on the club and the city:

Jürgen Klopp's legacy [...] will be felt and remembered by supporters for generations to come. He will be remembered in folklore just like Bill Shankly is still remembered. Ageing Reds will tell their grandchildren of this charismatic German who, like The Beatles, shook the world.

In years to come, when Jürgen and his coaching team look back on just what they achieved at Anfield, they will feel a sense of pride. Not just at Anfield, though. If you walked around the city, Jürgen's presence seemed to be everywhere, almost supernatural in a strange way. I walked past Anfield a week or so after he finally left and just stood and looked; it felt strange that come the new season we'll still be there, but Jürgen won't be. He has left Liverpool, but Liverpool will never leave him.

Danke, Jürgen. From all of us.